VOLUNTEER VACATIONS
IN LATIN AMERICA

AMY E. ROBERTSON

LATIN AMERICA

UNITED STATES

MEXICO

Gulf of
Mexico

Atlantic
Ocean

CUBA

HAITI
DOM. REPUBLIC

BELIZE
HONDURAS
JAMAICA

Caribbean Sea

GUATEMALA
EL SALVADOR
NICARAGUA

COSTA RICA
PANAMA

VENEZUELA

GUYANA
SURINAME
GUYANE

COLOMBIA

ECUADOR

PERU

BRAZIL

BOLIVIA

PARAGUAY

URUGUAY

ARGENTINA

CHILE

Pacific Ocean

Southern Ocean

© AVALON TRAVEL

Contents

▶ **Why Volunteer?** **6**
  Planning Your Trip 8
  How to Volunteer 13
   • Type of work 13
   • Questions to Ask Yourself 14
   • Choosing an Organization 16
   • Volunteers with
     Special Skills 18
   • Questions to Ask
     an Organization 20

▶ **Mexico** **21**
  Local Organizations 24
  Essentials 32

▶ **Guatemala** **34**
  Local Organizations 35
  Essentials 47

▶ **Honduras** **50**
  Local Organizations 51
  Essentials 62

▶ **Nicaragua** **64**
  Local Organizations 65
  Essentials 77

▶ **Costa Rica** **79**
  Local Organizations 82
  Essentials 91

▶ **Panama** **93**
  Local Organizations 96
  Essentials 100

▶ **Colombia** **102**
  Local Organizations 103
  Essentials 111

▶ **Ecuador** **113**
   Local Organizations 116
   Essentials 128

▶ **Peru** **130**
   Local Organizations 131
   Essentials 145

▶ **Bolivia** **147**
   Local Organizations 150
   Essentials 158

▶ **Brazil** **160**
   Local Organizations 161
   Essentials 169

▶ **Argentina** **172**
   Local Organizations 173
   Essentials 182

▶ **Chile** **184**
   Local Organizations 185
   Essentials 190

▶ **International
   Organizations** **192**

▶ **Resources** **213**
   Transportation 213
   Tips for Volunteers 214
   Suggested Reading and
      Internet Resources 218

▶ **Indexes** **223**

Why Volunteer?

"Never doubt that a small group of thoughtful, committed citizens can change the world. Indeed, it is the only thing that ever has."

– Margaret Mead

Volunteer vacations—combining travel and volunteer work—are becoming an increasingly popular way to see the world. Why spend your vacation *working*? It's not about work—it's about travel. Travel becomes transformative when you share experiences and integrate with the people, culture, and environment of the place. Volunteer vacations convert the tourist into the traveler, allowing you to experience a destination and connect with locals in a new way. It's about sharing talents and abilities, mutual learning, and pulling back the curtain that separates the foreigner from the country.

It's also about fun. You might find yourself drawn to the rich indigenous cultures of Guatemala, Bolivia, or Peru. The golden sands of Honduras, Panama, and Brazil may beckon. Are you captivated by the extraordinary wildlife of Costa Rica and Ecuador? Or do you long for the laid-back vibe of Nicaragua and Mexico? From the European-Latin fusion of Argentina to the beaches and colonial cities of less-traveled Colombia, Latin America offers something to entice any traveler.

Of course, it's also about need. Poverty figures in Latin America dwarf those of the United States and Canada. Most Latin American countries don't have social safety nets like welfare or Medicaid. Entire families

may live in one- or two-room homes with dirt floors and no running water. Children may go to school only 100 days a year—or not at all. Wildlife conservation and environmental protection is often left behind in the basic struggle for survival.

I took my first volunteer vacation when I was 13 years old, building homes with Habitat for Humanity in Washington State. The camaraderie that I shared—with both my fellow volunteers and the family whose home we were building—was amazing, and it was gratifying to be able to help people in need. Seeing the injustice of economic inequality up close, and feeling the satisfaction of participating in a solution, planted the seeds for my first career in international development.

Today I have built homes in Honduras, monitored presidential elections in Ecuador, and worked with marginalized youth in Bolivia. Each experience opened a window into a world different from my own, and I gained indelible memories in the process. Whatever you choose to do, volunteering will add a new dimension to your travels and will leave you with meaningful remembrances of your own.

Planning Your Trip

▶ WHERE TO GO

Encompassing 20 nations, 4 dependencies, 600 million people, and roughly 8 million square miles, Latin America is a big place with many possibilities. Once you've narrowed down your options, take the time to read up on your destination. A deeper understanding of the local culture, economy, and political context will not only help you find the right fit, but also greatly enhance your volunteer experience once you're on the ground.

Mexico and Central America

Mexico is Latin America's northernmost country, filled with bustling and sophisticated cities interspersed between lush countryside and ancient pyramids, as well as endless golden beaches. Heading south, Central America's "Northern Triangle" of Guatemala, El Salvador, and Honduras is next: a fertile region of mountains and cloud forests that is also rife with hardships. While Guatemala and Mexico are rich with indigenous cultures, the Maya and the Aztec the most famous among them, in compact Honduras a visit to Mayan ruins can be made in conjunction with a trip to its spectacular Caribbean archipelago. At the southern border of Honduras lies Nicaragua, the poorest country in Latin America (and second poorest in the Western Hemisphere, after Haiti), but volunteers may be surprised by the wealth of volcanoes, colonial architecture, and easygoing attitudes. The stable and more economically developed Costa Rica, Panama, and (English-speaking) Belize make up the rest of the region.

Guatemala, Honduras and Nicaragua have a large selection of locally based volunteer opportunities, from teaching English to protecting sea turtles, plus some unusual offerings, such as the promotion of green and alternative building practices in Guatemala, or training emergency responders in Nicaragua. Because of Mexico and Central America's proximity to the United States, flights there are frequent and generally much less expensive than those to South America.

South America

From the beaches of Brazil to the Andean mountains of Bolivia, the coffee farms of Colombia to the pampas of Argentina, South America evokes beauty and romance. Colombia, Venezuela, Guyana, Suriname, and French Guiana line the northern Atlantic coast of the continent. Along the Pacific, Ecuador, Peru, and Bolivia are famed for their Andean mountains, strongholds of the diverse Quechua people and home to many more indigenous groups as well. They also share the Amazon rainforest with their eastern neighbor, Brazil, whose beaches and fun-loving cities are as celebrated as its forests. Argentina, Chile, Paraguay, and Uruguay compose the Southern Cone region and are distinguished by a strong European influence and a love of the *asado,* or barbecue.

Colombia is emerging as a great offbeat destination for travel and voluntourism, while a more established path for volunteers has been worn to Ecuador, Peru, and Bolivia. As a result, these countries also offer the greatest number of locally based volunteer opportunities in the region. Southern Cone countries have stronger economies and less outreach to international volunteers, but existing opportunities are generally well organized. National regulations make volunteering in

Plaza de Armas, Lima, Peru

Brazil a trickier affair, but those wishing to practice their Portuguese or samba steps while volunteering will find plenty to do. Flights to South America are generally pricey, and advanced planning is recommended to make the most of a trip.

▶ WHEN TO GO

Latin America is a year-round destination: It's sunny *somewhere* in Latin America no matter what month it is. Top travel times for Latin Americans themselves are Semana Santa (Holy Week, the week leading up to Easter) and the days between Christmas and New Year's, so you can expect beaches to be packed (often bordering on mayhem) and most big cities to be quiet during those times. Prices for airline tickets and hotel rooms in the popular destinations spike significantly during these periods.

Across Latin America, altitude is as important as season in determining temperatures, so remember that it can be cooler, especially at night, in mountain cities such as Mexico City, Antigua, Quito, Cusco, or La Paz.

Mexico and Central America

Generally speaking December-April is the dry season (*verano*) in Central America,

with temperatures at their hottest in March and April. Spring break is a great time for students to visit—although if your break coincides with Semana Santa, book your airfare well in advance to get a reasonable price. Hotels and hostels in top tourist destinations such as Antigua, Guatemala, or Roatan, Honduras, are often booked months in advance.

On the Caribbean coasts of Mexico, Guatemala, Honduras, and Nicaragua, August-October is hurricane season. October tends to be the rainiest month (though it rarely rains all day) and is not the best choice if you are looking for sunshine.

Northern Mexico (above the Tropic of Cancer/the 24th parallel) is temperate and dry, with cool weather in the winter.

South America

The countries close to or crossed by the equator—Colombia, Ecuador, Peru, Bolivia, and Brazil—can have warm weather year-round, at least at sea level. Seasons are referred to by locals as *invierno* (winter) and *verano* (summer), but even within a country, the months that are wet or dry and warm or cool vary. Variations in temperature are defined more by altitude than by season. Cities like Quito, Ecuador (elevation 9,350 ft/2,850 m), Cusco, Peru (elevation 11,150 ft/3,400 m), and La Paz, Bolivia (elevation 11,975 ft/3,690 m) are much cooler than coastal areas, and they can get downright cold during the winter, especially at night.

Farther south, Argentina and Chile have climates similar to the United States and Canada—but in reverse. In winter the northern regions of Argentina and Chile enjoy fairly moderate weather, while the southern tips (the Patagonia region) are cooler and get snow. Summer is December-March, and winter is June-August.

▶ BEFORE YOU GO

Passports

Many volunteer organizations ask for your passport number. If you don't have a valid passport already, start the application process. Most countries in Latin America require passports be valid for six months beyond the date of entry into the country, so if you already have a passport, check the expiration date. Some countries may require visas—check the individual country chapters and/or with the local embassy of your destination.

As a precaution, scan your passport and birth certificate into your computer at home, then email the scans to yourself so that you can access them if your passport goes missing. Make a photocopy of your passport to take along as well. Visit the website of

The jaguar corridor runs from Mexico to Argentina; there are opportunities to support wildlife protection across the region.

your home country's embassy in the country you'll be visiting and find the 24-hour emergency citizen services number. Write this number down on your photocopy. Keep your passport in your handbag or backpack, and tuck the photocopy into your suitcase, so the documents are traveling separately.

Vaccinations

Ensure that routine vaccinations for tetanus, polio, and hepatitis B are up-to-date before traveling. Vaccinations for hepatitis A and typhoid are typically recommended for travel in Latin America.

Yellow fever is a mosquito-borne disease endemic in parts of Bolivia, Brazil, Colombia, Ecuador, and Peru, with some cases in Argentina and Panama. A safe and effective vaccine is available and may be required if you are traveling from a country where yellow fever is endemic (for example, from Peru to Bolivia).

Transportation

For many of the opportunities in this guide, the biggest expense will be airfare—and the farther you travel, the greater that expense will be. However, by booking well in advance or traveling at nonpeak times, you may be able to save money. Also consider other airports that could offer a better fare; you might find cheaper flights if you are willing to hop on a bus from a different airport to your destination. For example, travelers to western Panama may find cheaper flights to San José, Costa Rica. They can then reach the volunteer site via a relatively inexpensive bus ride, rather than a pricey domestic flight.

If you are not staying at the volunteer site, check whether or not local transportation is needed and provided. If not, include that in your estimate as well. Bus networks are comprehensive across Latin America, as well as a cheap way to travel. Intercity buses are generally reliable, but buses within some big cities in Latin America may not be safe; taxis are recommended instead.

Driving in Latin America is fairly easy, especially if you speak Spanish or have a GPS, and rental cars are available at all international airports. A valid driver's license from your home country is usually sufficient.

Language Skills

Even if you are planning to take foreign-language lessons, brushing up on those skills prior to departure will only enhance your experience. Enroll in a language course at your local institute or community college, or sign up for an online class. Self-learners can buy a study guide from companies such as Teach Yourself, Pimsleur, or Rosetta Stone; download language learning podcasts; or find conversation partners with whom to practice online or in your home community.

It's worth noting that English is the first language in the Bay Islands of Honduras, as well as in Belize, so if brushing up on your Spanish skills is a priority, volunteer opportunities in these places might not be the best fit. Portuguese is spoken in Brazil. It's possible to study the indigenous languages Quechua, Aymara, and Guarani while volunteering in Bolivia.

What to Take

Let's start with what *not* to take: Leave your valuables at home. The best way to avoid problems is to eliminate their possibility. If you do bring electronics, such as a tablet or music player, the more discreet you can be, the better. Do not use these devices while walking down the street or on public transportation. If you bring a laptop, leave the standard carrying case at home and pack your computer inside something less obvious. If your engagement ring is flashy, or your earrings could pass for real diamonds, leave them at home. Ditch

Sea turtles come to Latin American beaches and mangroves to lay their eggs.

the expensive watch and wear a cheap one for your trip.

Likewise, if you want to bring anything from school supplies to project materials, be sure to check first with your hosting organization to see what is really needed, and if it is available to purchase at your destination instead. Not only will you keep your luggage lighter, but you'll also help support the local economy with on-site purchases.

Now, for what *to* take. Many warm places feel surprisingly cool in the evenings, so a lightweight jacket or sweater is often handy. If you will be in the mountains, be prepared for cooler temperatures, and even downright cold nights. Once you've laid out on your bed all the clothes you want to bring, put half of them back in the closet. Do bring one nice outfit for the unexpected (a night on the town, an inauguration of your project, or even a local wedding—you just never know!). Remember that Latin Americans tend to dress up more than their northern counterparts, and that shorts are not usually worn except on the beach.

Think about the kind of work you will be doing, as well as any exploring you plan to do. Hiking boots can be great for agricultural and construction work. Closed-toed, strong-support sandals (such as those made by Keen, Chaco, or Teva) can be good for nighttime beach patrols for sea turtles. Lightweight and quick-dry long pants and long-sleeved shirts can be lifesavers in buggy jungle environments. A waterproof jacket or poncho is handy anywhere that rain threatens. If you will be staying in the jungle or on the beach, buy some biodegradable shampoo and soap, and environmentally friendly insect repellent and sunscreen. Bring a high-quality water bottle, such as a stainless-steel model that keeps water cool even if you leave it in the sun (and avoids increasing plastic waste). You may want to bring earplugs and Pepto-Bismol (the latter is available in some pharmacies in Latin America; the generic version is called bismuth), and a pair of flip-flops to wear into the shower. A few sites require that you bring your own sleeping bag. Be absolutely sure to bring a hat.

How to Volunteer

► TYPE OF WORK

Think about the type of work you want to do. Do you like working with people? Do you enjoy taking care of children? Are you passionate about women's rights? Is working with animals where your heart lies? If interacting with local community members and practicing foreign-language skills are priorities, you may want to put projects that benefit people at the top of your list. Many of the organizations in this guide offer a holistic approach to development, and as such, their work falls into multiple categories.

Development projects should aim to leave the beneficiary—whether an individual or a community—better equipped to confront the challenges than before. (Consider the adage of teaching someone to fish, rather than giving someone a fish for one day.) When working on a development project, it is important to bear in mind that many are ongoing efforts to address large problems, and volunteers must be able to accept that their efforts are "a drop in the bucket," or rather, a step forward along the development journey.

Agriculture

Agricultural work might be on a rural community farming or permaculture project. The best of these projects include local outreach—such as demonstration farms and educational workshops in schools—that support a community-wide change in thinking about agriculture.

Children and Youth

Volunteers might work with kids at an

Volunteers can participate in sports programs for marginalized youth.

Questions to Ask Yourself

Identifying the right experience depends greatly on knowing yourself and your own expectations. One volunteer told me she selected an organization precisely because it didn't seem structured – for others that would be a reason to run away. Here are a few questions to consider.

What are my top expectations?

Do you expect to change the world, or change yourself? Do you need to see a job get completed during your stay, or is it enough to know that your efforts are a drop in the bucket? Will you be crushed if you don't hear a thank you from the beneficiary of your efforts, or will it be enough to hear it from the organization hosting you? All of the organizations listed in this book are doing something worthwhile, but the best project for you will depend on your goals.

How much time do I have, and how much of it do I want to spend working?

Even if you only have one week and really want to spend some of it lazing on the beach or studying Spanish, there are volunteer opportunities available– some for as little as one day.

How far out of my comfort zone do I want to go?

Do you want to stay in a comfortable hotel and just visit the project during the day? Will you be at ease visiting a marginalized neighborhood? Do you want to find a placement where English is the primary language of communication, or can you cope with language barriers? Do you need to be somewhere with Internet access and cell phone coverage, or can you live without them?

What else do I want from this trip?

Do you want Spanish or salsa lessons, or just nature walks and time to read a book? Do you want to meet and socialize with other volunteers, or would you prefer to be the only international around? If you want to maximize your interactions with the local community, programs that offer homestays are a good choice. Those hoping to enjoy some of Latin America's famous sunshine need to be sure to check the season of their would-be destination.

How much structure do I prefer?

This applies to your volunteer work as well as your free time. Generally speaking, the larger agencies with programs in multiple countries offer greater structure (and consequently have higher fees). This may include language lessons, cultural outings, field trips, and other benefits that are well worth the fees, but you may prefer to organize such things on your own. Likewise, smaller organizations may have more flexibility in the type of volunteering they offer, tailoring it to the skills and interests of the individual volunteer, but they may also require significant initiative and resourcefulness on the part of the volunteer in order to maximize the experience.

What expectations do I have of the community where I will be working?

Will you be comfortable if you work with a community that has different gender roles and hygienic standards than what you are used to? Will local community members work side by side with your at your project, and if not, will that be okay with you?

What expectations do I have of myself?

What do you expect to have contributed to the local community through your volunteer efforts? Do you want to improve your Spanish (or Portuguese, or Quechua) language skills, and if so, will the volunteer opportunities you are considering and accommodation options you are considering lend themselves to that? How will you share your experience with others in order to maximize your impact?

orphanage or nursery, tutor teens in English or math, or organize sports activities for at-risk youth. The most effective child care centers are those that provide a quality education that prepares the children and youth for an economically viable future, and engaging alternatives to the temptations of drugs and gangs.

Community Development

This broad category includes everything from installing solar panels at a health clinic or water catchment systems at a school and training firefighters in emergency response to supporting the administration of microcredit programs. For those who prefer a tangible sign of progress, projects in the area of construction—from installing a better stove to building a house—may be especially satisfying.

Education

Educational programs range from lending a hand at an elementary school to teaching English to adults in order to improve their job opportunities. Volunteers might provide vocational training or health and hygiene education through workshops, or tutor struggling students at an after-school program.

Environment

Environmental projects may have volunteers working in an office preparing educational materials, outside creating trails (or recycling, or picking up trash, or planting and tending flora), or in schools or neighborhood centers providing community outreach. In a context where putting food on the table is a more urgent need than care of the environment for many families, volunteers should look for projects that combine community outreach and education with their efforts and know that their presence can help draw attention to an area that might have been overlooked by the local community in the past.

Volunteers can support women's weaving cooperatives in Peru or Guatemala.

Health

While opportunities abound for specialized skills, from first-aid training to heart surgery, you don't necessarily need to be a medical professional to assist in a community health clinic or public hospital. Volunteers may be able to help organize workshops, assist medical staff, provide translation skills, or raise awareness on issues such as HIV/AIDS.

Wildlife Protection

Volunteers can choose from activities such as protecting turtle hatchlings on their journey from nest to sea, supporting the rehabilitation of injured and trafficked animals, or restoring natural habitats for endangered species. Not all wildlife protection projects allow volunteers to work with their animals; work may instead be focused on the cleaning of cages, restoration of natural habitats, or visual monitoring of animal activity in the wild. Programs that help develop alternative sources of income generation for the community are especially interesting, turning many "wildlife protection" projects into a combination of environment, education, and community development.

Women's Empowerment

Volunteer opportunities that focus on women might include promoting associations of artisan weavers or supporting workshops on everything from civil rights to home finances. According to UN Women, "there is a direct link between increased female labor participation and growth," and World Bank studies demonstrate that women are more likely than men to spend their income on food and education for their children, making investments in women a critical part of development.

▶ CHOOSING AN ORGANIZATION

While all volunteer organizations have something positive to offer the community that they aim to serve, the programs offered, as well as the organizational structure and style, cover a wide spectrum. Large or small, highly organized or more flexible, grassroots or government sponsored, the variety of organizations is as great as the variety of volunteers. Whether you are a student or a retiree, a single or a family, a free spirit or someone who prefers structure, you can find a volunteer opportunity to meet your expectations.

In addition to asking yourself questions about what you want from this experience, you will need to ask the organizations that interest you plenty of questions to make sure you are getting what you want. Once you've narrowed your choices down, look for volunteer testimonials on their websites. If there aren't any, ask for the contact information of a former volunteer or two. Search online for other volunteer comments or reviews about the organizations, in particular comments that sound authentic and feedback that is voiced multiple times.

No matter which organization you select, remember that a spirit of adventure is required when you step off the beaten path in international travel. If the work or the organization isn't quite what you expected, do your best to remedy the situation rather than stewing in silence. Speak with your volunteer work supervisor and show initiative at your worksite in finding helpful activities that do fit your expectations. In extreme cases, a few volunteer placement agencies are able to reassign unhappy volunteers. If you've done your homework and have evaluated both the organization and your own expectations closely, you will find the experience rewarding.

The indigenous people of Latin America are among the most marginalized.

How Much Will It Cost?

Many organizations welcome volunteers and do not charge any fees—and in these cases, the volunteer is almost always then responsible for his or her expenses. Some volunteer organizations ask for a small fee in order to offset the staff time spent on organizing volunteer placements or to provide a donation to the project. A larger fee may cover many of your expenses, such as accommodations and meals, or other benefits such as Spanish lessons, dance classes, or even surf lessons. Look carefully at any fees and be sure to understand what they cover. Some organizations have hefty fees that represent significant contributions to the local community, such as solar panels, construction materials for a smokeless oven or a new house, or a tank for a water catchment system.

Other expenses to consider:

- airfare
- any in-country travel (Will you need a bus ride, taxi, or domestic flight upon arrival to reach your final destination? Will you need daily local transportation to reach your volunteer site?)
- Internet access (if not included at the volunteer site or accommodation)
- special equipment (Are you expected to bring a sleeping bag? Will you need closed-toed sandals?)
- travel insurance (If you have homeowners or renters insurance, check to see if it covers theft away from home. If you have medical insurance, does it cover travel abroad?)

LITTLE OR NO FEE

Budget travelers are often drawn to volunteer opportunities that are arranged directly with the volunteer site for little or no fee. However, these organizations often do not provide accommodations or meals. Be sure to estimate *all* your expenses—including travel, lodging, and food—when comparing the cost of volunteer opportunities. Organizations that do not cover these expenses for their volunteers should be able to provide an estimate

Volunteers with Special Skills

Professionals and students with specialized training, such as nurses, EMTs, doctors, and engineers, can find opportunities that capitalize on their skills and experience.

ENGINEERS
Engineers Without Borders (U.S. tel. 303/772-2723, www.ewb-usa.org) has active branches in many countries around the world. Water engineers in particular are in hot demand in Latin America.
Locations: Belize, Bolivia, Brazil, Ecuador, El Salvador, Guatemala, Honduras, Mexico, Nicaragua, Panama, Paraguay, Peru

MEDICAL PROFESSIONALS
Short-term medical brigades support underserved and often remote communities to provide general health care or specialty care, such as heart surgeries or repairing cleft palates, during one-week stays in a large city. Independent volunteers with more time might consider working at a public hospital or a community health clinic. Those wishing to be part of a brigade should contact:

Doctors Without Borders/Médecins Sans Frontières (www.doctorswithoutborders.org) does not generally utilize short-term volunteers, but it does recruit medical and nonmedical aid workers for paid positions in some 60 countries (minimum commitment 9-12 months). Surgeons, anesthesiologists, nurse anesthetists, and OB/GYNs may be accepted for shorter assignments. At the time of this writing, anesthesiologists, HIV/AIDS and TB specialists, nurse-midwives and certified midwives, and pharmacists were urgently needed.

Foundation for International Medical Relief for Children (FIMRC) (toll-free U.S. tel. 888/211-8575, www.fimrc.org) provides volunteers through innovative and self-sustainable programs, including clinical services, community outreach, and health education.
Locations: Costa Rica, El Salvador, Nicaragua, Peru

Project Hope (toll-free U.S. tel. 800/544-HOPE, www.projecthope.org) offers health care and education through ship-based care in partnership with the U.S. Navy, as well as through land-based missions.
Locations: Colombia, Costa Rica, Ecuador, El Salvador, Guatemala, Guyana, Honduras, Mexico, Nicaragua, Panama, Peru, Suriname

Volunteer Optometric Services to Humanity (www.vosh.org) provides eye exams and eyeglasses, and is working to eliminate preventable blindness.
Locations: Belize, Colombia, Costa Rica, El Salvador, Guatemala, Guyana, Honduras, Mexico, Nicaragua, Paraguay, Peru

STUDENTS
Global Brigades (www.globalbrigades.org) facilitates university students in the areas of architecture, business, dental, environmental, human rights, medicine, microfinance, public health, and water. There are 646 chapters in universities across the United States, as well as chapters in Canada, the United Kingdom, Ireland, Germany, and Switzerland.

VETERINARIANS
Vets can train local communities on animal health care, deliver vaccinations, or educate families about food production, nutrition, husbandry, and disease control. The following specialized organizations offer short-term missions:

Christian Veterinary Mission (Canadian tel. 250/590-3340, www.cvmusa.org)
Locations: Costa Rica, Honduras, Nicaragua

Veterinarians Without Borders (U.S. tel. 206/546-7569, www.vetswithoutborders.ca)
Locations: Chile, Guatemala

World Vets (toll-free U.S. tel. 877/688-8387, www.worldvets.org)
Locations: Belize, Colombia, Costa Rica, Ecuador, El Salvador, Guatemala, Guyana, Honduras, Nicaragua, Panama, Paraguay, Peru, Suriname

of transportation costs, lodging, and a meal in a restaurant; sometimes this is detailed on their website.

LARGER FEE-BASED ORGANIZATIONS

Larger organizations offer quite a bit more for a higher fee—accommodations and meals are usually included. Other benefits may be language lessons, salsa classes, movie nights, cultural excursions, and in-person support if the volunteer experience isn't going as you had hoped. Organizations with volunteer sites in more than one country often have the highest fees, but these often include a financial contribution to the volunteer project. If so, ask how much that is—not only will it be a good indicator of project transparency (no organization should be reluctant to tell you the amount if they claim to make a donation), but it will also be the easiest portion of your costs to ask friends and family to help contribute toward.

FUNDRAISING

After completing your budget estimate, think about where that money is going to come from. Determine how much of your volunteer fees go directly to the project and set that amount as your fundraising goal. In addition to saving up, there are a few more ways to put together the cash for your trip.

- In lieu of gifts, ask for a donation. If your birthday or a gift-giving holiday (Hanukkah or Christmas) falls before your departure date, consider asking friends and family to donate to your trip rather than buy a present.

- Host a fundraising event. Throw a dinner or party and ask guests to make a contribution toward your fundraising goal; you can even theme your event with food and music from the host country. Volunteer groups can organize larger events, such as a walkathon, a silent auction, a bake sale, or a car wash.

- Find a grant. Go Overseas (www.gooverseas.com) offers four US$1,000 scholarships per year for volunteer travel. Travelocity (www.travelocity.com) offers US$5,000 grants (one per quarter) to be applied to a voluntourism trip with one of their partner organizations.

- Raise funds online. Crowd-funding websites can help raise awareness about your trip while offering a way for friends and family to donate. All of the sites charge a small fee for their service and vary in the way they release funds. At VolunteerForever.com (www.volunteerforever.com), the funds you raise will be released to you, or your designated organization, even if they fall short of your goal.

How Long?

Perhaps you are a student with an entire summer at your disposal. Maybe you're a professional who has saved up enough vacation time to take a lengthy break for travel and volunteering. Then there are the rest of us, with commitments and obligations that don't permit long vacations. Rest assured, there are plenty of volunteer opportunities for those on tighter schedules.

Many organizations accept a commitment of one month or less from their volunteers (the minimum time commitment is listed for each). For organizations with "no minimum," volunteers can help out for as little as a few hours or one day. This can be especially appealing for people who want volunteering to be a part—rather than the sole focus—of their travels.

Questions to Ask an Organization

As important as knowing your own expectations is understanding how a volunteer opportunity is structured and what the organization is offering. The following are questions to ask an organization as you consider their volunteer opportunities.

What is the impact of this project?

Who determined the need for it: Was it a community request, or was it decided by the organization? If the latter, on what basis did they come to this decision? If it is a construction project such as a school or hospital, are there others in the area? If the project provides medical care, what other options do community members have? Does the local community support this project? (If so, how? If not, why not?)

What does the program fee cover?

A fee is not a bad thing in and of itself, and a small fee may simply cover the administrative cost of the placement. If any portion of the fee is deemed a contribution to the project, ask how much. For larger fees, ask for a breakdown of where the money goes – the organization you volunteer with should be transparent and should be able to provide this information.

While placement agencies and international organizations have administrative costs (covering staff time, advertising, and having an office), comparing this between organizations will help give you an idea of what is a reasonable expense and what might be extravagant.

What level of language skills do I need to really enjoy this project?

If your Spanish (or Portuguese) skills are little to none, read between the lines in their response. Will there be any translator nearby? On the other hand, if one of your goals is to improve your language skills, does the volunteer experience provide ample opportunity to do so?

What resources are there in-country for volunteers?

Is there a number you can call 24/7 if you need assistance with anything? If traveling with an international organization, do they have a contact person based in-country as well?

You may want to ask about the average age of their volunteers. This is also the time to ask if the organization can accommodate any special needs, such as a vegetarian diet or physical limitations.

ProWorld volunteers and local community members build a preschool in Agua Dulce, Peru.

MEXICO

Sharing its northern border with the United States, as well as Guatemala to the north and Belize to the south, Mexico is the Latin American country most visited by U.S. and Canadian citizens. Known officially as the United Mexican States, the 31 states that make up the country are home to a wealth of natural resources, a wide diversity of climates and ecologies, stunning Spanish colonial cities, endless sandy beaches, ancient Aztec pyramids and Mayan temples, rich indigenous culture, and plenty of volunteer opportunities for adventurous travelers.

With an estimated 113 million residents, Mexico is large both demographically as well as geographically, and it is the most-populous Spanish-speaking country. Mexico's rich culture includes more than 60 indigenous groups (with a population of more than 10 million, nearly 10 percent of the total population). The two largest and perhaps best-known indigenous groups are the Nauhatl (descendants of the Aztec) and the Maya, and the history of both groups lives on today in the form of towering pyramids and complex ruins. Yet despite a relatively high income (the World Bank calculates the gross national income at US$9,240 per capita), more than 50 percent of the population lives in poverty—a heartbreaking amount of people living with very little.

For those who prefer to volunteer independently through local organizations, there are opportunities to work with children (in day cares or orphanages), to work in medical clinics

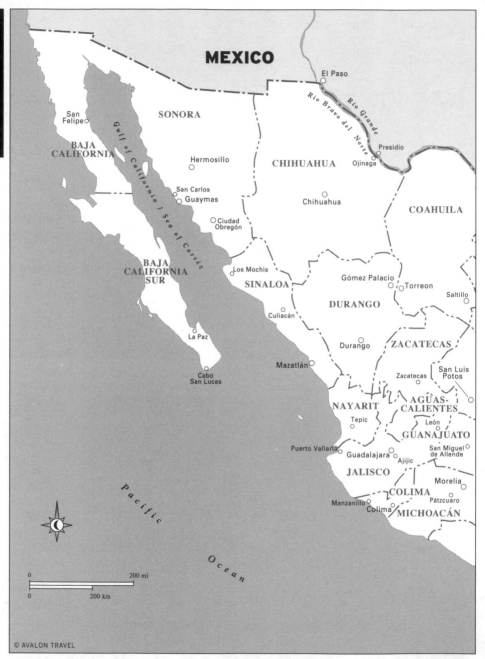

© AVALON TRAVEL

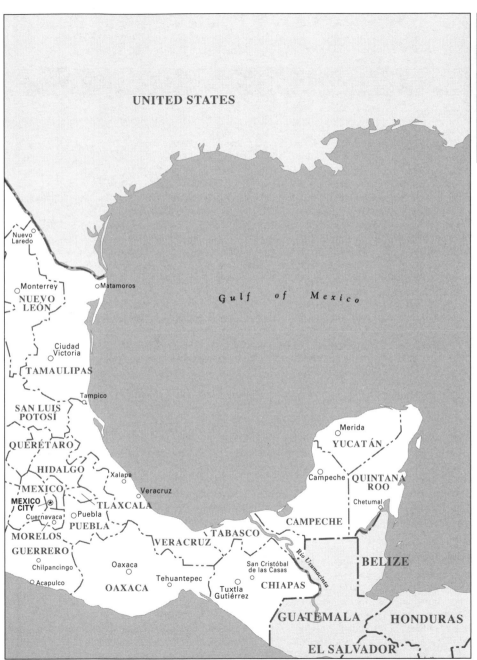

or conduct health workshops, and to work in botanical gardens or permaculture farms. There are also excellent volunteer placements available through international organizations (see listings in the *International Organizations* chapter).

Local Organizations

BECARI
Oaxaca, tel. 52/951-516-4634, www.becariqr.com
TYPE OF WORK: children and youth, education, health

Becari is a Spanish school in Oaxaca that places volunteers with six different organizations in Oaxaca (additionally, Becari has an agreement with the volunteer organization Oaxaca Streetchildren Grassroots). Volunteer work is mostly to support children in a variety of settings, from working in a preschool to supporting the "Teletón," which raises funds for children with cancer and disabilities. They also place volunteers in a health-focused nonprofit dedicated to the eradication of malnutrition.

During their free time, volunteers can study Spanish at Becari. Courses start at US$150 per week for 20 hours of group classes, and volunteers receive a 10 percent discount on their course. (It is not required to take a Spanish course in order to volunteer through Becari.)

The city of Oaxaca is home to lovely colonial buildings, Zapotec and Mixtec archaeological sites, museums, markets, parks, and gardens. Together with the archaeological site of Monte Albán, Oaxaca was named a World Heritage Site in 1987.

Application Process: An application form is available online.

Cost: Becari's registration fee is US$70, which is donated to the organization where volunteers are placed.

Placement Length: There is a minimum placement of one week.

Language Requirements: Varies by placement, but there are some programs available that do not require Spanish.

Housing: Becari can arrange for homestays (US$18/night) with 1-3 meals per day. They can also arrange for hotels and apartment rentals.

Operating Since: 1992

Number of Volunteers: 50 in 2012

CASA DE LOS ÁNGELES
San Miguel de Allende, tel. 52/415-154-0720, www.casadelosangeles.org
TYPE OF WORK: children and youth, education

Casa de los Ángeles was originally founded as a free day care center for children whose mothers work in San Miguel de Allende. It has since grown to include medical care for families, a food bank, and scholarship opportunities, as well as serving as a health clinic and a transitional shelter for poor families. At the time of this writing, the organization served 95 children.

Volunteers are assigned to particular areas at the day care: in the classroom, in the kitchen or babies' room, working one-on-one with a disabled child, or working with older children who come before or after school. Responsibilities include playing with the children, teaching arts and crafts, feeding babies and changing their clothes, and organizing field trips. Occasionally volunteers have the opportunity to help with other projects taking place during their stay, such as construction, painting, or fundraising events. Volunteers are asked to work full-time; however, there is flexibility to work mornings (9:30am-12:30pm) or afternoons (1:30pm-3:30pm) only with a long-term commitment.

Casa de los Ángeles is located in the beautiful city of San Miguel de Allende, in central Mexico. Tourists flock here for the centuries-old buildings of the well-preserved historic center, which, together with the nearby Sanctuary of Atotonilco, have been declared

VOLUNTEER PERSPECTIVE

Ariana Alvarez (age 19) is a student at Saint Mary's College of California in Moraga, California. She had this to say about her volunteer experience with the day care center **Casa de los Ángeles** (tel. 52/415-154-0720, www.casadelosangeles.org) in picturesque San Miguel de Allende, Mexico.

Before coming to volunteer at Casa de los Ángeles, I would have never imagined how blessed, humbled, and content I would feel by the end of my time there. Being greeted every morning by gorgeous smiles and tiny hands reaching for hugs was such a treasure. The mothers of Casa de los Ángeles have overcome domestic violence, economic hardships, and multiple other issues as they fight to put food on the table every day, all while raising beautiful children and learning to be strong and independent women. Being granted the opportunity to see, firsthand, how hard these women fight has inspired me as a woman. The children and mothers of Casa de los Ángeles shed a light of hope and happiness onto all who cross their path. My lens on life has been altered: I have grown to see that nothing is impossible, everyone deserves a chance, and that when one is doing good, one's actions will always be repaid (and little kisses, smiles, and hugs are the best repayment, if I say so myself). Every child I met at the center was a testament to the fact that one does not need great riches to be happy; being willing to give your time and get to know someone personally, sharing a laugh, and just being genuine has proved to be more than enough.

© DONNA QUATHAMER

A young boy enjoys his time at Casa de los Ángeles day care.

a World Heritage Site. The beauty of the town, its mild climate, and its low crime rates also attract a significant number of U.S. and Canadian retirees. There are plenty of cafés and restaurants, not to mention Spanish-language schools, where volunteers can spend their free time.

Application Process: Send an email to request an application form. Volunteers under age 18 must be accompanied by a parent or chaperone. Families with children old enough to help volunteer are welcome.

Cost: US$50 application fee. Accommodations are US$160/week or US$500/month (some meals included), and part of the accommodation fee benefits the program. Volunteers can also make their own living arrangements.

Casa de los Ángeles can arrange a pickup from the León airport for US$75 (up to three people).

Placement Length: Placement length is flexible. While volunteers who can stay a few weeks or more are especially appreciated, other volunteer placements have ranged from a few days to one year.

Language Requirements: Spanish skills are beneficial but not required. Casa de los Ángeles has hosted many English-only volunteers in the past and can help connect volunteers with Spanish classes and tutors.

Housing: Volunteers stay in a lovely 12-bed guesthouse (with a kitchen and wireless Internet) close to the city center and about one mile from the day care. (Beds in the guesthouse can fill up in advance, so best to apply early!) Breakfast and lunch are provided to volunteers at the day care on weekdays.

Operating Since: 2000

Number of Volunteers: approximately 150 in 2012

EN VÍA FOUNDATION

Oaxaca, tel. 52/951-515-2424, www.envia.org

TYPE OF WORK: children and youth, community development, education, women's empowerment

En Vía Foundation is "a non-profit organization working to fight poverty in Oaxaca, Mexico, by combining interest-free microloans, educational programs, and sustainable tourism." Their microloan program supports the creation or expansion of small businesses by women, their educational programs equip these women with financial knowledge, and their tourism program funnels resources into the community in a sustainable way while educating travelers about the power of microlending.

Volunteers are needed to teach English to women and children in small villages near Oaxaca. Many work in the town of Teotitlán del Valle, a small village 30 kilometers (19 mi) from Oaxaca known for its handwoven textiles. Volunteers may also be placed in Tlacochahuaya, Abasolo, Santo Domingo Tomaltepec, or Diaz Ordaz. Travel to these villages is by public bus (at the volunteer's expense), and the ride may take up to one hour.

En Vía provides training and support, so no previous teaching experience is required. Volunteers are expected to work on Tuesday and Thursday (9am-2pm or 2pm-7pm). There are opportunities to become further involved with leadership, fundraising, recruitment, and more.

There is plenty to explore in the Spanish colonial city of Oaxaca, where volunteers usually stay, as well as in the surrounding villages. Volunteers who want to improve their Spanish receive a discount at Instituto Cultural Oaxaca, the largest Spanish school in Oaxaca.

Application Process: Send an email with your résumé and a cover letter.

Cost: None. Volunteers are responsible for their own expenses.

Placement Length: Two days per week for a minimum of one month.

Language Requirements: No language requirement to teach English. Advanced to fluent Spanish is required for most of the other volunteer work.

Housing: En Vía can help volunteers find a hostel, apartment, or homestay.

Operating Since: 2010

Number of Volunteers: 54 in 2012

NATATÉ

San Cristobal de las Casas, tel. 52/967-631-6918, www.natate.org

TYPE OF WORK: agriculture, children and youth, community development, education, environment, health, wildlife protection

Nataté was founded by a group of Mexican and international volunteers interested in fostering development and peace in the state of Chiapas. The organization promotes voluntary service, intercultural learning, youth development and education, ecological and sustainable lifestyles, empowerment of minorities and the marginalized, and human rights. In addition to coordinating volunteer placements and brigades, Nataté also reaches out to local communities with training and seminars, community development and capacity building projects, and information and awareness-raising campaigns.

Nataté offers 2- to 3-week work camps, as well as midlength (1-6 months) and long-term (6-12 months) volunteer placements. Work camps are scheduled six months or so in advance. Volunteers work 30-35 hours per week. Meals are provided; volunteers work in small teams to prepare food and clean up after meals. At the time of this writing, scheduled camps included:

- working at a shelter for abandoned and mistreated dogs and cats

- creating a vegetable garden and henhouse

- providing cultural and educational activities for a group of disabled youth

- developing an urban permaculture demonstration center

- maintaining and improving an educational park dedicated to the protection, conservation, and exhibition of the flora and fauna of Chiapas

- supporting a rural cooperative dedicated to sustainable living by building cabins, learning about permaculture, and engaging in crafts like soapmaking

- supporting a two-week "Cinema with Meaning" event focused on recycling, where

volunteers participate in and lead community outreach and educational events

San Cristobal de las Casas is based in the state of Chiapas in southern Mexico. This is one of Mexico's best-preserved Spanish colonial towns, with an artsy vibe, theaters, coffeehouses, and hip bars. It is also home to a very significant indigenous presence, which makes it easy to visit small indigenous towns nearby (either independently or with a tour).

Those wishing to brush up on their language skills can study Spanish at La Casa en el Árbol (US$120 for 15 hours of group study in a week). Volunteers interested in traveling farther afield on the weekend might head to the famed Mayan ruins of Palenque.

Application Process: An application form is available online. Individual volunteers are usually age 18 or older; children age 12 and older are welcome as part of a work team. Families traveling with children of any age are always welcome.

Cost: US$233, including meals, basic accommodations, and project-related local transportation.

Placement Length: There is a minimum placement of two weeks.

Language Requirements: No language requirement for work camps; some Spanish may be required for certain mid- to long-term opportunities.

Housing: Basic, shared accommodations are provided, typically mattresses and sleeping bags in a school, house, or tent.

Operating Since: 2006

Number of Volunteers: 109 work camp volunteers in 2012; 62 mid- to long-term volunteers

OAXACA STREETCHILDREN GRASSROOTS

Oaxaca, tel. 52/951-501-1069, U.S. tel. 501/574-9040, www.oaxacastreetchildrengrassroots.org

TYPE OF WORK: children and youth, education

Oaxaca Streetchildren Grassroots was founded by an American couple who loved vacationing in Oaxaca but wanted to respond to the difficulties faced by many local children. They informally began a child sponsorship program, which eventually solidified into a children's charity that has continued since the founders' passing. The organization now supports more than 600 children, offering education, meals, medical care, and any other necessary support to "Oaxacan children living in extreme poverty."

Short-term volunteers may help out in the kitchen or the library, work with children in the computer lab, translate letters from Spanish to English, or work with children on art or other projects. In addition to these tasks, long-term volunteers may also help fundraise or reach out to beneficiary families.

Oaxaca is located in central Mexico and is famed for its silver and its beautiful colonial buildings. In addition to exploring the city, volunteers can study Spanish in their free time. The Spanish school Becari Q.R. offers a 10 percent discount on classes (from US$150/week), and the US$70 inscription fee is donated to Oaxaca Streetchildren Grassroots.

Application Process: There is a simple online form to initiate the application. Families are welcome.

Cost: None. Volunteers are responsible for their own expenses.

Placement Length: No minimum.

Language Requirements: Spanish language skills are always helpful but are not required. They have had many successful English-only volunteers.

Housing: Volunteers make their own arrangements. Volunteers may receive a 10 percent discount on homestays at a local Spanish school, Becari Q.R. (from US$18/night, including breakfast).

Operating Since: 1996
Number of Volunteers: 98 in 2012

RED SUSTAINABLE TRAVEL

Baja California, tel. 52/612-125-7824,
www.redtravelmexico.com

TYPE OF WORK: environment, wildlife protection

RED takes conservation projects and turns them into "Conservation Adventures." By incorporating economic alternatives for local communities in its efforts, RED promotes "a model of tourism for the region based on natural resource preservation." Volunteer trips encompass "ecotourism, community development, conservation, and true cultural interaction." Projects are located in four communities in Baja California (there is a fifth community near Mazatlán), all created in partnership with several locally based conservation organizations.

There are typically 6-16 volunteers per trip. Volunteers are taken to Magdalena Bay in Baja California, where they spend their days either on the beach or on a guided nature walk, and two nights monitoring black sea turtles. A slightly longer trip might include kayaking or whale-watching. Trips can also be customized for groups of middle or high school students. The project location is remote (part of the local travel is by boat); there is limited cell phone service and no Internet access.

Trips sell out well in advance. In early 2013, *National Geographic Adventure* magazine named RED Sustainable Travel one of "10 Great Adventures that Give Back," so they will likely grow in popularity. Plan this one well ahead of time.

Application Process: Contact RED (see website for details) to apply and receive an application form. A 20 percent deposit is required with the application. There is no minimum age; RED offers custom trips for families.

Cost: US$650 for three days, US$1,100 for a five-day trip with kayaking, and US$1,400 for a five-day trip with whale-watching. Prices include accommodations, meals, local transportation, and a 3 percent donation to RED's community conservation fund. Children under age 11 receive a 30 percent discount with a paying adult.

Placement Length: 3-5 days (3-7 for youth trips)

Language Requirements: None.

Housing: Volunteers stay right on the beach, in tents with mattresses and linens. Gourmet meals are included, with an emphasis on seafood. There are well-maintained dry composting toilets, and volunteers are given buckets of hot water to use in the shower facility.

Operating Since: 2009

Number of Volunteers: 85 in 2012

SEXTO SOL CENTER FOR COMMUNITY ACTION

Motozintla, Sierra Madre, Chiapas, www.sextosol.org

TYPE OF WORK: agriculture, community development, education, environment, health

Sexto Sol Center for Community Action (SSCCA) is named for the Sixth Sun of the Mayan calendar, a time of justice and emancipation of indigenous peoples. SSCCA "contributes to the elimination of poverty and the restoration of the damaged environment by promoting cooperative enterprise, environmentally sound agriculture, appropriate technology and conservation." They work in the Sierra Madre region of Chiapas, as well as across the southern border, supporting repatriated refugees in Guatemala. The organization assists with the creation of cooperative businesses, helps grow healthy food, improves neglected schools, protects the watershed, creates ecovillages, and helps community members heal from the trauma of armed conflict. SSCCA also advocates internationally for the respect of indigenous human rights and for environmental and economic justice.

Escuela de Agroecología y Permacultura Tierra Linda is its permaculture school, located in a mountainous region where subsistence farmers tend to plant only corn or beans and where malnutrition is widespread. The demonstration farm teaches people that, on a relatively small parcel, one can produce a variety of crops for a good diet. It is possible to grow food using soil-building techniques and other principles of permaculture even in places where deforestation has damaged the land. Tierra Linda is also the location of the founders' office and home. Sitting on a steep ridge above the city of Motozintla, Terra Linda has a spectacular view of the Sierra Madre and plenty of sunshine.

Sexto Sol tends to have more interested volunteers than space available, and it is better able to place volunteers closer to their travel dates rather than many months out as volunteer needs change. At the time of this writing, SSCCA was looking for volunteers to:

- help with permaculture and gardening work
- assist with online tech support
- install bottle lights in dark schools
- harvest coffee at a collective coffee farm in Guatemala
- train service and kitchen staff at a newly established ecolodge
- help with a future project for an ecovillage in Guatemala

They were also looking for someone with experience with rocket stoves to heat schools.

Motozintla is a quiet town. Volunteers can use their free time to read, study, or socialize. On the weekend, the surrounding mountains make a great day-trip destination. Volunteers are asked to abstain from drugs, alcohol, and cigarettes while at Tierra Linda, and to dress appropriately for rural Mexico.

Application Process: Send an email, noting availability, skills (including level of Spanish, if any), and interests. Volunteers must have finished high school and be able to travel independently. At the time of this writing, they were unable to accommodate families but hope to do so in the future.

Cost: None. Volunteers are responsible for their own expenses.

Placement Length: There is a minimum placement of one week.

Language Requirements: Depends on the work, but usually Spanish is not required for most tasks.

Housing: Accommodations are available at the Tierra Linda farm for a small donation and include a studio apartment with a shared bathroom. Volunteers must purchase their own groceries and prepare their own meals.

Operating Since: 1997

Number of Volunteers: eight in 2012

SOLIDARIDAD INTERNACIONAL KANDA A.C. (SIKANDA)

Oaxaca, tel. 52/951-201-4992, www.si-kanda.org

TYPE OF WORK: agriculture, children and youth, community development, education, environment, health

SiKanda's mission is "to facilitate and manage participatory processes of balanced and sustainable development in order to improve the quality of life in Mexico and other countries." Volunteer opportunities depend on the amount of time a volunteer can commit. Those with just a day or a week can help out at the earthworm farm or lend a hand in the gardens of the organic farm. Responsibilities include feeding the earthworms, watering the worm beds, collecting organic fertilizer, building vegetable gardens, preparing the soil with compost, planting and thinning, controlling pests, tilling the soil, and harvesting the vegetable gardens.

Those with a bit more time can get involved with the sale of the organic fertilizer, work as an agricultural assistant, or lend their skills in graphic design. Long-term volunteers (three months or more) can delve deeper into SiKanda's other projects, such as working with families who live at the city dump in the provision of economic alternatives and reduction of health risks, or working with high school students to raise awareness about the situation of the dump workers.

SiKanda seeks to ensure that all volunteers have the chance to meet the groups and communities with whom they work (including school visits). With a location just five minutes' walk from the center of Oaxaca, SiKanda also offers volunteers plenty to do in their free time, from exploring the colonial buildings and cafés to studying Spanish.

Application Process: Contact SiKanda via email to apply. Volunteers must be age 18 or older.

Cost: None. Volunteers are responsible for their own expenses.

Placement Length: Ranges from a one-day minimum (at the worm farm) up to one month or more at other placements.

Language Requirements: Basic to advanced Spanish is required, depending on the placement.

Housing: Volunteers are responsible for their own arrangements and expenses. SiKanda estimates local living costs as follows: rent US$160-240/month; food US$65-280/month; transport US$0.45 per bus ride or US$80 to buy a used bike; US$20 for a prepaid Mexican cell phone.

Operating Since: 2009

Number of Volunteers: seven in 2012

VOLUNTARIOS INTERNACIONALES MEXICO A.C. (VIMEX)

Mexico City, tel. 52/55-5566-2774, www.vimex.org.mx, blanca@vimex.org.mx

TYPE OF WORK: children and youth, community development, education, environment, health, wildlife protection

Based in Mexico City, VIMEX is a nonprofit organization that places international volunteers with opportunities throughout Mexico and sends Mexican high school and university students to volunteer placements abroad. Its mission is to "promote global solidarity, tolerance and mutual understanding between different cultures and races through International Volunteer Workcamps" and to be able to "detect the necessities of our country in social, educative and environmental areas."

Within Mexico, VIMEX works with several different organizations (including Nataté; see listing in this chapter) to place volunteers everywhere from one-week work camps to permanent volunteer positions. Short-term work camps typically last two weeks, and project dates are set well in advance.

Projects include:

• working at a Montessori school in Cuernavaca

• supporting an environmental education center at Chapala Lake

INTERNATIONAL ORGANIZATIONS

The following international organizations support volunteer efforts in Mexico:

Amizade Global Service Learning (U.S. tel. 412/586-4986, www.amizade.org), page 194.
Type of Work: agriculture, children and youth, community development, education, environment, health

Elevate Destinations (U.S. tel. 617/661-0203, www.elevatedestinations.com), page 199.
Type of Work: children and youth, community development, education, environment, wildlife protection

Global Communities: Partners for Good (U.S. tel. 301/587-4700, www.globalcommunities.org), page 200.
Type of Work: children and youth, community development, education, environment, women's empowerment

Global Volunteers (toll-free U.S. tel. 800/487-1074, www.globalvolunteers.org), page 200.

Type of Work: children and youth, community development, education

Global Volunteers International (toll-free U.S. tel. 888/653-6028, www.gviusa.com), page 201.
Type of Work: children and youth, community development, education, environment, health, wildlife protection

International Volunteer HQ (IVHQ) (toll-free U.S. tel. 877/342-6588, www.volunteerhq.org), page 203.
Type of Work: agriculture, children and youth, community development, education, environment, health, wildlife protection

TECHO (U.S. tel. 305/860-4090, www.techo.org), page 209.
Type of Work: community development

Wanderland Travel (toll-free U.S. tel. 866/701-2113, www.wanderland.org), page 212.
Type of Work: agriculture, children and youth, community development, education, environment

---

- providing environmental workshops for a "Society of Solidarity" made up of 21 rural communities on the Oaxacan coast

- working in a girls' home in Chiapas or for an AIDS support organization in Mexico City

For volunteers who would like to improve their language skills, Spanish classes are available in Mexico City with VIMEX (US$210 for 15 hours of lessons; includes accommodations for five nights and one local excursion).
Application Process: There is an application form available online, or email Blanca Jimenez, Vice-President of VIMEX, at blanca@vimex.org.mx. VIMEX requires all volunteers to obtain international health insurance if their home policy does not provide overseas coverage.
Cost: US$230 for two weeks, including housing
Placement Length: Most work camps require two weeks. Note that many opportunities listed as "permanent" require a minimum commitment of one month, so cast a wide net if utilizing their website's search function.
Language Requirements: Varies by placement; there are some work camps that do not require any Spanish.
Housing: The majority of the organizations where volunteers are placed provide accommodations (usually in a dorm room or cabin) and food.
Operating Since: 1982
Number of Volunteers: 90 in 2012

Essentials

BACKGROUND
Geography and Climate
Mexico's 31 states cover a territory of 1,972,550 square kilometers (761,606 sq. mi), making it nearly three times the size of the state of Texas. As might be expected with a country this big, Mexico is a diverse hot spot. It is home to more than 200,000 species of flora and fauna (more than 10 percent of the world's biodiversity) and is ranked second in the world in number of ecosystems.

The Tropic of Cancer, at roughly the 24th parallel (just above Mexico City), effectively divides the country into temperate and tropical zones. Northern Mexico tends to be dry with sporadic rainfall and becomes cool in winter, getting downright cold at night. In southern Mexico, the climate varies more according to altitude. Many large inland Mexican cities are set in valleys above 2,000 meters (6,500 ft), with mild days and cool nights. The southern coasts and the Yucatan peninsula are the hottest areas, with a yearly median temperature of 24-28°C (75-82°F). These areas are also subject to hurricanes in the summer and fall.

History and Economy
Drawn by the quest for gold and riches, Hernán Cortés was the first Spaniard to land in Mexico, arriving in 1519. Cortés quickly dominated the Aztecs, in large part due to a smallpox epidemic that ravaged the Aztecs while the Spaniards were largely immune. Spanish colonization lasted until Mexico declared independence in 1810. A series of conflicts followed: the 1846 Mexican-American War border dispute, a military occupation by France in the 1860s, and the Mexican Revolution in 1910, in which the population rebelled against social inequality and political repression. While the country's economy has seen ups and downs since

then, the political scene has remained fairly stable.

Trade with the United States and Canada is crucial to Mexico's economy, accounting for nearly half of both exports and imports. Mexico has surpassed both the United States and Canada in automobile production. It is home to the largest Spanish media company in Latin America, and it is the sixth-largest oil producer in the world. Resources, however, are not equally distributed. Mexico has the second-highest degree of economic disparity between the extremely poor and extremely rich in the world.

PREPARATION
Transportation
Mexico is home to more than 100 airports, roughly half of which receive international flights. The largest airport is **Benito Juarez International Airport** (MEX, www.aicm.com.mx) in Mexico City. Volunteers can usually get fairly close to their final destination by air. Departure taxes are usually included in the cost of airline tickets and range US$18-29, depending upon the airport.

Bus service is comprehensive across the country, but it is not always the safest route. Travelers should check with their volunteer organization about bus safety in the area and avoid traveling between cities after dark.

Passports and Visas
U.S. citizens can no longer travel to Mexico with only a driver's license. Passports are required by all travelers, except Canadians, who can enter Mexico with an official photo ID and proof of citizenship (such as a birth certificate).

Citizens of the United States who are under 18 years old and are traveling to Mexico without legal guardians or *both* parents must have a signed, notarized letter from the parent(s) or guardians granting permission to leave the country.

Money

Mexico's currency is the **peso**. Bills are printed in denominations of $10, $20, $50, $100, $200, $500, and $1,000. Coins have a face value of $0.50, $1, $2, $5, or $10. At the time of this writing, the exchange rate was about 13 pesos to one U.S. dollar. The symbol for the peso is $, the same symbol as the U.S. dollar. If you are unsure whether the price refers to dollars or pesos, please ask. Dollars are often accepted in tourist areas or anywhere near the U.S. border.

Health

Health concerns vary widely depending on destinations within Mexico. Check with your doctor or local travel clinic about vaccinations. There are vaccinations for both malaria and dengue in the tropical and subtropical areas of Mexico (Chiapas; and in rural areas of the states of Nayarit, Oaxaca, and Sinaloa; as well as a few other areas). Bring insect repellent and see a doctor if you get a high fever or find yourself with flu-like symptoms.

Safety

Safety concerns vary significantly from state to state; within each state, it varies between urban and rural areas. Due to ongoing drug wars, security in Mexico can be volatile. Always check with your volunteer organization for the current security situation in any destination you plan to travel. The **U.S. Department of State** website (www.state.gov) maintains travel information for Mexico, broken down by state. Despite its former notoriety, Chiapas did not have any travel advisory in effect at the time of this writing, but many other states did. Wherever you go, avoid traveling by road at night.

GUATEMALA

Guatemala is part of Central America's "Northern Triangle"—bordered by Mexico to the north and the west, by the Pacific Ocean to the southwest, El Salvador and Honduras to the southeast, and Belize to the east. Studded by volcanoes, much of southern Guatemala is mountainous highlands, descending to a tropical environment along the Pacific coastline. The low-lying northern region of Petén is sparsely populated in juxtaposition with its history of thriving Mayan kingdoms, as evidenced by the ruins at Tikal, Yaxhá, Quiriguá, and elsewhere. Fourteen ecoregions with a wide assortment of rivers, swamps, forests, and lagoons make Guatemala a biodiversity hot spot, home to 1,246 known species of fauna and countless more species of flora.

Guatemala's population is just as diverse. Approximately more than 50 percent of the population is indigenous, composed of 21 distinct Maya groups speaking 20 or more different languages, with Spanish the second language for many. Guatemala's population of 15 million is the largest in Central America. Unfortunately, more than half of those people live in poverty (the World Bank estimates the gross national income per capita is US$2,870).

As a result, most of the volunteer organizations working in Guatemala are focused on people, with many opportunities to teach and care for children at schools and orphanages, provide medical services such as checkups and dental care, help families improve homes through new construction (or the installation of less-polluting stoves), or empower women

© AMY E. ROBERTSON

and preserve culture through the development of textile weaving projects. Those interested in conservation can teach environmental education to children or participate in the construction of green schools, built with recycled waste such as used tires and discarded bottles.

With the chance to explore colonial towns and extravagant crafts markets, hike volcanoes and lake ridges, and visit Mayan ruins or Pacific beaches, volunteers will find in Guatemala a unique combination of cultural immersion and local opportunities.

Local Organizations

AKAZUL: COMMUNITY, CONSERVATION & ECOLOGY

La Barrona, Jutiapa, U.K. tel. 7715/304-600, www.akazul.org

TYPE OF WORK: environment, wildlife protection

Akazul is a U.K.-registered not-for-profit Community Interest Company (CIC) whose mission is "to utilise Guatemala's sea turtles as a 'flagship' species, engaging coastal communities in conservation practices through science and education." La Barrona is a key nesting site in Guatemala for olive ridley and leatherback sea turtles. The name Akazul is inspired by the Maya. According to ancient myth, *Ak* was the "great cosmic turtle," which is the constellation known today as Orion. Orion's belt represents a crack in the cosmic turtle's shell, from where the "Hero Twins" emerged to create all life on earth. *Azul* is the Spanish word for blue, which represents the ocean, home to the greatest biodiversity on Earth.

Akazul monitors the nesting beach in order to better understand Guatemala's sea turtle populations and provides educational activities and community initiatives (such as a sea turtle festival) to encourage local support for conservation. Volunteer responsibilities include:

- nightly beach patrols (minimum four hours per night)
- data collection and monitoring of nesting sea turtles
- hatchery management activities such as egg burial, hatchling release, and posthatching nest excavations
- community-based conservation activities such as environmental education classes,

capacity building workshops, social surveys, and learning local skills

Volunteers are welcome to contact Akazul with potential project or research ideas prior to arrival. While volunteers will have plenty of opportunities to practice their Spanish, formal lessons are not available locally and instead should be taken in places like Antigua or Quetzaltenango (commonly referred to as Xela) prior to arrival. There is plenty in the village to keep you busy—fishing or boating the mangroves, learning how to make hammocks or tortillas, bird-watching, and playing soccer with locals.

Application Process: To apply, send an email requesting a volunteer guide and application form. Volunteers must be age 18 or older.

Cost: A US$50 registration fee is due prior to arrival, which is used to help cover administration fees and the cost of volunteer materials and project equipment. Volunteers are responsible for their own expenses.

Placement Length: The suggested minimum placement is four weeks, although shorter stays may be considered. Placements are available July-December only.

Language Requirements: Basic Spanish is highly recommended.

Housing: Volunteers may stay in rustic dorm-style bunks at the Akazul project building (US$40 per week; no meals included). The project building includes use of a kitchen, and volunteers usually cook their own meals on a rotating basis. Homestays can be arranged (US$10-15 per day; includes three meals daily). Accommodations have electricity but no hot water.

GUATEMALA

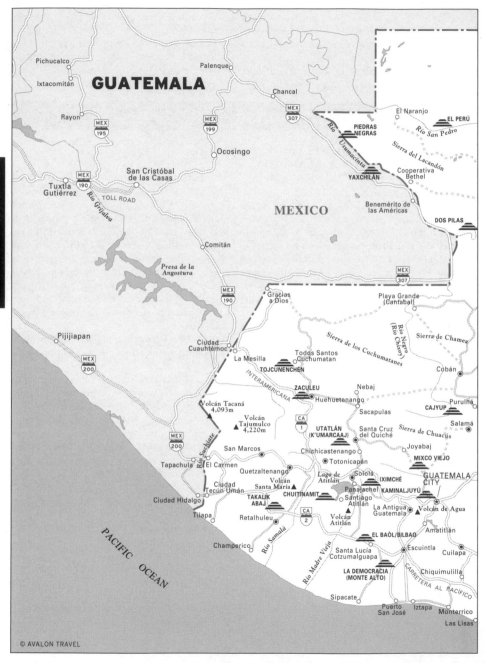

© AVALON TRAVEL

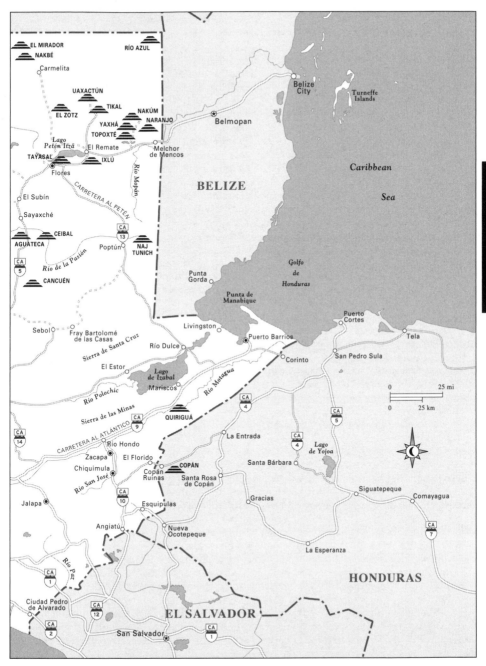

Operating Since: 2011
Number of Volunteers: approximately 20 in 2012

CASA GUATEMALA

Las Brisas, Río Dulce, tel. 502/2331-9408,
www.casa-guatemala.org, www.viajescasaguatemala.org
TYPE OF WORK: agriculture, children and youth, community development, education, health

Started by a Canadian couple in response to Guatemala's civil war, Casa Guatemala has provided a stable environment for disadvantaged children in Guatemala since the 1970's. Their mission is to provide a safe and loving home, along with adequate medical care and education, to Guatemalan children who are abused, abandoned, malnourished, or living in extreme poverty.

The primary center is in Las Brisas, 20 minutes from the town of Río Dulce, near the Caribbean coast of Guatemala, and is home to up to 250 children at a time. This is not your typical orphanage—in addition to housing, there is a primary school, medical clinic, library, carpentry shop, outdoor playing fields, a dining hall, and a farm. In an effort to move toward self-sustainability, Casa Guatemala operates both a hostel, Hotel Backpackers, and a butcher shop in Río Dulce.

Short-term volunteers are accommodated in the hostel and take a boat back and forth daily from Río Dulce to the orphanage. Volunteers typically work 7:30am-4pm and are involved in arts and crafts activities; reading with the children; helping in the library or kitchen; teaching English, computer, or PE classes; or working on maintenance projects on the farm. Those with a medical background can lend a hand at the center's clinic. Volunteers eat lunch with the kids and have the chance to play soccer or other games together.

Casa Guatemala is a few hours from the spectacular Mayan ruins of Tikal, Yaxhá, and Quiriguá. Volunteers can also tack on time for exploring nearby waterfalls, Garífuna villages, and nature reserves. While short-term volunteers pay for seven days of volunteering, it is possible to take one day off for nearby sightseeing as well. There is a Spanish school in Río Dulce, but volunteers typically help each other study rather than enroll in classes.

Application Process: An application form is available online. Short-term volunteers must be at least age 18; families are welcome as long-term volunteers.
Cost: US$250 per week
Placement Length: There is a minimum placement of one week.
Language Requirements: Basic Spanish is recommended but is not essential.
Housing: Accommodations and meals are included with the program fee. Short-term volunteers stay at the Hotel Backpackers in Río Dulce, where they have breakfast and dinner, while lunch is taken at the children's center.
Operating Since: 1977
Number of Volunteers: 45 short-term and 65 long-term in 2012

CONSTRU CASA

Antigua, tel. 502/7832-8348, www.construcasa.org
TYPE OF WORK: community development

Based in Antigua, Constru Casa seeks to provide basic, safe housing to families across Guatemala who live in extreme poverty. Similar to the model used by the international organization Habitat for Humanity, Constru Casa's recipients participate in the construction of their home and pay for a portion of it (roughly 25 percent) through an interest-free, four-year loan. The target beneficiaries are families whose income is US$65-270 per month. Volunteers and the home recipients work together under the supervision of a local mason to build a three-room, concrete and corrugated iron house in two weeks' time. Constru Casa also works with partners and individual families in a variety of support programs, such as helping with small-scale health care and educational projects, paying teacher salaries, offering improved stoves and water filters to beneficiary families, and carrying out home maintenance. They built or improved approximately 90 houses and community projects in 2012.

GUATEMALA

The town of Antigua, known for its cobblestone streets and colonial heritage, also offers many volunteer opportunities.

Volunteer workdays are 8am-5pm, with a break for lunch. Cultural experiences such as climbing a volcano, taking a tour to visit traditional weavers, visiting a coffee or macadamia nut farm, or making an excursion to Lake Atitlán can be organized for the weekend. The cost of weekend trips ranges from US$10 for a half-day excursion to US$45-250 for an overnight trip.

Antigua is a lovely historical town full of colonial churches and adobe-walled homes. Founded in the early 16th century, it was the capital of Guatemala until 1773. Locals flock to Antigua from Guatemala City on the weekends to walk its cobblestone streets, eat in its many restaurants and cafés, and shop for high-quality handicrafts. Although beautiful, Antigua still has some petty street crime, so volunteers should be careful with their personal belongings, avoid flashing expensive jewelry or electronics such as MP3 players, be discreet with their cameras, and avoid walking alone at night, especially on dark or quiet streets (taxis are inexpensive). When taking a hike or nature

walk outside of Antigua, it is recommended to go in groups rather than alone.

Application Process: To apply, send an email. Volunteer slots can fill up in advance, especially during busy times of the year. Individual volunteers must be at least age 18; those age 16 and 17 may volunteer with parental permission and an adult chaperone. Families with children age 13 and older are welcome.

Cost: Volunteers are asked to fundraise for the house they will work on: US$350 for individuals and US$4,000 for groups (which covers the entire cost of a house). There are no other program fees. Volunteers are responsible for their own expenses.

Placement Length: A minimum placement of at least two weeks is encouraged, in order to stay to see the house built.

Language Requirements: Spanish is useful but not required.

Housing: Constru Casa can arrange local accommodations, either in a homestay (US$90/week, meals included) or in a hostel or hotel (US$9/night and up). Volunteers who stay in a hostel or hotel are responsible for their own meals.

Operating Since: 2004
Number of Volunteers: approximately 220 in 2012

EL NAHUAL COMMUNITY CENTER

Quetzaltenango, 502/5606-1704,
www.languageselnahual.com

TYPE OF WORK: children and youth, community development, education

El Nahual is one of several Spanish schools in Quetzaltenango, but unlike the others, it is a nonprofit organization that is almost entirely staffed by volunteers. The language school provides the funding for its other projects, which focus on improving educational opportunities. Located on the outskirts of Xela (as Quetzaltenango is better known by locals), El Nahual seeks to serve the marginalized Guatemalans outside of the city center.

All Spanish-language students must spend at least four hours per week volunteering. While volunteers are certainly welcome to combine a volunteer work experience with Spanish classes, El Nahual is also unique in offering a volunteer-only program. Volunteers are needed to teach English to children and adults; to lead art, drama, music, and sports activities; and to assist with tasks that range from repairing bicycles to maintaining computers to working in the community garden. Volunteers can also support the school's educational projects by helping to organize a fundraising event or working on publicity and overseas promotion. The program is flexible, and volunteers can opt to spend anywhere from 4 to 30 hours per week working.

Besides studying Spanish, volunteers can spend their free time exploring the center of Xela, which is a 20-minute walk away. El Nahual can help arrange weekend hikes to the volcanoes surrounding Xela, to the coast, and to popular destinations such as Antigua, Semuc Champey, Lake Atitlán, and Chichicastenango.

Application Process: An application form is available online. Families are welcome.
Cost: None. Volunteers are responsible for their own housing.
Placement Length: There is a three-week minimum for volunteers only. For those taking Spanish classes, the minimum is one week.
Language Requirements: Advanced beginner Spanish skills are required. Non-Spanish speakers can take a Spanish-language course at El Nahual before starting their volunteer work.
Housing: El Nahual offers homestays (US$10 per day, US$65 per week, US$170 per week w/Spanish class, meals included). Volunteers can choose to stay in a hostel or hotel in the center of town, if they prefer. El Nahual can help arrange transportation from the airport in Guatemala City to Xela.
Operating Since: 2004
Number of Volunteers: 40-50 per year (most in June-August).

HOGAR MIGUEL MAGONE

Guatemala City, tel. 502/5306-2113,
www.hogarmiguelmagone.com

TYPE OF WORK: children and youth, education

More than 80 children between the ages of 3 and 16 call Hogar Miguel Magone home. A refuge for children who have suffered abuse or neglect, Hogar Miguel Magone is located outside of Guatemala City, about 20 minutes by taxi (US$10). The home oversees the children's education (at nearby public and private schools), hygiene, health, and recreational activities. They also attend to the children's emotional needs with loving staff and a professional psychologist, as well as prepare them for productive futures through visits by skilled locals who teach the children valuable skills like baking, carpentry, art, and computers.

In the mornings, volunteers help prepare lunch or spend time with the children who attend school in the afternoons—playing, helping out with homework, and teaching English. After serving lunch, volunteers continue their work with the children who were at school in the morning. After dinner, the children usually go to bed around 8pm.

Volunteers usually stay in the lovely colonial town of Antigua, which is 20 minutes away by car. Weekends can be spent on visits to Lake Atitlán or on trips farther afield. Nearly all of the home's volunteers come on group trips, but individual volunteers are also welcome.

Application Process: To apply, send an email, detailing your expectations, skills, interests, level of Spanish, reason for interest in Hogar Miguel Magone, a résumé, and a photo. Individual volunteers should be age 22 or older; families are welcome.

Cost: US$15 per day, which covers electricity, food, the use of Internet, local phone calls, and water.

Placement Length: A minimum of two weeks and maximum of one month are recommended.

Language Requirements: Intermediate Spanish or higher is required to be able to effectively interact with the children and staff.

Housing: Volunteers are responsible for their own accommodations and meals, and typically stay in Antigua.

Operating Since: 1997

Number of Volunteers: more than 100 in 2012 (all in groups of 12 or more)

LONG WAY HOME

San Juan Comalapa, tel. 502/5703-5238, U.S. tel. 936/275-7807, www.lwhome.org

TYPE OF WORK: children and youth, community development, education, environment

Located in a small town in the southwestern highlands of Guatemala, Long Way Home uses "sustainable design and materials to construct self-sufficient schools that promote education, employment and environmental stewardship." Founded in 2004 by a former Peace Corps volunteer, Long Way Home has since received international attention for its innovative leadership in combating waste. In addition to alternative construction, their projects include environmental education and water distribution.

The organization's focus is on the promotion of green and alternative building practices. Their current primary project is the construction of an elementary and vocational school using rammed-earth tires and polypropylene bags, water harvesting, and trash-filled bottles. The project is scheduled for completion in 2014, and some classrooms have already opened. Long Way Home has also partnered with Engineers Without Borders to help bring running water to rural villages near Comalapa; they have built wood-burning cookstoves and water storage tanks for families who do not consistently have running water.

Volunteers work 7am-4pm Monday-Friday, and the tasks are physically demanding: pounding dirt, plastering walls, creating art, or offering engineering services. Alternatively, volunteers who can commit to two months or more can choose to support Long Way Home's educational efforts by teaching English, environmental education, or other skills in local schools. Long Way Home also suggests ways for supporters to volunteer from home, either before or after their trip. Volunteers can sign up for Spanish lessons as well as day trips, for an additional fee.

Application Process: An application form is available online, which requires three references (at least two of which should be professional). The minimum age for individual volunteers is 18. Spots can fill up well in advance.

Cost: Individuals pay US$75 per week or US$300 per month, which includes the accommodations (volunteers are responsible for their meals). One-week group trips are US$600 per person and include accommodations and meals, as well as transportation between Guatemala City and Comalapa, one town tour, one cultural night, and one overnight excursion to Antigua or Lake Atitlán.

Placement Length: The recommended placement length is 1-3 months for individuals and one week for groups.

Language Requirements: There are no language requirements for building projects. Intermediate Spanish is required for teaching.

Housing: Volunteers stay at a guesthouse at the community park. The guesthouse has a kitchen, and volunteers typically purchase and

GUATEMALA

VOLUNTEER PERSPECTIVE

Ashley Mihle is from Houston, Texas. When she was 26 years old, Ashley spent two months working with **Long Way Home** (San Juan Comalapa, tel. 502/5703-5238, U.S. tel. 936/275-7807, www.lwhome.org), a nongovernmental organization (NGO) dedicated to sustainable design and materials.

I volunteered at Long Way Home in the midst of a carefully calculated career change. I was shaking up my life and trying to find a way to change the world. I expected hard work and manual labor, some chaos, and the often slow pace of development work. I did not expect Long Way Home to steal my heart and soul. But it did. I fell in love with the incredibly strong and beautiful things you can build with trash. I fell in love with red dirt and corn fields, with waking up at sunrise, and with the knowledge that you really only need one bucket of water to bathe. I fell in love with the smiling people who say hello to you on the street and with our neighbor Fidelia, who takes care of the volunteers as if they are her own children. Mostly, I fell in love with the commitment and purpose of Long Way Home's employees, and with the noticeable impact they make on the community. I saw locals trained, educated and employed, children become environmental stewards, school walls finished, and mothers cry in appreciation. I left Long Way Home with renewed hope, having learnt that change might be hard, but it is certainly never impossible.

© ASHLEY MIHLE

Long Way Home supporters Haley, Fidelia, and Ashley.

prepare food communally (meals at the guesthouse are mostly vegetarian). There is electricity but no hot water. Homestays are available for an additional fee (US$10 per week), or volunteers can stay in a simple hotel (US$20 per week).
Operating Since: 2004
Number of Volunteers: approximately 200 in 2012

MAYAN FAMILIES

Panajachel, tel. 502/7762-2390,

U.S. tel. 619/550-2608, www.mayanfamilies.org

TYPE OF WORK: children and youth, community development, education, environment, health, women's empowerment

Mayan Families was founded by an American and an Australian resident in Panajachel in response to the devastation wreaked by Hurricane Stan in 2005. The mission of Mayan Families is to provide "opportunities and assistance to the indigenous and impoverished people of Guatemala." Their work is multipronged: They run seven preschool nutrition centers, as well as a nutrition and health needs program for the elderly; have sponsored thousands of children to go to school; managed medical, dental, and veterinary brigades; built and repaired schools; and installed hundreds of fuel-efficient stoves. That's just a partial list.

As Mayan Families works in a variety of areas, volunteer tasks too are varied. Opportunities include: carpentry; information technology; assisting in preschools; fundraising and marketing; supporting Mayan Families' student sponsorship/education program; working with the family aid program; volunteering photography; videography, or medical services; and working on monitoring and evaluating programs. Workdays are 9am-5pm Monday-Friday, including the occasional weekend day, depending on the project. For those who would like to get involved either prior to their arrival in Guatemala or after they leave, Mayan Families can suggest several ways to volunteer from anywhere.

Mayan Families welcomes service trips for individuals and families as well. For groups of 8-12 volunteers, stays are typically one week. In addition to the price of the trip, a minimum donation of US$200 per person is required. Local transportation and accommodations are included.

Panajachel is in the southwestern highlands of Guatemala, about three hours from Guatemala City. Located on the rim of Lake Atitlán, Panajachel is popular with day-trippers from Antigua and is a destination in its own right; it makes a convenient jumping-off point for explorations of a nearby nature reserve and villages. In town, volunteers can study Spanish or backstrap weaving, enjoy the lake, or spend some time browsing the best handicraft selection in the country. Panajachel has very low crime rates and is a safe place to visit and volunteer.

Application Process: To apply, send an email with your résumé attached. Individual volunteers must be at least age 18; families are welcome.

Cost: None for individual volunteers, who are responsible for their own expenses. Group trips require a US$200 per person donation; in addition, there is a fee for accommodations and local transportation.

Placement Length: There is a minimum placement of two weeks, although there is some flexibility. Group trips are usually for one week.

Language Requirements: None, although a translator may be needed if volunteers want to work in or visit an indigenous community.

Housing: Individual volunteers are responsible for their own accommodations and meals, although Mayan Families can point volunteers in the right direction or arrange a homestay. Local accommodations range US$125-600 per month; past volunteers have spent an average of US$125/month on groceries.

Operating Since: 2005
Number of Volunteers: approximately 100 in 2012

GUATEMALA

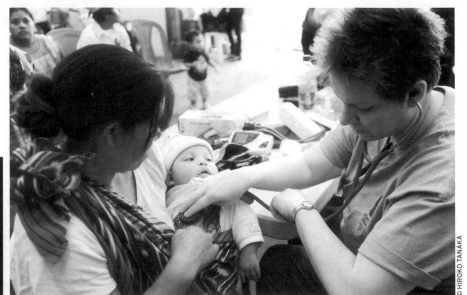

© HIROKO TANAKA

A young Guatemalan benefits from a check-up thanks to one of Mayan Families' medical brigades.

MORE THAN COMPASSION/ FUNDACIÓN SALVACIÓN

Huehuetenango, tel. 502/7762-7529,
www.morethancompassion.org,
sandrasalvacion@yahoo.com

TYPE OF WORK: children and youth, education

Fundación Salvación is a private, Christian orphanage that is "committed to rewriting the stories of orphans in Guatemala"; More Than Compassion is the U.S.-based fundraising counterpart. The orphanage is home to approximately 90 children between the ages of 6 months and 18 years and runs completely on donations. In addition to providing a home, food, and clothes, the orphanage also makes sure the children attend school and receive tutoring if needed, as well as any professional psychological support. The orphanage also seeks to meet the children's spiritual needs with Vacation Bible Schools organized by local churches and visiting groups, as well as prayer times. More Than Compassion is in the process of building a bilingual elementary school,

designed so that the tuition fees of children from outside the orphanage will cover the tuition of children from the orphanage, as well as operating costs.

Volunteers help take care of the children (from babies to teenagers); teach English, computers, or arts and crafts; tutor children after school; work on a special construction/repairing project; or simply organize activities for the kids. Working hours are normally 8am-6 pm. In the mornings, most volunteers help in the School of Hope (a bilingual elementary school) that the children from the orphanage attend, and then return to the orphanage to help out in the afternoon. Volunteers typically spend their free time with each other and with the children. There is a Spanish school roughly 20 minutes' walk from the orphanage if a volunteer is interested in formal lessons. Weekdays there is a strict 8:30pm curfew that volunteers are required to respect.

While MTC/FS are Christian organizations, they are not affiliated with a specific church, nor do they "limit or restrict the religious expression of its team members or followers."

Application Process: To apply, send an email to sandrasalvacion@yahoo.com. Individual volunteers are usually age 18 or older, but families are very much welcome.

Cost: None. Volunteers may be able to stay at the orphanage for free but are responsible for their own meals.

Placement Length: There is no minimum.

Language Requirements: None.

Housing: There are apartments in the back of the orphanage campus that are used to house volunteers. Space is limited and beds fill up quickly, so reservations should be made as far in advance as possible. There is a kitchen where volunteers can cook and store their own food, and there is wireless Internet. Volunteers typically spend US$100-200 per month on food and cooking gas.

Operating Since: 1998

Number of Volunteers: more than 200 individuals and groups in 2012

NIÑOS DE GUATEMALA

Ciudad Vieja, Antigua, tel. 502/7832-8033, www.ninosdeguatemala.org

TYPE OF WORK: children and youth, education

Founded by a Dutch expatriate, Niños de Guatemala seeks to "build a better future for Guatemala and its children through education." They emphasize community involvement and design projects with plans for self-sufficiency in five years.

The organization runs two elementary schools in Ciudad Vieja, a poor community about 15 minutes outside Antigua, one of Guatemala's tourist hubs. Volunteers with intermediate to advanced Spanish can work five mornings a week as teaching assistants. Those with basic (or advanced) Spanish can work afternoons in the after-school arts and sports program, Expresión Artística, or perform one-on-one tutoring with students who need reinforcement in the school's core subjects (the number of afternoons worked per week is flexible). Volunteers who wish to work

both mornings and afternoons can certainly do so. Responsibilities will be tailored to the volunteer's skills, but the primary options are teaching computers, sports, English, music, or art.

For volunteers who cannot commit to four weeks but would still like to check out Niños de Guatemala's work, there is a three-hour Experience Guatemala tour that departs from the volunteer center in Antigua on Tuesday, Thursday, and Friday. The tour takes visitors to see the community of Ciudad Vieja and their projects in the morning, then shares a lunch with students at the school. (Volunteers go on this tour during their first week with Niños de Guatemala; the price is included in their volunteer fee.)

Niños de Guatemala opened a nonprofit Spanish school offering affordable lessons, whose proceeds go directly back to Niños de Guatemala. Volunteers who come with a less than intermediate or advanced level of Spanish are encouraged to take one-on-one lessons in order to maximize their volunteer experience. In addition to volunteering, there is plenty to explore in and around town. Antigua offers centuries-old churches, cobblestone streets, and a lively scene of funky cafés, elegant restaurants, and busy bars. Visits to Lake Atitlán and the market at Panajachel are popular on the weekends, as are hikes to the nearby volcanoes.

Application Process: An application form is available online; your passport number and an emergency contact are required. The minimum age to volunteer is 18, but 16- and 17-year-olds can volunteer with a signed letter of permission from their parent or guardian.

Cost: US$38, which includes the Experience Guatemala tour. The tour only is US$25, and students receive a 50 percent discount. Volunteers are responsible for their own accommodations and meals.

Placement Length: There is a minimum placement of four weeks at the schools. Those with less time can work at Niños de Guatemala's Volunteer Center in Antigua.

GUATEMALA

Three-hour Experience Guatemala tours are also available.

Language Requirements: Volunteers with less than intermediate to advanced Spanish skills will be encouraged to take one-on-one lessons. No Spanish is required for the experiential tour.

Housing: Volunteers make their own arrangements. Niños de Guatemala can help with homestays (US$95 per week; includes three meals daily Mon.-Sat.). A guesthouse is US$200 per month with a shared bath, US$300 per month with a private bathroom, and there is a shared kitchen for making meals. A portion of the rate is donated to Niños de Guatemala. Volunteers usually stay in Antigua (not in Ciudad Vieja).

Operating Since: 2006
Number of Volunteers: 79 in 2012

TRAMA TEXTILES

Quetzaltenango, tel. 502/7765-8564,
www.tramatextiles.org

TYPE OF WORK: community development, women's empowerment

TRAMA Textiles is a women's weaving association in Guatemala's second city, Quetzaltenango (more commonly referred to by its indigenous name, Xela, or SHAY-la). Xela's population of 225,000 is just over 60 percent indigenous. The association works with 17 weaving cooperatives representing roughly 400 women from five regions of the Guatemalan highlands. Their mission is to "create work for fair wages for the women of Guatemala."

Volunteers work in the TRAMA office in Xela. Possible responsibilities include: helping out in the store, fundraising or marketing, researching international sales possibilities and updating the product catalog, managing the website and graphic design, or, for those with multiple language skills, translating. Volunteers who learn how to weave may assist students in the weaving classes. While there are no minimums in terms of time commitment or language skills, the longer one can stay and the more advanced the Spanish skills, the more complex the projects volunteers can take on.

For those who want to start or improve their Spanish, there are many language schools in Xela. Through the schools or independently, volunteers can visit nearby indigenous villages and markets, take salsa classes, play soccer, visit hot springs and volcanoes, and learn the ancient art of backstrap loom weaving. TRAMA offers weaving courses that range from one hour (US$5) to 30 hours (US$130).

Application Process: An application form is available online, which must be downloaded and then submitted via email. Families are welcome.

Cost: None. Volunteers are responsible for their own expenses.

Placement Length: There is no mimimum.

Language Requirements: None.

Housing: Volunteers must make own arrangements.

Operating Since: 1988

Number of Volunteers: approximately 75 in 2012

INTERNATIONAL ORGANIZATIONS

The following international organizations support volunteer efforts in Guatemala:

A Broader View (U.S. tel. 215/780-1845, toll-free U.S. tel. 866/423-3258, www.abroaderview.org), page 193.
Type of Work: agriculture, children and youth, community development, education, environment, health, wildlife protection, women's empowerment

Cross-Cultural Solutions (CCS) (toll-free U.S. tel. 800/380-4777, www.crossculturalsolutions.org), page 195.
Type of Work: children and youth, community development, education, health, women's empowerment

Habitat for Humanity International (toll-free U.S. tel. 800/422-4828, www.habitat.org), page 202.

Type of Work: community development

International Volunteer HQ (IVHQ) (toll-free U.S. tel. 877/342-6588, www.volunteerhq.org), page 203.
Type of Work: agriculture, children and youth, community development, education, environment, health, wildlife protection

TECHO (U.S. tel. 305/860-4090, www.techo.org), page 209.
Type of Work: community development

VOFAIR (www.vofair.org), page 211.
Type of Work: agriculture, children and youth, community development, education, environment, health, wildlife protection, women's empowerment

GUATEMALA

Essentials

BACKGROUND
Geography and Climate
Guatemala's ethnic and biological diversity is packed into 109,000 square kilometers (42,000 sq. mi), an area about the size of the state of Tennessee. While Guatemala's climate is tropical, it can vary greatly between regions. In the mountainous highlands, temperatures are mild and pleasant during the day and cool at night, so visitors should be sure to pack a sweater. The plains and lowlands to the north and south are warm year-round, with an average temperature around 27°C (80°F). Seasonal variations can be important, with the coolest season November-February, when mountain travelers will need a jacket, and the warmest weather in March and April, when temperatures in the Petén can hover around 38°C (100°F) during the day.

The rainy season is May-November, but the only time that rains can really be unpleasant is at the height of hurricane season—two devastating hurricanes, Stan and Mitch, both fell in October (Stan arrived in Guatemala on October 1, 2005, and Mitch hit Guatemalan territory on October 26, 1998).

History and Economy
Mayan civilization thrived in Guatemala, and visitors today can rediscover the ruins of countless temples, ball courts, and stelae (carved statues), which are mostly concentrated in the northern region of Petén. Regional kingdoms were present in Guatemala after the collapse of the Mayan empire around AD 900. While powerful, they never reached the strength and size of the classic Mayan civilization.

Spaniards arrived in Guatemala in the mid-1500s, lured by precious metals, land for cash crops like sugarcane and coffee, and cheap labor, which they exploited mercilessly. Three centuries later, on September 15, 1821, the Captaincy-General of Guatemala, an alliance formed of Guatemala, El Salvador, Honduras, Nicaragua, Costa Rica, and Chiapas, officially proclaimed its independence from Spain. The alliance dissolved two years later, and Guatemala became an independent country.

In the 1950s, Guatemala became a pawn in the Cold War between the Soviet Union and the United States, and CIA-backed dictators were encouraged to overturn land reform, while U.S. Special Forces transformed the Guatemalan Army into a modern counterinsurgency force. The 1960s saw massacres by the army, guerrilla groups that formed in response, and the outbreak of a civil war that lasted from 1960 until 1996. During the war some 200,000 people were killed, and 40,000-50,000 more went missing. Guatemala is still coming to terms with this violent history, with a U.N.-sponsored Truth Commission, and the first convictions related to the war beginning just in 2009. At the time of this writing, Efrain Rios Montt, former president of Guatemala, was standing trial for charges of genocide.

Guatemala's economy is dominated by remittances (money sent back to Guatemala by emigrants), which exceeded US$4 billion in 2010. Manufacturing is another pillar of the economy, while tourism, along with exports such as sugar, coffee, and bananas, also play an important role.

PREPARATION
Transportation
Most volunteers will arrive at **La Aurora International Airport** (GUA, tel. 502/260-0311) in Guatemala City. Many volunteer organizations can help with transportation from there; if not, there is a tourist information kiosk that can help you out. Note that there is a second international airport in northern Guatemala, **Mundo Maya International Airport** (IATA) in Flores, but U.S. and Canadian airlines do not service this airport. The US$30 airport departure tax is usually (but not always) included in the price of airfare.

Groups with flights landing in Guatemala City at night are advised to contact **Programa de Asistencia al Turista** (PROATUR, dial 1500 within Guatemala or 502/2421-2810 outside Guatemala, asistur@inguat.gob.gt) for an escort. Individual travelers should use the Taxi Seguro service within the airport.

Within Guatemala, travelers can choose between so-called chicken buses (refurbished school buses that travel just about everywhere, with the occasional chicken or farm animal on board), first-class buses, and shuttle buses (which connect the most popular tourist destinations). Do your best to avoid the chicken buses. Crime has been increasing on them— from pickpocketing to armed hijacking—and they have an alarming accident rate. First-class buses are much safer and are quite reliable; the shuttle buses are even better and are highly recommended. It is also possible to arrange private transportation. Taxis may be hired for long-distance trips, as well as by the hour, by the day, or for several days.

Passports and Visas
For U.S. travelers, passports must be valid for at least six months after the start date of your trip (or they won't even let you get on the plane in the United States); you will be granted a 90-day visa upon arrival. For Canadian and E.U. travelers, passports must be valid for at least three months after your arrival date; you will be granted a 30-day visa.

Visas are valid for the CA-4 countries of Guatemala, El Salvador, Honduras, and Nicaragua. If you are planning to stay beyond the length of your visa, you must exit the entire CA-4 region, which is most easily achieved from Guatemala by a quick trip to Belize or Mexico.

Money
The currency is the **quetzal** (currency symbol Q), which comes in bills of Q1, Q5, Q10, Q20, Q50, Q100, and Q200 (with bills of Q500 and Q1,000 pending congressional approval). The quetzal is pegged to the U.S. dollar at a rate of Q7.9 to US$1 at the time of writing.

Dollars are often accepted in tourist-oriented establishments. If you are staying at a hotel, you can usually change currency there; otherwise you will need to head to a bank with your passport. Travelers checks can be changed in larger urban and tourist areas, although it can be a bureaucratic hassle (going to a bank to make the exchange and showing your original purchase receipt). However, it's still a good idea to bring a few along for backup, as ATMs aren't as widely distributed as in other Latin American countries.

Health

Malaria (and to a much lesser extent, dengue) can be found in the northern lowlands and along the southern coast. However, these mosquito-borne diseases are not problems in the highlands, as the insects don't like moderate altitudes.

Safety

Crime rates are high in many parts of Guatemala, fueled by police corruption and a flourishing drug trade. Locals are your best source of information on current safety recommendations. Visitors should be vigilant about their belongings and personal safety. No matter where you are headed, take as few valuables as possible and be discreet with those you must have: Put your camera out of sight between shots, and do not use your cell phone on the street (unless it's old or cheap). Men and women alike are advised to take cabs after dark; women should avoid taking a cab alone. The U.S. Embassy reports a high rate of passport theft in Guatemala and recommends keeping a photocopy of your passport with you at all times and the passport itself in a safe place.

In an effort to keep visitors safe, the Guatemalan government has established an efficient and reliable tourist police force. To obtain emergency aid, contact **Programa de Asistencia al Turista** (PROATUR, dial 1500 within Guatemala or 502/2421-2810 outside Guatemala, asistur@inguat.gob.gt).

GUATEMALA

HONDURAS

Honduras lies at the heart of Central America, bordered by Guatemala, El Salvador, and Nicaragua. The country boasts a long Caribbean coast, as well as a short Pacific one, with palm trees, golden sands, intricately carved Mayan ruins, jungle and cloud forests studded with wildlife, sleepy colonial towns, and bustling cities. While each region offers unique experiences, the warm, easygoing attitude of the *catrach,* as Hondurans call themselves, is found everywhere.

More than 90 percent of Hondurans are *mestizos,* also called *ladinos* (persons of mixed European and Central American Indian ancestry). An estimated 7 percent are of indigenous descent. Roughly 4 percent of the population is black (mostly Garífuna, who trace their ancestors to the island of San Vincente). The Garífuna live along the north coast and speak the Garífuna language, as well as Spanish and English. Black Caribs are English speaking and trace their ancestors to Jamaica; they live mostly on Roatan. Roughly half of the population still lives in rural areas, and just over 50 percent of the population is under 18 years old. In 2011, the World Bank calculated the gross national income per capita at US$1,970, ranking Honduras the third-poorest country in the Western Hemisphere (after Nicaragua and Haiti). This means that it's a good place to work side by side with people striving for a better life.

Volunteer opportunities are spread across the country and include even the most touristed spots: the Mayan ruins of Copán, the idyllic Bay Islands, and along the palm-lined

north coast. Volunteers can choose between projects in construction or conservation, teaching children English or playing sports, or working on an organic coffee farm. A few days of rest can easily be tacked onto trips anywhere along the north coast. Spanish is the country's official language, but English is spoken as often as Spanish on the Bay Islands, and the culture is more closely related to the Caribbean than the rest of Honduras. Adventurous volunteers can head off the beaten track to one of countless small towns dotting the countryside to work in education or agriculture, while urbanites may prefer to work with disadvantaged youth in one of Honduras's two major cities, San Pedro Sula and Tegucigalpa.

Whichever opportunity you choose, you'll soon realize that you're not alone—as soon as you spot a group of folks in matching T-shirts proclaiming your medical brigade or church mission on your flight.

Local Organizations

BAY ISLANDS CONSERVATION ASSOCIATION

Utila, tel. 504/2425-3260, www.bicautila.org

TYPE OF WORK: education, environment, wildlife protection

Bay Islands Conservation Association (BICA) is involved with a number of conservation activities on Utila and the surrounding waters, including scientific research, management of protected areas, sea turtle conservation, lionfish eradication, and environmental education. The range of activities for volunteers can vary, although it can generally be divided into two types: research and education.

Research volunteers can be active in managing the office, patrolling and monitoring reefs, managing the dive site database, organizing ecotours on foot or by boat, developing communication materials, or working in BICA's Information Center providing information to tourists on Utila environment and tourist attractions. Education volunteers participate in environmental education in local schools; work on organizing field trips, community workshops, and beach and underwater cleanups; and can be active in reforestation efforts and fish house construction.

While those studying toward or with a degree in environment, biology, or ecotourism are especially welcome, all that is required is an interest in nature and a flexible attitude. Volunteers are welcome to work on related personal projects while working with BICA.

There is a large and eclectic group of international expats on Utila, resulting in plenty of restaurants and a lively nightlife. Volunteers can snorkel or scuba dive in their free time, or study Spanish (English is the native tongue for many Utilians, but Spanish lessons are available).

Application Process: To apply, send an email and include the reasons for your interest, your expectations and qualifications, any previous experience, and the intended duration of your stay. Applicants must be at least age 21 and an undergraduate- or graduate-level student.

Cost US$350 per month, which includes accommodations and Internet access. Volunteers are responsible for their own meals.

Placement Length The average placement length is 1-3 months.

Language Requirements: For research volunteers, Spanish is helpful but not crucial. For education volunteers, strong Spanish skills are necessary.

Housing: Accommodations are in a volunteer house, and rooms may be shared. Meals are not provided, but the dorm has a fully equipped kitchen.

Operating Since: 1991

Number of Volunteers: 53 in 2012

HONDURAS

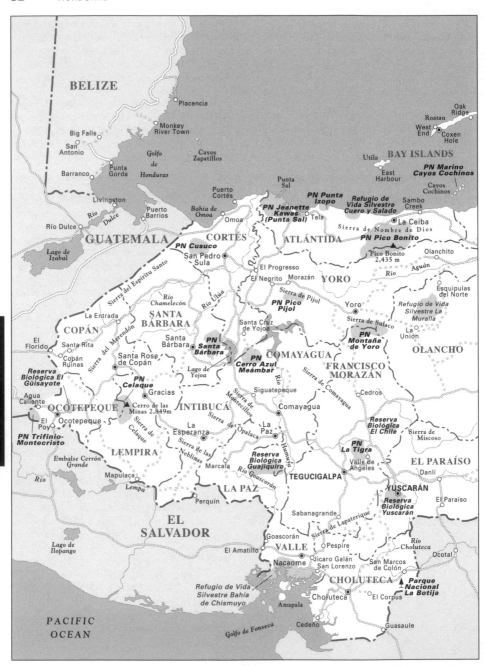

BELIZE

Placencia

Big Falls

Monkey
River Town

San
Antonio

Golfo
de
Honduras

Cayos
Zapatillos

Utila

BAY ISLANDS

Oak
Ridge

Roatan

West
End

Coxen
Hole

Barranco

Punta
Gorda

**PN Marino
Cayos Cochinos**

East
Harbour

Punta
Sal

Cayos
Cochinos

Livingston

Puerto
Barrios

Puerto
Cortés

Bahía de
Omoa

Omoa

**PN Jeanette
Kawas
(Punta Sal)**

Tela

**PN Punta
Izopo**

Refugio de
Vida Silvestre
Cuero y Salado

Sambo
Creek

La Ceiba

Río Dulce

Río
Dulce

Lago de
Izabal

GUATEMALA

CORTÉS

PN Cusuco

San Pedro
Sula

ATLÁNTIDA

Sierra de Nombre de Dios

PN Pico Bonito

Pico Bonito
2,435 m

Olanchito

El Progresso

El Negrito

Morazán

YORO

Río

Aguán

Esquipulas
del Norte

Sierra del Espíritu Santo

Río
Chamelecón

Río Ulúa

Sierra de Pijol

**PN Pico
Pijol**

Yoro

Refugio de Vida
Silvestre La
Muralla

La Entrada

SANTA
BARBARA

Santa Cruz
de Yojoa

Sierra de Sulaco

La
Unión

COPÁN

Santa
Bárbara

**PN
Santa
Bárbara**

**PN
Montaña
de Yoro**

OLANCHO

El
Florido

Santa Rita

Sierra del Merendón

Santa Rose
de Copán

Lago de
Yojoa

COMAYAGUA

Copán
Ruinas

**PN
Celaque**

Gracias

**Cerro Azul
Meámbar**

Río

Sierra de Comayagua

FRANCISCO
MORAZAN

Cedros

Reserva
Biológica El
Güisayote

Agua
Caliente

OCOTEPEQUE

Cerro de las
Minas 2,849m

INTIBUCÁ

Sierra de
Montecillos

Siguatepeque

Comayagua

El
Poy

Ocotepeque

Sierra de
Celaque

La
Esperanza

Sierra de
Opalaca

La
Paz

Reserva
Biológica
El Chile

Sierra de
Miscoso

**PN Trifinio-
Montecristo**

LEMPIRA

Sierra de las
Neblinas

Marcala

Humuya

**PN
La Tigra**

Valle de
Angeles

EL PARAÍSO

Embalse Cerrón
Grande

Mapulaca

**Reserva
Biológica
Guajiquiro**

Río Goascorán

TEGUCIGALPA

Danlí

Río

Lempa

LA PAZ

Perquín

YUSCARÁN

**Reserva
Biológica
Yuscarán**

El Paraíso

EL
SALVADOR

Sabanagrande

Sierra de Lepaterique

Ocotal

Lago de
Ilopango

Goascorán

VALLE

Pespire

Río
Choluteca

El Amatillo

Nacaome

Jícaro Galán
San Lorenzo

San Marcos
de Colón

CHOLUTECA

Parque
Nacional
La Botija

**Refugio de Vida
Silvestre Bahía
de Chismuyo**

Amapala

Choluteca

El Corpus

PACIFIC
OCEAN

Golfo de Fonseca

Cedeño

Guasaule

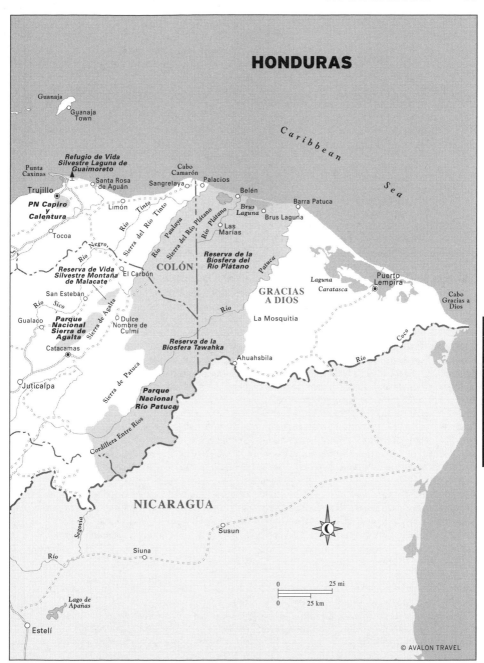

HONDURAS

Guanaja
Guanaja
Town

Caribbean

Sea

Punta
Caxinas
**Refugio de Vida
Silvestre Laguna de
Guaimoreto**
Santa Rosa
de Aguán
Cabo
Camarón
Sangrelaya
Palacios
Belén
Barra Patuca

Trujillo
**PN Capiro
y
Calentura**
Limón
Río Tinto
Brus
Laguna
Brus Laguna

Tocoa
Río del Río Tinto
Río Paulaya
Sierra del Río Plátano
Río Plátano
Las
Marías

Río Negro

**Reserva de Vida
Silvestre Montaña
de Malacate** El Carbón
COLÓN
**Reserva de la
Biosfera del
Río Plátano**
Río Patuca
Laguna
Caratasca
Puerto
Lempira
Cabo
Gracias a
Dios

San Esteban
Río Sico
**GRACIAS
A DIOS**

Gualaco
**Parque
Nacional
Sierra de
Agalta**
Sierra de Agalta
Dulce
Nombre de
Culmí
Río
La Mosquitia
Río Coco

Catacamas
**Reserva de la
Biosfera Tawahka**
Ahuahsbila
Río

Juticalpa
Sierra de Patuca
**Parque
Nacional
Río Patuca**

Cordillera Entre Ríos

NICARAGUA

Río Segovia
Susun

Siuna

Río

Lago de
Apañas

Estelí

0   25 mi
0   25 km

© AVALON TRAVEL

HONDURAS

COFRADÍA BILINGUAL SCHOOL

Cofradía, tel. 504/2509-2666, www.cofradiaschool. com, volunteer@cofradiaschool.com

TYPE OF WORK: children and youth, education

Cofradía Bilingual School is a small bilingual school located roughly 40 minutes from San Pedro Sula. This private school serves more than 200 students, from pre-K through the eighth grade, and tries to accommodate as many children in need as possible through scholarships (currently more than half the students receive them).

Volunteers spend 2-12 weeks working as teacher's classroom aides; they can also take responsibility for lesson planning and leading the class if they so desire. There is also a five-week summer school program, during which volunteers work mornings only. Long-term volunteers commit to work the entire school year (August-June) and are responsible for teaching classes, organizing school events, and performing community outreach.

During their free time, volunteers can grab a coffee at Cafe Click (Cofradía's first coffee shop), learn how to cook Honduran food, and get to know the Cofradía kids better by visiting their homes and meeting their families. Weekends can be spent exploring Honduras— visiting Lago de Yojoa (Honduras's largest lake) and the nearby Pulhapanzak Falls, recharging on urbanity with dinner and a movie in San Pedro Sula, exploring the Mayan ruins of Copán, or heading to the beach near Tela or La Ceiba.

Application Process: To apply, send an email to volunteer@cofradiaschool.com and include a résumé listing relevant educational, professional, volunteer, or travel experience, as well as any specific experience teaching or working with children. Applicants must be at least 21 years of age.

Cost: Short-term costs are US$100 per week; there is no fee for long-term volunteers. Most long-term volunteers spend roughly US$100 per month on living expenses. Summer school costs US$250 for five weeks.

Placement Length: There is a minimum placement of two weeks.

Language Requirements: No Spanish skills are required, as the classes taught by volunteers are in English.

Housing: Short-term volunteers receive accommodations with a local family; three meals a day are included. Long-term and summer school volunteers share rooms in a volunteer house; lunch on school days is included.

Operating Since: 1997

Number of Volunteers: 12 long-term and 2 short-term volunteers in 2011-2012 school year; 13 long-term volunteers for the 2012-2013 school year

EL HOGAR PROJECTS

Tegucigalpa, U.S. tel. 781/729-7600, www.elhogar.org

TYPE OF WORK: children and youth, community development, education

El Hogar is a faith-based organization founded by members of the small English-speaking congregation of the Episcopal church in Tegucigalpa. The organization operates a home for children in grades 1-6 in the heart of Honduras's capital, Tegucigalpa, and three secondary education schools in small towns nearby, offering an alternative to gang life. El Hogar provides food, clothing, shelter, education, and Christian development to 250 children (ages 5-18).

The volunteer experience at El Hogar is designed for service teams rather than individuals, so be prepared to put together your own travel group of up to 15 persons (of whom at least one must speak Spanish). While many of the service groups that visit El Hogar come from Episcopal churches, the home has hosted corporate service teams since October 2006. Participation in religious activities by service team members is optional, although it's encouraged as a way to share in the children's life.

Volunteers typically work on construction projects, painting, or gardening, and usually help the children with their homework, play games with them (such as soccer, marbles, basketball, cards), or read, draw, and just talk together. Specialized teams can help with dental and health care or teacher training. There are usually visits to the neighborhoods where the children are from.

Note: Tegucigalpa has some of the highest crime rates in the country. As a matter of safety, volunteers are not allowed to leave El Hogar's property without permission. While there is free time for relaxing in the evenings, there is limited time for sightseeing.

Application Process: An application form is available online. It is advisable to contact El Hogar as early as possible. Applicants should initiate the process a minimum of 4-6 months before the travel dates. Service teams are accepted February-October, and dates such as spring break can fill quickly. The minimum age for volunteers is 15 (or a freshman in high school).

Cost: US$150 a week per person for room, board, and local transportation, and US$2,000 per service team for project expenses, plus airfare to Tegucigalpa.

Placement Length: one week

Language Requirements: At least one person in each service team must speak Spanish.

Housing: Volunteers stay at either a guesthouse at the children's home or at the organization's farm outside the city (if that is the work site). The guesthouses have dorm rooms, a living room, and a kitchenette. Meals are included; any meals out are optional and at the participant's expense.

Operating Since: 1979

Number of Volunteers: more than 300 in 2011

EL MAESTRO EN CASA

La Esperanza, tel. 504/2783-2728,
www.lencaeducation.org, lencaeducation@gmail.com
TYPE OF WORK: education

Founded with the assistance of a retired secondary school teacher from the United States, El Maestro en Casa is a program that serves the rural poor, many of whom have never finished the primary grades. Students also include those wishing to continue past the sixth grade. Most students are aged 16-25, and almost all are Lenca, an indigenous group of southwest Honduras (and eastern El Salvador). The area of La Esperanza is one of the poorest of Honduras.

The organization's four teachers travel by motorcycle on a weekly basis to six rural student centers outside of La Esperanza, as well as teach weekly classes in the school center in La Esperanza. Short-term volunteers work with organic strawberry and vegetable production in the center's greenhouse, or in construction, repairing roofs and laying tile or building fences. Volunteers who can commit to 2.5 months may work as academic teachers or in outreach, teaching classes in basic English, computers, art, music, crafts, and practical skills such as bicycle mechanics or cooking.

La Esperanza is a quiet town, but there are several restaurants for volunteers who want to spend an evening out. There are natural thermal baths nearby and plenty of hiking in the surrounding hills.

Application Process: An application form is available online. To apply, email the completed form to lencaeducation@gmail.com.

Cost: None. Volunteers are responsible for their own accommodations and meals.

Placement Length: For short-term volunteers, there is a minimum placement of two weeks; for long-term volunteers, the minimum placement is 2.5 months.

Language Requirements: Basic to intermediate Spanish skills are required for short-term volunteers; intermediate to advanced Spanish skills are required for long-term volunteers.

Housing: Volunteers may choose between staying in the center's dorm (US$25/week, no meals), with a local family (US$50/week, two meals daily), or in separate accommodations in La Esperanza, with meals in a local restaurant (weekly costs range US$75-100).

Operating Since: 1995

Number of Volunteers: eight in 2012

HONDURAS

GUACAMAYA

Copán Ruinas, tel. 504/2651-4360,
www.guacamaya.com

TYPE OF WORK: agriculture, children and youth, community development, education, health

Located in northwest Honduras, Guacamaya is a Spanish school in the eponymous village of Copán Ruinas, mere steps away from the ancient Mayan ruins of Copán. It has run volunteer programs since its inception and is an ideal place for combining volunteer work with language learning. Volunteers typically work four or five hours in the morning and study Spanish in the afternoon (or vice versa).

There is a wide variety of volunteer work available, depending on the skills and interests of the volunteer. Projects include: working with children in an orphanage, painting and repairing schools in indigenous villages (or building play equipment for those schools), creating family and school vegetable gardens, and building homes and schools through partnership with a local nongovernmental organization (NGO).

Volunteers may also work in an elementary school serving the indigenous (Chortí) population and assisting the teacher; there is the option to teach classes in math, history, and art. Volunteers also work with youth or community groups in conjunction with either Catholic or Protestant churches. Working on an organic coffee farm is a popular option and may include anything from elaborating organic fertilizer to drying and grinding coffee beans. Volunteers who wish to work as a doctor's assistant must have a medical background or be studying medicine. Tasks are in accordance with the volunteer's knowledge.

Application Process: An application form is available online. Applicants must be at least 15 years of age.

Cost: US$135 a week, including accommodation, meals, and one local tour. Spanish lessons are available (US$140 for 20 hours).

Placement Length: There is a minimum placement of one week.

Language Requirements: An intermediate level of Spanish is required for most

Volunteers at Guacamaya can explore the Mayan ruins of Copán in their free time.

© AMY E. ROBERTSON

volunteer opportunities; strong Spanish skills are required for others. Beginning Spanish is acceptable for volunteers in agriculture or construction.

Housing: Volunteers are placed in homestays (three meals daily). Vegetarians can be accommodated. It is possible to arrange to stay in a hostel, if preferred.

Operating Since: 1999

Number of Volunteers: 93 in 2012

ISLAND FRIENDS–ROATAN CHARITIES

Roatan, www.islandfriendsroatan.com,
islandfriendsroatan@yahoo.com

TYPE OF WORK: children and youth, community development, education, environment, health, wildlife protection

Island Friends—Roatan Charities is a umbrella organization run on a volunteer basis by local expats to connect volunteers with suitable organizations based on skills, interests, and availability. They are expanding exponentially as the number of organizations working on the island grows. (At the time of this writing, Island Friends was working with 35 different organizations.)

Two of Island Friends' partners are Partners in Education and Roatan Daycare and Learning Center (see listings in this chapter). You may contact those organizations directly or work through Island Friends, who can place you in another organization if your first choice doesn't work out. Volunteer opportunities include: working at a community health clinic; supporting college-prep efforts for local high school students; increasing awareness about AIDS prevention and treatment; teaching arts, sports, music, and English to local youth; working with an organization that teaches steel drum music or with the local humane society; and supporting the marine park's conservation efforts.

Travelers to Roatan will have plenty to do in their free time—from swimming, snorkeling, and scuba diving to fishing, zip-lining, and hitting the nightlife. Although there has been an increase in Spanish speakers moving to Roatan from the Honduran mainland in recent years, the island is still primarily English speaking, so there are few Spanish lessons available—but it *is* possible to find them. Many of the volunteer opportunities, however, are working with the Spanish-speaking population.

Application Process: To apply, send an email and include your education and background information, reasons for choosing the organization, and any relevant experience or skills. Volunteers must be old enough to travel to and stay in Honduras by themselves. Families are welcome.

Cost: None. Volunteers are responsible for their own expenses.

Placement Length The minimum placement varies from half a day to one week (working half days), depending on the project. Placements are adjusted to fit the skills and time constraints of the volunteers.

Language Requirements: Some projects benefit Spanish speakers, but Spanish is not required.

Housing: Volunteers are responsible for their own accommodations and meals. There are hotels and restaurants at all price points on Roatan, and transportation by public minibus is cheap and easy.

Operating Since: 2007

Number of Volunteers: approximately 70 in 2012

Partners in Education–Roatan (PIER)

Sandy Bay, tel. 504/2651-4360, www.pierroatan.org, PartnersInEducationRoatan@yahoo.com

TYPE OF WORK: PIER runs the Sand Castle Library & Community Education Center, based in the village of Sandy Bay at the western end of the Bay Island of Roatan. PIER needs "English and Spanish language tutors, basic math tutors, and science lovers." Volunteers can expect to lead hands-on activities with the kids. The Brain Spaces Center has computer and board games, and lots of hands-on activities intended to foster self-directed independent learners. There are a few hotels and a dive shop or two right in Sandy Bay, and it is a short ride from West End.

Application Process: To apply, contact Island Friends or send an email to PartnersInEducationRoatan@yahoo.com with a brief summary of experience and education, time available to volunteer, and areas of interest.

Operating Since: 2006

Number of Volunteers: more than 20 in 2012

Roatan Daycare and Learning Center (RDLC)

Coxen Hole, www.roatan-daycare.com

Volunteering with RDLC offers a chance to see another face of Roatan. RDLC provides bilingual early education and a nurturing environment for children of working parents, most of whom are living at or near the poverty line. Volunteers can read to children, teach art, engage in a craft project, play games, or teach songs. Many of the children at the day care are Spanish speaking, but Spanish is not required to volunteer. Although the airport, ferry terminal, and two cruise ship terminals

VOLUNTEER PERSPECTIVE

Larry and Julie Guyette, and their children Hailey (age 15), Rachel (age 12), and Molly (age 10), are from central Florida and spent two days of their weeklong vacation to Roatan working at the **Roatan Daycare and Learning Center** (Coxen Hole, www.roatan-daycare.com).

When we were searching the Internet for travel spots combining mission with vacation, we happened upon Roatan, Honduras. Upon further research, we came upon the Island Friends of Roatan. The site and volunteer opportunities were the deciding factors for us to go to Roatan. We felt especially led to the day care center and the clinic. After emailing both organizations with our dates of travel and inquiring about volunteering with them, they both provided their needs, which made the preplanning easy.

Our friends were happy to donate items, and it became our goal to "leave" the majority of our luggage contents in Roatan. With five of us, we were able to take suitcases and leave behind the contents of three at the day care and the clinic.

Initially, we were going to spend one day each at the day care and the clinic. The first visit went to the day care. Initially we were worried about interrupting the normal day care schedule, but the staff was gracious, and it was easy to plug all of our ages into "helper" spots. The books, school supplies, crafts, and light sticks that we brought were appreciated. We colored, played puppets, read books, and even helped celebrate a birthday. Despite a small language barrier, we all had such a grand time, we went back the next day!

Although we didn't end up volunteering at the clinic, we delivered a suitcase full of over-the-counter medicines and medical supplies to them. For us, this trip was an impactful experience. We had been told many times that children couldn't serve in a volunteer position the way adults could, but we proved that wasn't true. The staff at the Roatan Daycare and Learning Center made all of us feel welcomed and helpful. Our daughters were especially vocal about their experience when we returned home. Our support for the Roatan Daycare and Learning Center continues today as we send supplies and donations. This trip was the beginning of a long-term relationship, and we hope to return one day!

are in and around Coxen Hole, there are few tourist attractions in town. Volunteers who will be working in Coxen Hole should find a hotel elsewhere on the island, as the small port city does not have any tourist-friendly hotels.

Application Process: To apply, contact RDLC via their online form, introducing yourself and including your background information, experience with children, and your reasons for choosing the RDLC.

Operating Since: under current management since 2006

Number of Volunteers: approximately 30 in 2012

PROTECTIVE TURTLE ECOLOGY CENTER FOR TRAINING, OUTREACH AND RESEARCH (PROTECTOR)

North Coast, South Coast, and the Bay Islands,
U.S. tel. 909/558-1000, ext. 48903,
www.turtleprotector.org

TYPE OF WORK: wildlife protection

ProTECTOR is a relatively young organization, dedicated, as its name suggests, to the

Volunteering at the Roatan Daycare and Learning Center shows visitors another side of the island.

HONDURAS

protection of sea turtles. It supports projects along both the northern and southern coasts of Honduras, as well as in the Bay Islands.

Volunteers work each day, but the type of work depends on the project location and type, as well as the time of year. Volunteers may monitor beaches for turtle nests, work at egg hatcheries, assist in tagging sea turtles, clean up beach debris, help track turtles in the water, or participate in underwater behavioral observations. (Volunteer responsibilities may include some amount of diving, but not necessarily.) Volunteers may also be involved in education outreach (teaching about turtles, the environment, or English), as well as assisting community members in food preparation, building, and community and beach cleanups. Service teams are welcome.

Application Process: To apply, contact ProTECTOR online at www.turtleprotector. org. Applicants must be a minimum age of 16 if accompanied by an adult volunteer or age 18 if unaccompanied.

Cost: US$250/week program fee, plus accommodation and meals (which varies US$210-680/week), as well as transportation costs.

Placement Length: There is a minimum placement of 1 week-2 months.

Language Requirements: On some projects no Spanish is required, while in other areas, there is little to no English spoken. Volunteers will never be left alone at a research site without a project participant or national assistant (or student), so while Spanish is advantageous, it is not a requirement.

Housing: ProTECTOR makes arrangements for the volunteer, but the cost is not included in the program fee. Accommodations vary depending on project location and may be very basic, such as a small dorm, or a family-style resort.

Operating Since: 2007, with volunteers since 2010

Number of Volunteers: six in 2012

STUDENTS HELPING HONDURAS / CENTRAL AMERICAN CHILDREN'S INSTITUTE

El Progreso and Villa Soleada, U.S. tel. 703/445-5497, www.ceciskids.org

TYPE OF WORK: community development, education

Founded by a Japanese student whose life was transformed by a volunteer trip to Honduras, Students Helping Honduras (SHH) has turned the shantytown of Villa Soleada into a sustainable village; created a children's home for orphaned, abandoned, and abused children; and works with rural villages to build and equip schools, with a goal of building 1,000 schools. They also provide university scholarships for girls.

Short-term volunteers, together with local community members and professional masons, work in groups on construction sites to build rural schools. Volunteers visit projects their first day, work the following four days, and spend their last day at the beach. There are cultural activities organized every evening. While the villages where SHH works are marginalized, they are also generally safe. Volunteers benefit from the organization's strong connections with the local communities.

SHH offers trips 12 weeks per year: four in December/January, four in March/April, and four between May and August. If you organize your own group of 10 or more, you can arrange to travel on other dates.

Application Process: A registration form is available online, and a US$150 deposit is required. English-teaching applicants must send an email with their résumé, a cover letter, and a short essay.

Cost: US$650 for one week if registering more than two months in advance; US$750 for one week if registering less than two months in advance. Each additional week costs US$375. English-teaching volunteers pay US$1,200 for five weeks. Airfare is not included.

Placement Length: Construction placements last 1-4 weeks. Volunteers interested in staying five weeks can teach English, but dates are

The Utila Iguana Conservation Project works to protect the swamp iguana, *Ctemosaura baberi.*

© AMY E. ROBERTSON

limited to late June-July to coincide with the local summer camp.

Language Requirements: No Spanish-language skills are required; there is always a translator with each group.

Housing: Volunteers stay either in a dorm-style volunteer lodge in the village of Villa Soleada or in shared accommodations in modest hotels in El Progreso.

Operating Since: 2006

Number of Volunteers: 500-750 per year

UTILA IGUANA CONSERVATION PROJECT

Utila, tel. 504/2425-3946, www.utila-iguana.de

TYPE OF WORK: education, wildlife protection

The Utila Iguana Conservation Project operates the Iguana Station, located on the island of Utila. Several species of swamp iguana (*Ctemosaura baberi*) are found only in the mangrove swamps of Utila and are in danger of extinction due to overhunting (for consumption) and the cutting of mangroves.

All that is needed to volunteer is a passion for nature. The work includes caring for the iguanas, butterflies, tarantulas, geckos, and other animals at the station, but it can also include teaching, public relations, gardening, maintenance, or ecological research, depending on the interests and skills of the volunteer. Volunteers are expected to work Monday-Friday (8:30am-noon and 1:30pm-5pm) and Saturday (8am-noon). The iguana breeding season is February-August and can be an especially interesting time to visit.

English is the primary language spoken on the island (although Spanish is useful if you are interested in teaching and community outreach). Free time can be spent snorkeling and scuba diving. There is a large and eclectic group of international expats on Utila, resulting in plenty of restaurants and a lively nightlife.

Application Process: An application form is available online. Applicants must be at least 18 years of age.

Cost: US$75 per week, which includes a shared room at the Iguana Station (US$90 for

---

INTERNATIONAL ORGANIZATIONS

The following international organizations support volunteer efforts in Honduras:

A Broader View (U.S. tel. 215/780-1845, toll-free U.S. tel. 866/423-3258, www.abroaderview.org), page 193.
Type of Work: agriculture, children and youth, community development, education, environment, health, wildlife protection, women's empowerment

Biosphere Expeditions (toll-free U.S. tel. 800/407-5761, www.biosphere-expeditions.org), page 195.
Type of Work: environment, wildlife protection

Elevate Destinations (U.S. tel. 617/661-0203, www.elevatedestinations.com), page 199.

Type of Work: children and youth, community development, education, environment, wildlife protection

Global Communities: Partners for Good (U.S. tel. 301/587-4700, www.globalcommunities.org), page 200.
Type of Work: children and youth, community development, education, environment, women's empowerment

Habitat for Humanity International (toll-free U.S. tel. 800/422-4828, www.habitat.org), page 202.
Type of Work: community development

TECHO (U.S. tel. 305/860-4090, www.techo.org), page 209.
Type of Work: community development

a private room), drinking water, and use of bicycles. Meals are not included.
Placement Length: There is a minimum placement of three weeks.
Language Requirements: Spanish is not required. An intensive Spanish-language course is available at a local language school (US$100 for 20 hours).

Housing: Volunteers stay in a dorm at the Iguana Station and are responsible for their own meals, but there is a fully equipped kitchen.
Operating Since: 1997
Number of Volunteers: 55 in 2012

Essentials

BACKGROUND
Geography and Climate
Honduras is generally warm, with March and April the hottest months. September-November is the rainy season, with October the rainiest month of the year. Roatan and Utila are warm year-round, and rain rarely lasts all day. Tegucigalpa is slightly cooler, thanks to its position 1,000 meters (3,280 ft) above sea level, while the western highlands are the highest and coolest part of Honduras. (La Esperanza can be downright cold during the cooler months.)

History and Economy
Honduras is home to several indigenous cultures. The most notable are the Maya, who left their mark with intricately carved pyramids and sculptures at Copán, and the Lenca, whose *guancasco* celebrations symbolizing the bonds between communities continue to be held in villages and towns across western Honduras.

The first Spanish arrived in Honduras and eventually incorporated it into the Spanish Kingdom of Guatemala. Honduras obtained its independence in 1821, nearly 300 years later. Since independence, Honduras has been fraught with political conflict. In the early 20th century, Honduras became the original banana republic, with foreign-owned fruit companies financing political uprisings when it suited their needs. Foreign involvement, especially American, remained strong throughout the century—including the notorious use of Honduras as a launching pad for the U.S.-financed and U.S.-directed

"counterrevolution" against the Sandinistas in Nicaragua in the 1980s. Political turmoil has continued since then with the hotly debated removal of Manuel "Mel" Zelaya in June 2009 and a December 2012 Congressional bill dismissing the nation's Supreme Court judges. Despite these problems, Honduras prides itself on avoiding the type of full-blown civil war that devastated its northern neighbors Guatemala and El Salvador.

Honduras is one of the poorest countries in the Western Hemisphere; many say that its development was set back 25 years by the devastation wreaked by Hurricane Mitch in 1998. Agriculture is the largest sector in the economy, with exports of shrimp, coffee, sugar, and bananas dominating. *Maquilas* (sweatshops) are also important to the economy, with textile exports to the United States leading the manufacturing sector. Sadly, the industry on the rise is the drug trade—planes from South America land in hidden airstrips (located primarily in the Mosquitia and Olancho) to discharge their goods, which continue north by land.

PREPARATION
Transportation
Honduras has three international airports (www.interairports.hn): **Toncontín** (TGU) in Tegucigalpa, **Ramón Villeda Morales** (SAP) in San Pedro Sula, and **Juan Manuel Galvez** (RTB) in Roatan. All are serviced by American Airlines, Delta, and United Airlines, as well as local and regional airlines. Spirit Airlines also flies to San Pedro Sula. There are charter

flights from Canada and Italy to Roatan as well. The city of La Ceiba and the island of Utila both have regional airports.

At the end of your trip, be sure to have cash on hand for the Honduran airport departure tax (US$39.24 as of April 2013), payable in lempiras or dollars (but change is given only in lempiras).

Utila and Roatan are connected to the mainland by twice-daily ferry service, while private boat service connects the Cayos Cochinos with Honduras's north coast. Bus service on the mainland is inexpensive and reliable, although it is recommended to spring for the "luxury" bus lines, which are both safer and more comfortable.

Main roads between cities and towns are in generally good condition, but if your volunteer site is in a remote village, expect bumpy dirt roads that take three times as long to traverse.

Note that Utila and Roatan can be bursting at the seams during Semana Santa (the week leading up to Easter) and in the week between Christmas and New Year's. If you are looking for a quiet island escape, you may want to consider different travel dates.

Volunteers in Tegucigalpa or southern Honduras will need to plan on either a long bus ride or a short but pricey flight in order to add on a visit to one of the country's tourist highlights.

Passports and Visas

The expiration date on your passport must be at least six months after the date your trip begins, or you will not be able to enter the country (or even board your plane). Honduras, Guatemala, El Salvador, and Nicaragua have formed a single immigration region—the CA4 region—which grants tourists from North America and many European countries an automatic 90-day visa. If you plan to travel or volunteer in these countries longer than 90

days, you must exit and reenter the region. (Belize is the easiest non-CA4 country to reach from Honduras.)

Money

The official currency in Honduras is the **lempira** (the symbol for the lempira is L). At the time of writing, the lempira was pegged to the U.S. dollar at roughly L$19.5 to US$1. Bills are printed in denominations of L1, L2, L5, L10, L20, L50, L100, and L500. Coins are worth so little that they're more of an annoyance than an asset. Dollars are accepted at most hotels around the country. Shops and smaller hotels may accept dollars, but don't count on it. In the Bay Islands, dollars are accepted everywhere.

Health

There is some risk of malaria and dengue fever in most of Honduras. Bring insect repellent, but please make sure it is DEET-free if you are planning to take a swim (DEET kills coral).

Safety

A stark income divide and high rates of poverty have opened the door to a lucrative drug trade, which has resulted in a dramatically increasing crime rate in Honduras. However, crime is concentrated in the urban centers, and tourists and volunteers have not been the primary targets of violent crime. Most volunteer sites are very safe, and volunteers should follow any security advice given by their host organization. Keep your street smarts about you at all times as a preventative measure.

Muggings are not unheard of in Roatan, Copán, or any of the big cities, so keep all valuables out of sight. Flashing valuables is never a good idea, nor is walking alone late at night. In the big cities, travel by taxi rather than bus. If traveling around Honduras, stick to the bigger bus lines when possible.

NICARAGUA

Nicaragua is the largest country in Central America, sharing a border with Honduras to the north and Costa Rica to the south, while the Pacific Ocean lines its western edge and the Caribbean lies to the east. Yet Nicaragua is also Central America's least densely populated country. Although it is not nearly as touristed as its neighbor to the south, Costa Rica, its colonial towns, two enormous lakes, and 40 volcanoes make it an ideal destination for adventurers who want to get off the beaten path.

Nearly a third of Nicaragua's six million people live in the nation's capital, Managua. Roughly 70 percent of Nicaraguans are *mestizos* (persons of mixed European and Central American Indian ancestry), and about half of the population is under 18 years old. More than 45 percent of the population lives below the national poverty line, making Nicaragua the second-poorest country in the western hemisphere. (The World Bank calculated the gross national income per capita at US$1,170 in 2011.)

Nicaragua's scarce resources mean that tourist amenities may not be as well developed as in more prosperous Latin American countries, but volunteer efforts are warmly welcomed, and opportunities abound. Volunteers might teach English, arts and crafts, or even surf lessons to local youth, or support a community clinic or school near one of Nicaragua's colonial towns. Free time can be spent exploring the country's volcanoes, lagoons, canyons, rivers, and valleys; swimming in the cool Caribbean or the bold Pacific surf; and taking in the cafés and cathedrals of colonial towns

© AMY E. ROBERTSON

like León and Granada. There are high-quality, low-priced Spanish-language schools in the towns and cities, as well as a few scattered in rural areas and along the beach, so volunteers can also opt to ramp up their language skills before or while volunteering.

While resources might be limited for many Nicaraguans, one thing most have in abundance is a friendly, laid-back attitude. Wherever you choose to spend your volunteer vacation, you can be sure you'll leave having made friends.

Local Organizations

BRIDGES TO COMMUNITY

Ossining, NY, U.S. tel. 914/923-2200,
www.bridgestocommunity.org
TYPE OF WORK: children and youth, community development, education, environment, health

Bridges to Community's mission is "to build a more just and sustainable world through service learning and community development by engaging volunteers to work in developing countries—building community and changing lives." The emphasis is on shared work and community empowerment, and Bridges to Community makes long-term commitments to the communities where it works. At their beginnings in 1992, they ran a single trip to Nicaragua; for 2013, they organized 50 trips. Many of these trips are organized for private groups (students, youth groups, colleagues from a corporation, a group of neighbors and friends), but others are open to individual volunteers. Open trips often have a particular focus, such as "friends and family," "college student leaders," "young professionals," or "business leaders."

Bridges to Community has four programmatic areas of focus: housing, health, education, and economic development. In addition to building low-income housing, Bridges to Community helps secure land titles and repair existing structures. Health projects have an emphasis on preventative care as well as clinic work, and have included installing smokeless stoves, building water systems to deliver potable water, and constructing and repairing medical facilities. The education program focuses on the construction of classrooms, libraries, and other school buildings, as well as scholarships, workshops, and adult education programs. The economic development program runs training workshops in basic arithmetic, accounting, and small business administration. Bridges to Community also provides grants for small cooperative business ventures, like fair-trade organic farming.

Evening activities might include a soccer or baseball game with other volunteers and members of the community. There are also evening meetings. Some are organized with local leaders who speak to volunteers about the needs in their community and how they are currently working with Bridges to Community. Other meetings are group reflections where the issues of poverty, globalization, fair trade, international affairs, Nicaraguan history, and other topics are discussed to enrich the volunteers' understanding of the challenges that community members face. There is usually a chance for one or two days of sightseeing sometime during the week.

Bridges to Community works in five regions of Nicaragua, including many rural or semirural communities, as well as in Masaya, Nicaragua's second-largest city. In 2012 Bridges to Community began a program in the Dominican Republic, with six trips planned for 2013.

Application Process: To apply, send an email to indicate your interest in an existing trip or discuss organizing a group trip. A US$250 deposit is required 90 days prior to your trip; full payment must be received one month before travel. Volunteers with youth/student groups must be age 15 or older; those under the age of 18 must provide a signed parental permission form. Families with children of any age are welcome.

NICARAGUA

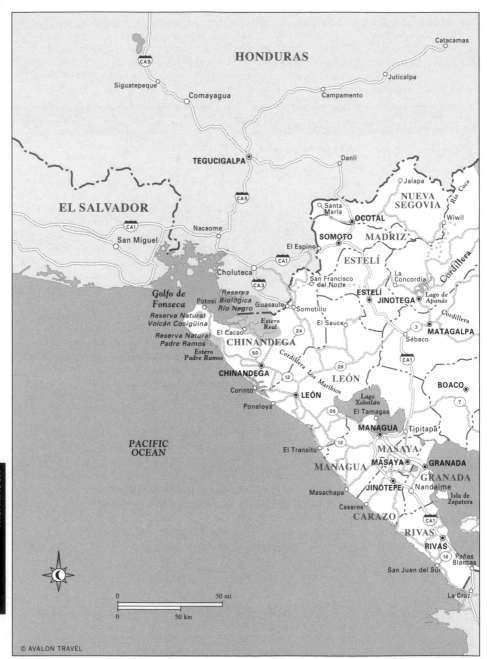

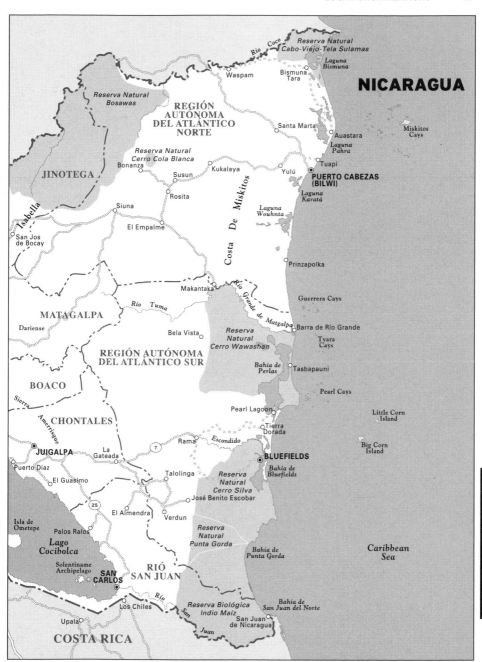

Cost: US$1,295, including all meals, lodging, transportation, hotels, project fees, and entrance fees to sightseeing venues.

Placement Length: The average placement length is nine days.

Language Requirements: None, although Spanish study prior to the trip is always encouraged.

Housing: Typically cots in community centers; volunteers must bring their own sheets and blanket. Meals are included, even those at restuarants.

Operating Since: 1992

Number of Volunteers: 900 in 2012

EL PORVENIR

Boaco, Jinotega, León, and Matagalpa,
tel. 505/2268-5781, U.S. tel. 303/861-1499,
www.elporvenir.org

TYPE OF WORK: community development

El Porvenir's mission is to improve the lives of Nicaraguans by establishing access to clean water, thereby "improving family living standards, reducing disease and child mortality, freeing girls' and women's time, as well as improving school attendance and performance." Projects are selected in response to requests for assistance from rural villages. El Porvenir provides technical expertise and training, tools, and funding to complete the project. The organization's integrated approach extends to the provision of fuel-efficient stoves (to help protect the watersheds by reducing the need for firewood) and health and hygiene education (so that communities reduce water and sanitation-related illnesses).

Volunteers work in small groups of 10-15 people together with Nicaraguan families to build a *lavandero* (a community laundry and bathing facility) or latrines, or to reforest the watershed around the village where the project is located. Most work sites are in rural villages without electricity, plumbing, or running water. Volunteers stay in a modest hotel in a nearby town, traveling to the village each day in the back of a truck.

Trips are typically one week in length, with dates set well in advance. At the time of this writing, there were just two work trips scheduled for 2013 (El Porvenir also organizes educational/cultural trips). During the workweek, afternoons and evenings are tailored to the interests of the group and may include meeting with local politicians, teachers, or health workers; visiting an artist's workshop; or going to a museum. After the workweek, trips include time for sightseeing; a weekend at the beach, in the mountains, or in Granada; and hiking, swimming, visiting a crafts market, or attending a concert. Those interested in expanding their trip can sign up through Road Scholar (www.roadscholar.org), which offers an enhanced itinerary and more educational aspects for a bit more money.

Application Process: An information form is available online. Volunteers of all ages are welcome; those under 18 must be accompanied by a parent or guardian.

Cost: US$925-1,135, including all in-country expenses (and health insurance), as well as materials for the project the volunteer will work on.

Placement Length: Usually one week; sometimes two weeks.

Language Requirements: No Spanish is required; project staff are bilingual.

Housing: Accommodations are in a modest hotel; breakfast and dinner is in town, while lunch is simple food on the work site.

Operating Since: 1989

Number of Volunteers: close to 200 per year

EMERGENCY RESPONSE SERVICES FOR LATIN AMERICA (ERSLA)

northwest Nicaragua, U.S. tel. 478/787-4889,
www.ersla.org

TYPE OF WORK: community development

ERSLA is a unique organization that seeks to address three fundamental needs to improve emergency response services in Nicaragua: (1) emergency response equipment; (2) first responder training; and (3) community integration of emergency service preparedness and response. At the time of this writing, current projects included the provision of firefighter equipment and training, a water filter program, building smoke-free stoves, and burn prevention education. ERSLA is committed to creating sustainable solutions, and its work focuses on training Nicaraguans. Volunteers support the trainer and, when possible, train the trainer.

Volunteers without specific emergency response skills (and, particularly, language skills) who will be visiting for one month or less are welcome on "familiarization trips." These volunteers can assist with projects such as first-aid training or water filter distribution. Those without Spanish skills, or with basic Spanish only, usually work as assistants for a staff member or other volunteer. Volunteers with emergency response skills, such as a firefighter who knows extrication or brush fire techniques, or a nurse who understands first-aid training, will have a greater opportunity to apply those skills on a short visit, depending on their knowledge level and Spanish skills.

Volunteer responsibilities are explained in an on-site orientation upon arrival in Nicaragua. ERSLA's project coordinator works with the volunteers to ensure that expectations are met and also that the volunteer feels useful. ERSLA can arrange Spanish lessons (at the volunteer's expense) for those wishing to improve their language skills. (ERSLA also receives team visits, but these are usually learning opportunities for the team members rather than volunteer opportunities.)

Application Process: Volunteers must complete a three-page application form (sent to them by ERSLA) that indicates skills and interests. ERSLA follows up with an interview to ensure the best placement.

Cost: ERSLA works with each volunteer to develop a budget that covers airport pickup, administration costs, transportation (private or public vehicles, depending on project and comfort level), and a personal cell phone with minutes added each week. This can vary significantly depending on the volunteer's ability or willingness to take public transportation such as buses, or the need to transport equipment for the project.

Placement Length: There is no minimum.
Language Requirements: Spanish skills are helpful but are not required.
Housing: ERSLA can make accommodation arrangements for volunteers, or volunteers can make their own.
Operating Since: 2009 (incorporated as a nonprofit in 2012)
Number of Volunteers: three volunteers and two interns in 2012

FABRETTO CHILDREN'S FOUNDATION
San José de Cusmapa, Estelí, and Managua, tel. 505/2266-8772, U.S. tel. 703/525-8716, www.fabretto.org
TYPE OF WORK: children and youth, education, health

Based in Managua, with offices in the United States and Spain as well, Fabretto aims to end poverty in Nicaragua through "hope, health and education." Most projects are in the region surrounding the town of San José de Cusmapa, but there are projects near the cities of Managua and Estelí as well.

Fabretto works to improve elementary education through teacher training, parent outreach, nutritional education, and enrichment activities such as tutoring, sports, art, and computers. Fabretto also offers a specialized tutoring support system for secondary students in rural communities, life skills and vocational training for young adults, and nutritional education for all ages.

Projects are assigned to service groups according to the group's size, skills, and trip length. Responsibilities may include painting schools, building kitchens, helping tend school gardens, repairing playgrounds or school fences, or cooking school lunches alongside local mothers. Volunteers typically work 4-6 hours per day, then visit a project or program for 1-2 hours.

Volunteers are encouraged to engage with the communities they serve by participating in local events, visiting microenterprises or shops, attending churches, and exploring the towns. While the main focus of each trip is to meet

NICARAGUA

the children and complete the service project, Fabretto can suggest and coordinate tourist activities as well.

Application Process: There is a service group application form available online. Volunteers ages 11-20 must have an adult chaperone to participate in a service group. Individual volunteers are welcome.

Cost: US$300 donation per person to cover the project cost, plus US$75 per day, which covers meals, housing, in-country transportation, and the cost of Fabretto team leader and translator.

Placement Length: Approximately one week for service groups; four months for individual volunteers.

Language Requirements: None.

Housing: Accommodations are in Fabretto's guesthouse in San José de Cusmapa if working nearby, or in small bed-and-breakfasts if working near Managua or Estelí.

Operating Since: 1948

Number of Volunteers: 23 individual and 17 service groups in 2012

Weekends provide an opportunity for busy volunteers to explore the colonial towns dotted across Nicaragua.

© AMY E. ROBERTSON

GUARDABARRANCO, S.A.

Ocotal, tel. 504/8367-0679, www.eco-nic.com

TYPE OF WORK: agriculture, community development, environment

Guardabarranco's mission is to "improve the local economy and quality of life by creating a venue for an exchange of knowledge, culture, and skills between the people of the region and individuals from around the world." The focus is on strengthening the connection between the residents of Nuevo Segovia and their farms by "encouraging the use of permaculture techniques." In case you're not familiar with it, permaculture is about sustainable and self-maintaining horticultural systems, modeled after those found in the natural world.

Volunteers willing to commit a month or more can work on Guardabarranco's demonstration permaculture farm. Volunteer responsibilities depend on the season, but generally the work is distributed between the cultivation of corn and beans, the care of farm animals, and the development of the project. Permaculture is new and unknown in the area, so Guardabarranco focuses on working with families to demonstrate how permaculture supports "coexistence with our surroundings." Volunteers do not need to have agricultural expertise, just a desire "to be part of the project, to share with families and the community." If the volunteer has skills other than related to agriculture, such as art, music, or languages, he or she can develop and participate in projects with children and youth in the community.

Workdays in either program are 7am-2pm Monday-Friday. November-January volunteers are needed to lend a hand with the coffee harvest. It is hard work that starts early and ends late in the day, but volunteers are welcome to take the weekend off to relax and travel. In their free time, volunteers can cycle, hike, take Spanish classes, swim at the local pool, enjoy live music, take boxing lessons or guitar lessons, or participate in pottery classes.

Application Process: An application form is availavle for download from Guardabarranco's website. Families are welcome.

Cost: US$30 per week, including accommodation and meals.

Placement Length: The minimum placement is two weeks.

Language Requirements: Basic to intermediate Spanish, depending on the type of work.

Housing: Volunteers can choose between a local homestay (with a private room, electricity, river water for washing, and chlorinated water for cooking and drinking) or a volunteer guesthouse. Volunteers are responsible for purchasing bottled water.

Operating Since: 2006

Number of Volunteers: 12 agricultural volunteers and 20 coffee harvest volunteers in 2012

LA ESPERANZA GRANADA

Granada, tel. 505/8913-8946,
www.la-esperanza-granada.org

TYPE OF WORK: children and youth, community development, education, health

The brainchild of a handful of dedicated travelers and resident expats in the colonial city of Granada, La Esperanza's mission is to improve access to and quality of education in the villages outside of town. Since its founding in 2002, La Esperanza has "built 18 classrooms, a clinic, a community center, and renovated two schools"; paid the salaries of extra teachers, a school nurse, and an educational psychologist; provided dental treatment for more than 1,500 children and eyeglasses for 150 children; given school supplies, arts and crafts supplies, and sports supplies; and provided scholarships.

Most volunteers will work in primary education, as an assistant in a kindergarten or elementary school classroom or as an English teacher (in which case the volunteer will have a teaching assistant that supports him or her in the classroom). Volunteers are also needed for "summer school" (Dec.-Jan.), where they will have full responsibility for planning and teaching lessons. Those willing to make longer commitments can help with communications and promotion or grant writing.

Volunteers work 5-7 hours per day (usually 9am-3pm) 4-5 days per week and must attend a weekly evening meeting. Weekends and other evenings are free. As Nicaragua's most picturesque town, Granada is a great place to hang out, exploring its colonial architecture and funky cafés, studying Spanish, and taking day trips to the *isletas* (little islands) of Lake Cocibolca or to the Mombacho volcano. Volunteers often take advantage of long weekends to visit other parts of Nicaragua.

Note: Obvious foreigners can be perceived as easy targets for petty theft in Granada, so keep your street smarts about you and avoid flashing valuables or walking alone after 9pm.

Application Process: There is an application form online. There is no minimum age for volunteers in groups; individual volunteers must be at least age 18.

Cost: There is a onetime US$20 contribution requested to cover administration fees. Volunteers must buy La Esperanza T-shirts (US$5) to wear while working.

Placement Length: The minimum placement is four weeks or more February-November; a minimum of three weeks in December or January. Long-term volunteers are welcome and encouraged.

Language Requirements: Intermediate Spanish or better for most positions; basic Spanish is acceptable for English teachers.

Housing: Volunteers are responsible for accommodations and food. La Esperanza offers housing for US$23 per week in a dorm-style room, US$43-46 in a single room, or US$100-120 in a homestay. Volunteers are also welcome to make their own accommodation arrangements in any hostel or hotel in Granada. According to La Esperanza, most volunteers live on US$35-100 per week, excluding rent.

Operating Since: 2002

Number of Volunteers: 185 individual and 640 with groups in 2012

NICARAGUA

NICARAGUA CHILDREN'S FOUNDATION

San Juan del Sur, Canadian tel. 604/926-5323, www.nicaraguachildrensfoundation.com

TYPE OF WORK: children and youth, community development, education, environment, health

After their 2006 vacation to San Juan del Sur, the Donovan family decided to invest in schools in the area. They believe that every child has a right to an education and to the tools that will enable learning, and that each of us has the ability to make a positive difference in the lives of others. Nicaragua Children's Foundation now supports two elementary schools and has opened a school for children with special needs. In addition, Nicaragua Children's Foundation works with partners to establish dental and veterinary brigades to the area. Nicaragua Children's Foundation registered as a Canadian charity in 2009.

Nicaragua Children's Foundation's volunteer program allows for significant flexibility both in commitment and activities. Volunteers might teach English to children or adults; assist with physiotherapy at the school for those with special needs; help out at a preschool; lead a beach cleanup; participate in school improvements such as painting, gardening, carpentry, plumbing, or installing solar panels; work on an environmental education program; teach an art workshop to children or a health workshop in the community; help out with an after-school sports program or start a new one; or head to Isla Omotepe to lend a hand at the orphanage. Some tasks require greater Spanish skills than others; there is a local Spanish school that offers classes (US$8/hour or US$120/week for 20 hours).

Besides studying Spanish, volunteers can spend their free time lazing around on the beach and hitting the surf, while activities such as dance classes, canopy tours, fishing, cooking classes, and weekend day trips can be arranged through the Spanish school.

Application Process: There is an application form available online, which requires two personal references. The organization is family run and welcomes families as volunteers.

Cost: None. Volunteers pay for their own housing.

Placement Length: There is no mimumum.

Language Requirements: Most opportunities require basic Spanish. Nicaragua Children's Foundation works with a local Spanish school and can arrange inexpensive, personalized lessons for those in need.

Housing: Volunteers are responsible for their own accommodations and meals, but Nicaragua Children's Foundation can help arrange a homestay or give hotel recommendations.

Operating Since: 2006

Number of Volunteers: 10 in 2012

POWER TO THE PEOPLE

Boaco, Granada, Matagalpa, and Rivas, www.powertothepeople.org

TYPE OF WORK: community development

Power to the People is an aptly named nonprofit that helps disadvantaged communities install solar electric systems on community buildings such as schools, libraries, health clinics, and orphanages. Power to the People works closely with the communities it serves to ensure that in addition to need, there is a community desire to have the project and the ability to actively participate in its preparation, installation, and maintenance. While the organization is based out of California, it works in rural communities across Nicaragua.

Power to the People offers three week-long service trips per year where volunteers travel with the organization to install solar panels. Trip dates are set well in advance and are available online. With guidance from a professional solar company, volunteers work side by side with local community members to install the solar panels. Specific installation tasks may include: installing the solar modules and the racking on the roof, mounting the battery rack and hooking up the batteries, hanging and wiring the inverter and charge controller on the wall, and installing and wiring all of the light sockets, outlets, and switches inside the building. Other tasks may include training community members,

Nicaragua's small towns boast plenty of colonial charm.

moving equipment, entertaining the kids in the community, organizing components, drilling holes in the wall, pulling wires, hanging conduit, and measuring the battery voltage. Volunteers usually work from morning to evening for 2-3 days to complete the installation.

Due to the remote locations of Power to the People projects, there may not be many opportunities for traditional tourism while at the project site. However, trips always include a couple of days of sightseeing, including activities such as a visit to a crafts market or one of Nicaragua's colonial towns, a lake tour by boat, nature hikes to a waterfall or on one of Nicaragua's volcanoes, dinner out, a music performance, and a trip to a coffee plantation or a cigar factory.

Application Process: To apply, send an email followed by a 50 percent deposit to hold your spot. There is no minimum age to volunteer, just the ability to walk long distances and tolerate the heat. Former volunteers have ranged in age from 9 to 65, and families are welcome.

Cost: Usually US$1,600, covering all in-country expenses.
Placement Length: eight days
Language Requirements: None.
Housing: Accommodations vary, from a high-end hotel in Managua to a very basic homestay (without electricity or running water) in the rural community where the project is located. After installation, volunteers move to a modest hotel for a couple of days of guided sightseeing. Meals range from restaurant fare to basic meals with rice, beans, and tortillas in the rural community.
Operating Since: 2008
Number of Volunteers: 44 in 2012

PROJECT BONA FIDE

Balgue and Ometepe, Lake Nicaragua,
www.projectbonafide.com
TYPE OF WORK: agriculture, community development

Project Bona Fide is "a non-profit organization working toward sustaining culture through organic agriculture, community

NICARAGUA

correlated outreach, and reforestation projects in Nicaragua." To this end, the project has established a pilot farm on Ometepe, an island formed by two volcanoes that rise out of Lake Nicaragua. Through outreach, education, and financial and technical support, Project Bona Fide works to create organic cooperatives and fair trade markets to benefit local farmers.

Volunteers work on the farm five hours a day Monday-Friday. Activities vary with the season and the needs of the farm, but they may include planting trees, harvesting, carpentry, construction, working in the garden or nursery, building terraces, digging swales, weeding, compost management, building raised beds, or watering plants. Volunteers will also spend part of their week at the organization's Mano Amigo Community Center in Balgue, which is home to a children's nutritional program, a community library, a learning center with computers and workshop spaces, and even a bread oven for a local women's cooperative.

Volunteers can spend afternoons and weekends exploring the island or may get involved with more farm work or volunteering at the community center. Spanish lessons are also available at the center. As one person put it, the farm tends to attract "WWOOFers, hippies, and botanists," but no experience in agriculture is required.

Application Process: To apply, send an email. All ages are welcome at the farm, as long as they are willing to put in five hours of work Monday-Friday.

Cost: Costs vary depending on length of stay, from US$15 per day to US$250 per month.

Placement Length: There is a minimum placement of two weeks, although exceptions may be made, especially in the low-season months (May, September-October).

Language Requirements: None, unless the volunteer wants to take on a coordinating or leadership position.

Housing: Volunteers can stay in tents on the farm (bring your own tent) or arrange for a homestay with a Nicaraguan family (US$14/

day). Vegetarian meals at the farm are included in the cost, and volunteers are welcome to help themselves to the products of the farm and vegetable garden. Homestay volunteers eat dinner during the week, and all meals on the weekends, with their host families.

Operating Since: 2001

Number of Volunteers: 170 in 2012

RANCHO ESPERANZA

Jiquillo, tel. 505/8879-1795,
www.rancho-esperanza.com

TYPE OF WORK: agriculture, children and youth, community development, education

Located on the northwest Pacific coast of Nicaragua, Rancho Esperanza is a low-key, sustainable beach getaway that combines tourism with community development. Their mission is to "create and support social and environmental community-based programs, while providing a sustainable and positive eco-hostel destination for travelers and volunteers alike."

Volunteers stay in one of the Rancho's properties and help children with their homework, play games, or teach arts and crafts in the community center; teach surf lessons or English classes; or share their gardening, carpentry, or artistic skills on the Rancho's property. Fluent Spanish speakers are needed to help build a homestay program, provide small business assistance, or develop the community tours. Volunteers are expected to help out with daily chores around the Rancho plus work on their project three hours a day, so there is plenty of free time to swim, surf, kayak, or further support the local community through cultural excursions (tortilla making, coconut tree climbing, or a community tour). All excursion fees go directly to the local guide.

Application Process: To apply, send an email and include your interests and experience. Long-term volunteers may be asked for references and a résumé.

Cost: Accommodation rates only; there are no additional program fees.

Placement Length: The minimum placement length starts at two weeks and depends upon the type of volunteer work.

VOLUNTEER PERSPECTIVE

Barbara Pavie (age 29) is from France. Here's what she had to say about her volunteer experience in Nicaragua with **Project Bona Fide** (Balgue and Ometepe, Lake Nicaragua, www.projectbonafide.com).

Volunteering for Project Bona Fide was a great experience. I worked mainly on the farm, learning a lot about the local culture and the permaculture approach. The team is really knowledgeable, helpful, and always here to answer questions. Food was delicious, and I appreciated it even more knowing that it was coming from the farm. We harvested it in the morning and ate it for lunch. While cooking dinner, whatever we needed, we could find around the kitchen. It was fresh, home grown, organic, sustainable, and tasted amazing. I learned about different tasty vegetables, leaves that you can eat, mysterious and colorful fruits, how to take care of a garden...I believe their work really supports the local community in becoming more self-sufficient, and I was proud to be part of it.

© BARBARA PAVIE

Volunteers at Project Bona Fide might harvest organic produce, such as these mangos.

Language Requirements: From none to fluent Spanish, depending on the type of work chosen.

Housing: Accommodations range from bamboo cabins (US$28/day) and dorms to tents and hammocks (US$4/day). Two cabins have private half baths; the rest use shared bathrooms. All showers are shared. Meals are available (with a vegetarian option) but are not included.

Operating Since: 2005

Number of Volunteers: 44 in 2012

SEEDS OF LEARNING

Ciudad Dario, tel. 505/776-3877,
U.S. tel. 707/939-0471, www.seedsoflearning.org

TYPE OF WORK: community development

Seeds of Learning is dedicated to "improving educational opportunities in rural Latin America." It achieves this by building and equipping schools in underserved communities.

Community engagement is a cornerstone of Seeds of Learning's approach: Projects are considered only when a written request has been made by the community and community involvement in all stages of project implementation is required. Past projects have included constructing or remodeling classrooms; building or repairing thousands of school desks and furnishings; developing three learning resource centers; sponsoring more than 1,000 scholarships for primary, high school, and university education; supporting literacy and adult education programs in over 20 rural communities; and developing sister school partnerships between classrooms in the United States and Central America. Seeds of Learning serves more than 300 students a day in the learning resource centers, equipped with 3,500 books for students and teachers, and offers classes in dance, music, sewing, embroidery, crafts, English, and computer basics, as well as tutoring. Seeds of Learning sends 10-16 teams each year to support these projects and learn from the local communities.

Cultural and educational opportunities for volunteers are built into the daily schedule. There are both open and closed work groups available; anyone can apply to the former, while closed groups are intended for those who organize their own group (of fellow students, colleagues, or church or synagogue members). In early 2013, Seeds of Learning had 19 trips to Nicaragua planned. Seeds of Learning has programs and occasional work trips in El Salvador as well.

Application Process: There is an online

INTERNATIONAL ORGANIZATIONS

The following international organizations support volunteer efforts in Nicaragua:

A Broader View (U.S. tel. 215/780-1845, toll-free U.S. tel. 866/423-3258, www.abroaderview.org), page 193.
Type of Work: agriculture, children and youth, community development, education, environment, health, wildlife protection, women's empowerment

Amizade Global Service Learning (U.S. tel. 412/586-4986, www.amizade.org), page 194.
Type of Work: agriculture, children and youth, community development, education, environment, health

Earthwatch (U.S. tel. 978/461-0081, toll-free U.S. tel. 800/776-0188, www.earthwatch.org), page 196.
Type of Work: environment, wildlife protection

Eastern Pacific Hawksbill Initiative (ICAPO) (U.S. tel. 619/818-0041, www.hawksbill.org), page 198.
Type of Work: education, environment, wildlife protection

Global Communities: Partners for Good (U.S. tel. 301/587-4700, www.globalcommunities.org), page 200.
Type of Work: children and youth, community development, education, environment, women's empowerment

Habitat for Humanity International (toll-free U.S. tel. 800/422-4828, www.habitat.org), page 202.
Type of Work: community development

TECHO (U.S. tel. 305/860-4090, www.techo.org), page 209.
Type of Work: community development

application form for open work groups. A copy of your passport and a US$600 deposit are also required. There is no minimum age to participate, and families are welcome. **Cost:** US$1,300 for a 10-day work group; housing and in-country transportation are included, as well as a donation to Seeds of Learning's programs. Travelers under the age of 30 can apply for small scholarships (around US$250), and family discounts are available.

Placement Length: 1-2 weeks
Language Requirements: None.
Housing: Volunteers stay in simple shared accommodations, such as retreat centers or small hotels. Meals are included in the program cost, and may be self-prepared breakfasts and packed lunches, while dinners are often catered or at local restaurants.
Operating Since: 1991
Number of Volunteers: 210 in 2012

Essentials

BACKGROUND
Geography and Climate
Nicaragua's tropical climate makes it a year-round destination. Temperatures do vary significantly from the mountains, where you'll need a sweater in the evening, to the low-lying valleys, where daytime highs can reach 38°C (100°F). The rainy season is roughly May-October; in areas closer to the Atlantic coast or down the Río San Juan, it may last longer. October is the wettest month, but it rarely rains all day or every day.

History and Economy
Nicaragua won its independence from Spain in 1821 and became fully independent when it withdrew from the Central American Federation in 1838. After a century of U.S.-backed governments, the Somoza family took power and held onto it tightly until 1979. The Sandinista revolution (named after a renegade general from the early 1900s) followed, complicated by U.S. funding of the "contras." The conflict lasted more than a decade and ended with the election of Violeta Chamorro in 1990. Regular elections and peaceful (if often corrupt) governance have been the norm since then.

Although Nicaragua has seen significant improvements since 1990, the decades of corruption and war were compounded by the effects of 1998's devastating Hurricane Mitch, during which an estimated 70 percent of the country's infrastructure was destroyed. Nicaragua's struggling economy is based almost entirely on the agricultural export of primary goods, the most important of which are coffee, beef, and sugar. Bananas, shellfish, tobacco, onions, and fruit are other important exports, along with clothing from the country's *maquilas* (sweatshops).

PREPARATION
Transportation
Nicaragua's international airport is **Augusto César Sandino International Airport** (MGA, www.eaai.com.ni), located in the capital city of Managua. Air Canada, American Airlines, United, and US Air all fly to Managua, as well as domestic, regional and European airlines. There is a US$35 airport departure tax (cash only, payable in U.S. dollars or local currency), which may or may not be included in your ticket price—be sure to check.

Within Nicaragua, small prop planes service domestic airports, while bus networks crisscross the country. Bus service is safe and cheap, albeit slow; if you have a choice between a "luxury" bus (without stops) or an old yellow school bus (stops whenever anyone hails), spring for luxury.

Passports and Visas
The expiration date on your passport must be at least six months after the date your trip begins, or you will not be able to enter the country (or even board your plane). Honduras, Guatemala, El Salvador, and Nicaragua have formed a single immigration region—the

NICARAGUA

CA4 region—which grants tourists from North America and many European countries an automatic 90-day visa. When arriving to Nicaragua by air, visitors must pay US$10 at the airport for a "tourist card," which is the visa. In Nicaragua, it is usually possible to renew your visa for an additional month (US$25). Alternatively, you will need to exit and reenter the region (Costa Rica is the easiest non-CA4 country to reach from Nicaragua).

Money

Nicaragua has two official currencies: their own **cordoba** (C$) and the U.S. dollar. Travelers carrying other Central American currencies should exchange their money at the border. Visitors from countries other than the United States should bring dollars, as exchanging anything else (including travelers checks) can be a real challenge.

Health

There is some risk of malaria and dengue fever in much of Nicaragua. Bring insect repellent, and consider whether you wish to take a malaria prophylaxis.

Safety

Nicaragua is fortunate to have a low crime rate. However, obvious foreigners can make tempting targets for would-be thieves, so keep your valuables out of sight. In towns and cities, take a taxi rather than walking at night (after 9pm or so). Always check with your host organization for the latest on safety recommendations in the place you will stay and work.

Unlike its neighbors to the north, Nicaragua has been able to keep the drug trade more or less out of its borders, and as a result, it remains one of the safest countries in Central America.

COSTA RICA

Bordered to the north by Nicaragua, to the south by Panama, and sandwiched between the Pacific and Atlantic Oceans, Costa Rica is diminutive yet ecologically diverse, encompassing a variety of forests (rain, deciduous, and cloud), volcanoes, valleys, swamps, and savannas. For decades Costa Rica has been one of Central America's most popular tourist destinations, a lush paradise of golden coastlines and tropical jungles, with well-developed amenities for travelers, including those looking to give something back while here.

As significant as its natural beauty is the stability and effectiveness of its democracy. Costa Rica is one of the most developed countries in the region, with a highly educated populace, long life expectancies, and potable water and electricity throughout the country. Most of Costa Rica's 4.7 million inhabitants are middle class and of European descent. The Guanacaste region is home to a large portion of Costa Rica's *mestizo* population, descendants of Spanish conquistadores and the indigenous Chorotega Indians. Puerto Limón, on Costa Rica's northern coast, is home to the majority of the country's 40,000 Afro-Caribbeans.

According to the World Bank, the gross national income per capita in Costa Rica is US$7,640. However, its relatively high income hides significant pockets of need: nearly one in four Costa Ricans live below the poverty line, while one in seven live in extreme poverty. High literacy rates mask equally high drop-out rates, with 40 percent of Costa Ricans dropping out of school by the sixth grade.

Fortunately, there are a few programs that

© ANITA BORAY

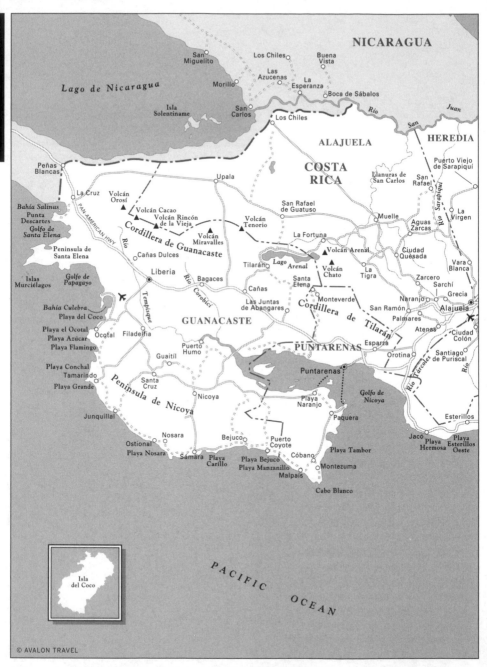

© AVALON TRAVEL

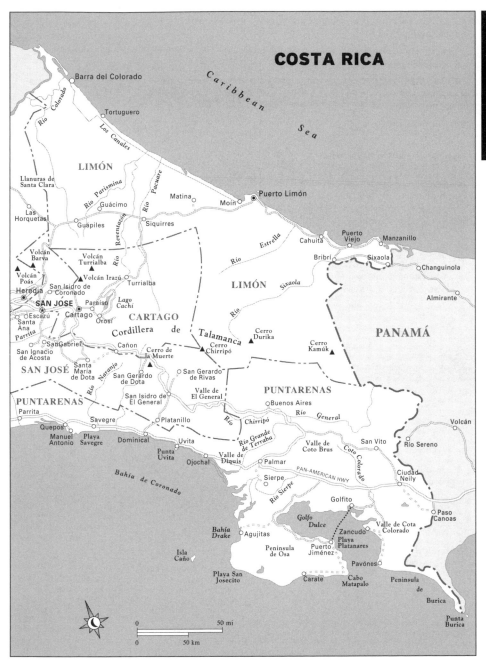

COSTA RICA

Caribbean Sea

Barra del Colorado

Tortuguero

Los Canales

Río Colorado

LIMÓN

Llanuras de Santa Clara

Las Horquetas

Río Parismina

Guácimo

Matina

Moín

Puerto Limón

Guápiles

Río Pacuare

Siquirres

Río Reventación

Estrella

Cahuita

Puerto Viejo

Manzanillo

Volcán Barva

Volcán Turrialba

Río

Río

Bribrí

Sixaola

Changuinola

Volcán Poás

Volcán Irazú

San Isidro de Coronado

Turrialba

LIMÓN

Sixaola

Almirante

Heredia

SAN JOSE

Paraíso

Lago Cachí

PANAMÁ

Escazú

Cartago

Orosí

CARTAGO

Santa Ana

Parrita

Cordillera de

Talamanca

Cerro Durika

Cerro Kamúk

SanGabriel

Cañon

Cerro de la Muerte

Cerro Chirripó

San Ignacio de Acosta

SAN JOSÉ

Santa María de Dota

San Gerardo de Dota

San Gerardo de Rivas

Río Naranjo

San Isidro de El General

Valle de El General

PUNTARENAS

PUNTARENAS

Buenos Aires

Parrita

Savegre

Platanillo

Río Chirripó

Río General

Volcán

Quepos

Manuel Antonio

Playa Savegre

Dominical

Uvita

Río Grande de Terraba

Valle de Coto Brus

San Vito

Río Sereno

Punta Uvita

Ojochal

Valle de Diquis

Palmar

Coto Colorado

Ciudad Neily

Bahía de Coronado

Sierpe

PAN-AMERICAN HWY

Río Sierpe

Golfito

Paso Canoas

Bahía Drake

Agujitas

Golfo Dulce

Zancudo

Valle de Cota Colorado

Isla Caño

Península de Osa

Puerto Jiménez

Playa Platanares

Pavónes

Playa San Josecito

Carate

Cabo Matapalo

Península de

Burica

Punta Burica

0   50 mi

0   50 km

support community development and education efforts–and a wealth of options for volunteers interested in working with wildlife. In addition to famed projects to protect sea turtles (nesting season is March-October, with hatchlings spotted through December), there is a unique opportunity to work with macaws, the emblematic birds of Central America.

Local Organizations

THE ARA PROJECT
Arajuela, tel. 506/8389-5811, www.thearaproject.org
TYPE OF WORK: wildlife protection

Based 30 minutes outside of San José, the ARA Project is dedicated to the conservation of Costa Rica's two native macaws (parrots): the endangered great green macaw (*Ara ambiguous*) and the scarlet macaw (*Ara macao*). ARA released more than 80 scarlet macaws into the wild between 1999 and 2012, and in 2011, it achieved the first great green macaw reintroduction in the world. The breeding center, which has about 100 of each type of macaw, is located near the San José airport, while the birds are reintroduced to the wild in five conservation areas across the country.

The ARA Project plans to move its breeding center to the release site at Punta Islita, south of Samara on the Nicoya Peninsula, pending funding.

Short-term volunteers are welcome at the breeding center. Those who can commit two months or longer can also consider the program for reintroduction to the wild, at three release sites located near beautiful beaches and jungles teeming with plants and animals. At the center, volunteers work 7am-5:30pm, six days per week. Responsibilities include feeding the macaws and cleaning their aviaries, observing the bird behavior, maintaining the grounds, and, if volunteers are interested, participating in conservation education.

© THE ARA PROJECT

The ARA Project works to protect Costa Rica's native scarlet and great green macaws.

Application Process: Send an email to. Volunteers must be age 18 or older.
Cost: US$23 per day at the breeding center, which covers a homestay and a US$5/day contribution to the project. Volunteers at the release sites pay US$10/day and are responsible for their own meals.
Placement Length: Minimum of two weeks.
Language Requirements: Basic Spanish is recommended but not required.
Housing: Short-term volunteers are placed in homestays near the breeding center (in either private or shared rooms). Three meals per day, plus laundry, are included. Volunteers at the release sites have shared rooms and are responsible for their own meals.
Operating Since: 2009
Number of Volunteers: 42 at the breeding center and 18 at the release sites in 2012

ASSOCIATION SAVE THE TURTLES OF PARISMINA

Parismina, tel. 506/2798-2220,
www.parisminaturtles.org
TYPE OF WORK: wildlife protection
Association Save the Turtles of Parismina (ASTOP) is a sea-turtle conservancy program, unique in that it was founded by the local community. Along with protecting sea turtles and their eggs from poaching, ASTOP economically supports roughly one-third of the village of Parismina, and since 2001 it has successfully redefined within the community the cultural importance of turtle conservation.

Volunteers are critical to ASTOP's work. On nightly patrols volunteers help guard nesting turtles, learn to identify turtle tracks, count the number of eggs, record tag numbers, and assist with relocating eggs. During the day, volunteers monitor the hatchery, help clean up the beach, watch over the hatchlings on their journey to the ocean, participate in nest exhumations, teach English or do arts and crafts projects with local children, help in the recycling center, or create community improvement projects based on personal skills and interests. Free time is spent relaxing, swimming, horseback riding, exploring the town and rainforest,

or learning how to dance salsa and merengue. While volunteers are welcome at any time, turtle nesting season starts in March and ends in September or October.

ASTOP welcomes families and can arrange for shorter patrols for those with kids who might not be able to make the entire four-hour patrol. Kids have especially enjoyed watching hatchlings, whose race to the sea generally starts in the month of May.
Application Process: Send an email. Volunteers under 18 must be accompanied by a parent. Families are welcome.
Cost: There is a US$35 registration fee. Homestays are US$27/day for the first 10 days, US$22/day thereafter, and it includes participation in the volunteer program. Volunteers who choose other accommodations must pay a program fee of US$10/day for the first 10 days, US$5/day thereafter, and they are responsible for their own meals. For groups, there are packages available.
Placement Length: Minimum of five nights.
Language Requirements: None.
Housing: Volunteers can stay in homestays, hotels, cabins, or camping areas. Homestays include three meals per day and laundry service, as well as the daily program fee, and there are a few homestays available with an English-speaking family member. Hotels range from basic to luxury.
Operating Since: 2001
Number of Volunteers: about 150 individuals in 2012, plus student groups

CPI SPANISH IMMERSION SCHOOL

San Joaquín de Flores, Monteverde, and Flamingo Beach, tel. 506/2265-6306,
toll-free U.S. tel. 877/373-3116, www.cpi-edu.com
TYPE OF WORK: children and youth, community development, education, environment, health, wildlife protection, women's empowerment
CPI's primary focus is on teaching Spanish, but it also has a volunteer program that can be a good option for anyone who wishes to combine serious language study with volunteering. There are three locations across Costa Rica:

VOLUNTEER PERSPECTIVE

Anita Boray (age 37) is from Montreal, Canada. She had this to say about her experience protecting sea turtles with **ASTOP** (Parismina, tel. 506/2798-2220, www.parisminaturtles.org) in Costa Rica.

One of the most authentic experiences of my travels in Central America was volunteering for ASTOP, a grassroots organization founded by local teenagers living on the small island of Parismina. They saw the detrimental effects of consuming turtle meat and eggs by locals and poachers alike, and decided to do something about it. Parismina is off the beaten track; you will find next to no tourists and few volunteers. (Groups sometimes come to work with ASTOP, but I traveled by myself. During my stay, we were never more than 10.) Anywhere else, you would have to pay the big bucks to see turtles laying eggs. Here, patrolling the beaches at night is a normal part of everyday life, for volunteers and locals alike. Other duties included relocating eggs, surveying the hatchery, and exhuming nests. These duties were as much of a highlight as living with my host family in a small, but cozy, two-bedroom house. They did everything to make my stay comfortable. It was fantastic to experience what Costa Rican rural life is like, connect with locals, and be able to practice Spanish. I might be a little partial to my experience because I am a science teacher and love seeing wildlife, but watching tiny turtles emerge from the sand and make their way to the ocean is a humbling sight for anyone. Parismina is so special to me that I decided to organize a volunteering trip for my high school students this summer.

I can't wait to go back!

"Heredia" is located in the small, typical town of San Joaquín de Flores; Monteverde is in the cloud forest; and Flamingo Beach is on the northern Pacific coast. At Heredia, volunteers can assist with English lessons at an educational center for preschoolers and elementary-aged children, or at a technical high school that prepares students for bilingual careers in tourism, accounting, and IT; female volunteers can also choose to volunteer at a home for impoverished girls. At Monteverde, volunteers can work with children or make building improvements at a missionary school, develop arts and crafts projects at a women's handicrafts cooperative, or lend a hand at one of several nature reserves, working on trail maintenance, environmental outreach, and more. At Flamingo, volunteers can choose to work at one of two schools, assisting with classroom activities, helping teach English, giving private tutoring to kids who need extra help, and helping out with administrative activities. Volunteers are also needed at CEN CINAI Huacas, a public institution that provides social services to children.

Free time activities vary with the location and include hiking, swimming, and, of course, studying Spanish (20 hours per week).
Application Process: To apply, register via an online form or send an email. Volunteers must be at least 18.
Cost: US$720-990 for two weeks of Spanish classes, plus a US$50 fee for the volunteer placement. Volunteers are also responsible for housing, but a few free activities, such as dance and cooking classes, are included, as is transportation from the San José airport to the chosen location.
Placement Length: Minimum of two weeks.
Language Requirements: None, but Spanish classes are required.
Housing: CPI encourages homestays, which

are US$150/week and US$23/night for additional nights. Volunteers are given private rooms, as well as breakfast and dinner. CPI can help arrange studio apartments for US$350-375/week, or students can stay in residences for US$150-250/week, depending on location and if the room is shared.

Operating Since: 1991

Number of Volunteers: In 2012 CPI received 927 students in Heredia, 808 in Monteverde, and 903 in Flamingo, including both individual students and groups. Of the individual students, around 50 participated in the volunteer program, primarily in Monteverde, while more than 500 volunteers came in groups (high school and college students, as well as professionals).

ENDANGERED WILDLIFE TRUST

Pacuare Nature Reserve, tel. 506/2234-5890, www.turtleprotection.org

TYPE OF WORK: education, wildlife protection

Endangered Wildlife Trust is a British nonprofit that owns the Pacuare Nature Reserve, 10.5 square kilometers (2,600 acres) of tropical rainforest on Costa Rica's northern coast, near Tortuguero. The reserve's 6 kilometers (nearly 4 mi) of beach is said to be the most important nesting site in the country for the giant leatherback turtles, and hawksbill and green turtles occasionally make their nests there as well. In addition, there are some 30 species of mammals, 230 species of birds, and countless reptiles and insects that call the reserve home.

In February, volunteer activities are related to the preparation for the nesting season: doing repairs on the facilities, such as painting, beach cleanup, and so on. At the height of the season, March-September, the beach is patrolled at night in three- to five-hour shifts. On the patrols, volunteers will have the chance to help biologists monitor the nesting turtles, recording nest location, dimensions, and other data. During the day, volunteers can help out with composting and the vegetable garden, or help with environmental education, either by accompanying a biologist on a local school

visit or by working with children who come to the reserve to learn about the turtles and the forest. March-June is the leatherback turtle season, and July-September is the green turtle season.

In their free time, volunteers can walk or bicycle in the reserve, take a guided night hike, look for monkeys near the lagoon, take a boat ride along the canal to look for caimans and crocodiles, or just hang out in a hammock.

Application Process: To apply, send an email, and you'll be sent an application form. There is no minimum age to volunteer (as long as minors are accompanied by an adult); families are very welcome.

Cost: US$25 per day, including housing, if staying in the volunteer cabins. There is also a US$20 charge for boat transportation from the canal to the reserve. US$85-95 per person, per night, if staying at the Casa Grande, and boat transportation is included.

Placement Length: Minimum of two nights if staying at the Casa Grande; otherwise minimum of one week.

Language Requirements: None.

Housing: Volunteers normally stay in simple cabins, 2-3 to a room, and bathrooms/showers have cold water and are outside of the cabins. There is also a more private, three-bedroom

Volunteers measure sea turtles as part of their research and monitoring.

house called the Casa Grande, which has solar-heated hot water for the shower; it can be rented by room or in its entirety for a two-night minimum. There is no electricity on the reserve. Three meals per day are included with both accommodations.

Operating Since: 1989
Number of Volunteers: around 60 in 2012

EVOLC (ENGLISH VOLUNTEERS FOR CHANGE IN COSTA RICA)

Central Valley, 506/2248-0237, www.evolc.org
TYPE OF WORK: education

EVOLC is the offspring of a government initiative to create a bilingual Costa Rica by 2020, thereby equipping communities across the country to reap the benefits of the country's thriving ecotourism industry. Its focus is on improving English education in rural/impoverished areas and in public schools, in order to provide more opportunity for disadvantaged Costa Rican citizens and to support sustainable tourism in rural communities.

While most of EVOLC's volunteer programs are long-term, they do have a community service program where volunteers can choose to stay between 2 and 12 weeks. For short-term volunteers, the first day is spent in San José, the capital of Costa Rica, where volunteers are put up in a hotel and receive an orientation. After that, volunteers in the community service program remain in the Central Valley region, working full-time with local organizations and/or schools to improve the English-language skills in nearby communities, working with both children and adults. These short-term volunteers are usually placed as assistants to English teachers, and exact responsibilities will depend on the volunteer's skills, interests, and experience: More experienced volunteers may prepare and teach lessons, while less experienced volunteers will tutor and conduct conversation classes. Unlike the long-term volunteer programs, the short-term one does not require any teaching certification.

As short-term volunteers are located in or around San José, there is plenty to do in their free time, from Spanish lessons to dance classes, visits to the National Museum, and other cultural activities. Volunteers have the option of taking three-day weekends and can easily hop a bus from San José to the volcanoes, forest, or beach.

Volunteers are also permitted to teach up to 10 hours per week of private lessons as a way to offset the program expense.

Application Process: There is a downloadable application form on their website, which must be completed and emailed back, along with a copy of your résumé/cv, a cover letter, and a one-page essay. Individual volunteers must be 18, but families who want to travel/volunteer with children can be accommodated.

Cost: From US$900 for 2 weeks up to US$2,550 for 12 weeks, which covers housing and transportation from San José to the work site and back.

Placement Length: 2-12 weeks
Language Requirements: None.
Housing: Volunteers are placed with host families, who provide three meals per day.
Operating Since: 2009
Number of Volunteers: 15 in 2012

SEA TURTLE CONSERVANCY

Tortuguero, toll-free U.S. tel. 800/678-7853, www.conserveturtles.org
TYPE OF WORK: wildlife protection

Founded in 1959 by renowned expert Dr. Archie Carr, the Sea Turtle Conservancy (STC; formerly known as the Caribbean Conservation Corporation) is the world's oldest sea turtle research and conservation group. Although their trips are pricey, they are highly regarded. Based in Gainesville, Florida, STC runs "eco-volunteer adventures" to Costa Rica March-October. All trips head to the remote island of Tortuguero, which is located off the Atlantic coast and home to a national park. There is a village on the island with shops, restaurants, and hotels.

STC offers a variety of trips, focused on leatherback or green turtles, on birds, or on a combination. Leatherback adventures are available March-May, and volunteers help find turtles, count turtle tracks, and tag nesting turtles. Leatherbacks are the world's largest turtles, can weigh nearly 700 kilograms (up to 1,500 lb), and measure over 2 meters (up to 7 ft). Green turtle adventures are available June-October, and volunteers will work with researchers to measure these "gentle giants" (green turtles can weigh up to almost 160 kg/350 lb), count eggs, mark nests, and count tracks. Bird adventures are available March-October. Volunteers will learn to identify the local and migrant birds in the area, and the basics of bird handling and data collection. They will assist researchers at (temporary) capture stations and with bird censuses and migration counts. Trips can be added one after the other, so those interested in working with leatherbacks and birds can come March-May, while those interested in green turtles and birds can plan a trip for August-October.

Tortuguero has been called "Costa Rica's Amazon" for its rainforest and abundance of wildlife. It's such a popular destination for ecovacations (turtle conservancy in particular) that they have even developed their own website (with the help of a Peace Corps volunteer) at www.tortuguerovillage.com, which has a "must-do" list of activities that, in addition to checking out the turtles on the beach, includes hikes in the rainforest, boat tours in the island canals, a visit to the turtle museum, a tour of the village, ocean swimming, and a jungle zip line tour.

Application Process: There is an online application form. Individual volunteers must be 18; 16- and 17-year-olds are welcome if accompanied by an adult.

Cost: Prices range US$1,439-1,999 per person for one week and include accommodations, meals, laundry service, in-country transportation (including a domestic flight Tortuguero-San José at the end of the trip), and either a boat excursion through Tortuguero's canal system or a guided hike through the rainforest.

Placement Length: One week minimum.

Language Requirements: None.

Housing: Volunteers can choose between a rustic dorm, the scientific residence with private bedrooms and bathrooms, or ecolodges a five-minute walk away. Meals are hearty Costa Rican food.

Operating Since: 1959

Number of Volunteers: 130 in 2012

SEA TURTLES FOREVER

Punta Pargos, U.S. tel. 503-739-1446,
www.seaturtlesforever.com

TYPE OF WORK: environment, wildlife protection
Founded by Marc and Rachel Ward, and based out of Oregon, Sea Turtles Forever (STF) runs conservation programs both in Costa Rica and on the Oregon coast. Their work in Costa Rica is on the Pacific coast near Punta Pargos, on the Nicoya Peninsula. STF focuses on the conservation of leatherback, green, hawksbill, and olive ridley turtles; the protection of nesting sites and hatchlings; the removal of marine plastic; and education and collaboration with local communities on all aspects of conservation. It averages about 8,000 live hatchlings annually.

Volunteers go on beach patrols, which are conducted 6pm-6am and last 3-6 hours each night. On the patrols, volunteers will assist in locating nests, taking and recording egg and turtle measurements, and monitoring hatchlings. Days are free for volunteers to swim, snorkel, and sleep, while interested volunteers can also help out with environmental outreach at the local schools, beach cleanup, and nest monitoring and reclamation.

Dates for the one- and two-week volunteer options are generally December-March, making for a good winter alternative to the spring-fall sea turtle programs elsewhere. There is also the possibility of volunteering for just one or two nights through their Research Expedition program.

Application Process: Send your résumé/cv via email. Individual volunteers must be juniors in college or older; those younger can volunteer through the one-day Research Expedition program if accompanied by a parent.

Cost: US$350 for one week; US$600 for two weeks. Accommodations are included, and two meals a day can be added for US$20 per day.

Placement Length: Usually a minimum of one week. Occasionally exceptions for shorter-term placements can be made.

Language Requirements: None.

Housing: Volunteers stay in several small, rustic cabins with communal bathrooms. The housing is coed. There is a small fridge and a stove that volunteers can use to prepare food, there are restaurants in town, and volunteers can also arrange for two meals per day.

Operating Since: 2002

Number of Volunteers: 24 signed up for two- to eight-week sessions during the 2012-2013 season; around 60 Research Expedition volunteers were hosted in the 2011-2012 season

TROPICAL ADVENTURES

Hojancha (Guanacaste), tel. 506/8868-0296, toll-free U.S. tel. 800/832-9419, ext. 302, www.tropicaladventures.com

TYPE OF WORK: children and youth, community development, education, environment, wildlife protection

Tropical Adventures (TA) seeks to support the empowerment of individuals and communities through the reduction of poverty and injustice, creation of safe environments, support of sustainable growth, and the promotion of international learning and cooperation. Very lofty goals, supported by very practical means: "volunteer and voluntour packages for individuals, families and groups interested in exploring the culture, language and natural beauty of Costa Rica."

TA partners with local nonprofit organizations in the areas of community development, children and education, and conservation and wildlife, providing them with volunteer labor and material donations. They have projects with partners across the country. Volunteers may stay on the beach to help monitor sea turtles and collect turtle eggs, clean up beaches, provide environmental outreach, maintain trails, and work in a garden at a conservation center. Others might monitor sea turtles from the water, assist with reef surveys, capture/tag/release

turtles, and rescue injured turtles. Those who are fans of land-loving fauna may choose to work at a wildlife rescue center where birds, caimans, monkeys, boars, herons, ducks, raccoons, dogs, cats, and even a kinkajou are being rehabilitated. Volunteers who prefer to spend their time helping people can head to Hojancha, a small town in the region of Guanacaste, where TA is based, to implement plans for community development that include developing a recycling program, building a technology center, and giving classes in nutrition, dance, health, and sports.

Most trips are planned on a four-day workweek so that volunteers will have plenty of time to explore Costa Rica's celebrated nature and adventure activities—volcanoes, waterfalls, rainforests, beaches, kayaking, snorkeling, surfing, and more. TA can help make plans and arrangements, and it offers a few tours of its own that volunteers can add onto their package. TA also offers special "voluntour" packages that combine sightseeing with a few days of volunteering.

Application Process: There is an online form, which requires your passport number. Individual volunteers must be at least 16, and those under 18 require parental authorization. Families of all ages are welcome (and encouraged!).

Cost: The cost depends on the project and length of commitment. One-week commitments range from US$140 to volunteer with sea turtles to US$1,195 for a week's volunteering at a wildlife rescue center. The cost includes airport pickup, bus transportation to your project site, and one night's hotel in San José if your flight schedule makes it necessary. Volunteers in Hojancha do not pay any program fee but are asked to fundraise US$200 toward the project and are responsible for the cost of their lodging and food.

Placement Length: Anything from one day onward.

Language Requirements: None.

Housing: Many volunteers stay with host families and are usually given their own room and private bathroom. Homes have electricity, but not always hot water. Meals are included with homestays. Some Caribbean families speak both English and Spanish, while others are Spanish only. Hostels and hotels are available in some project locations, and volunteers with the sea turtle programs stay in volunteer guesthouses or cabins.

Operating Since: 2005
Number of Volunteers: typically over 250 per year

TURTLE TRAX

Nicoya Peninsula, www.turtle-trax.com
TYPE OF WORK: children and youth, community development, education, environment, wildlife protection

Turtle Trax (TT) has been contracted by the highly regarded sea turtle conservation agency, Pretoma (Programa Restoracion de Tortugas de Marina), to manage its volunteer program. The mission is to "provide a unique community based volunteer experience immersing volunteers within local traditions and cultures, providing important economic benefit to coastal communities with aiding in the direct conservation of endangered marine turtles." The project sites are roughly six hours by bus (or a short flight) from San José, either in tiny beach communities along the Pacific Ocean or near uninhabited beach. The volunteer program runs July 15-December 15 (the project opens a few days earlier at the Corozalito site, on July 10).

Volunteers join Pretoma staff on nightly three-hour beach patrols to search for adult female nesting turtles. Responsibilities include collecting eggs and relocating them to project hatcheries, measuring and tagging nesting turtles, monitoring project hatcheries, and registering data. If volunteers are interested, they can also get involved with the local community, teaching English, environmental education, or arts or sports programs at local schools.

In their free time, volunteers can take community-run tours to go fishing, visit waterfalls, ride horses, and more. TT can make arrangements for a hotel upon arrival in San José, and transportation to and from the project site, if needed.

Application Process: There is a downloadable application form to complete and return by email. Recommended minimum age for volunteers is 12.

Cost: US$375 for one week, US$1,300 for four; staying in a private cabin is US$50 more.

Placement Length: Recommended minimum of two weeks.

Language Requirements: None, although Spanish certainly helps for interacting with the local community.

Housing: Varies by location. Volunteers may stay at a volunteer house, in private cabins, or in a rustic base camp. Meals are provided.

Operating Since: Pretoma was founded in 1997; Turtle Trax began working with Pretoma in 2011.

Number of Volunteers: roughly 70 in 2012

INTERNATIONAL ORGANIZATIONS

The following international organizations support volunteer efforts in Costa Rica:

A Broader View (U.S. tel. 215/780-1845, toll-free U.S. tel. 866/423-3258, www.abroaderview.org), page 193.
Type of Work: agriculture, children and youth, community development, education, environment, health, wildlife protection, women's empowerment

Cross-Cultural Solutions (CCS) (toll-free U.S. tel. 800/380-4777, www.crossculturalsolutions.org), page 195.
Type of Work: children and youth, community development, education, health, women's empowerment

Earthwatch (U.S. tel. 978/461-0081, toll-free U.S. tel. 800/776-0188, www.earthwatch.org), page 196.
Type of Work: environment, wildlife protection

Elevate Destinations (U.S. tel. 617/661-0203, www.elevatedestinations.com), page 199.
Type of Work: children and youth, community development, education, environment, wildlife protection

Global Volunteers (toll-free U.S. tel. 800/487-1074, www.globalvolunteers.org), page 200.
Type of Work: children and youth, community development, education

Global Volunteers International (toll-free U.S. tel. 888/653-6028, www.gviusa.com), page 201.
Type of Work: children and youth, community development, education, environment, health, wildlife protection

Habitat for Humanity International (toll-free U.S. tel. 800/422-4828, www.habitat.org), page 202.
Type of Work: community development

International Volunteer HQ (IVHQ) (toll-free U.S. tel. 877/342-6588, www.volunteerhq.org), page 203.
Type of Work: agriculture, children and youth, community development, education, environment, health, wildlife protection

Spanish at Locations (toll-free U.S. tel. 877/268-3730, www.spanishatlocations.com), page 208.
Type of Work: agriculture, children and youth, community development, education, environment, health, wildlife protection

TECHO (U.S. tel. 305/860-4090, www.techo.org), page 209.
Type of Work: community development

Wanderland Travel (toll-free U.S. tel. 866/701-2113, www.wanderland.org), page 212.
Type of Work: agriculture, children and youth, community development, education, environment

Essentials

BACKGROUND
Geography and Climate

In an area roughly the size of Vermont and New Hampshire together, Costa Rica is home to 12 distinct ecological zones, which has resulted in a rich array flora and fauna, with more than 10,000 species of vascular plants and some 850 species of birds. Sadly, hunting and habitat destruction have reduced the mammal population, and there are now "only" 200-odd species, roughly half of which are types of bats. (But hey, there are some 300,000 species of insects!) There are also over 200 species of reptiles, and crocodile-spotting excursions, as well as turtle viewing and protecting, are popular activities with visitors to Costa Rica.

Although Costa Rica is wholly tropical, there are markedly diverse microclimates in the different ecological zones. In most places, the dry season, or *verano* (summer), is December-April, while the wet season (*invierno*, or winter) lasts May-November. While some months are wetter than others, temperatures are fairly stable, ranging from lows of 16-21°C (61-70°F) at night to daytime temperatures in the low 20s during the day in San José, and highs of 27-32°C (81-90°F) along the coasts.

History and Economy

Like so many of its neighbors, Costa Rica was colonized by Spain in the late 1500s, and it remained under its rule until its independence in 1821. Despite its peaceful reputation, Costa Rica has faced civil war twice since then (in 1823 and again in 1948, not to mention a "War of the League" in 1835). However, progressive politics with development and reform agendas have dominated Costa Rica's modern political history, and they have paid off with the highest literacy rates (96 percent) and lowest poverty rates (which nevertheless hover around 19 percent) in the region.

With nearly two million visitors to Costa Rica per year, tourism is the number-one income earner in the country, followed by technology (Intel, the computer chip manufacturer, has dubbed it "Silicon Valley South"), then agriculture (with particularly strong coffee and banana exports).

PREPARATION
Transportation

Costa Rica has four international airports. Most travelers arrive at **Juan Santamaría** (SJO, www.aeris.cr) in the capital of San José, served by some 20 international airlines. A second airport, **Daniel Oduber Quirós** (LIR, www.liberiacostaricaairport.net), is outside the city of Liberia in Guanacaste in western Costa Rica. Air Canada, American, Delta, JetBlue, United service both aiports, while Spirit and USAir fly only to San José. Domestic flights are relatively inexpensive, and buses connect every corner of the country for cheap.

Upon departure, visitors must pay a US$28 airport tax.

Passports and Visas

Ninety-day tourist cards are issued to visitors from the United States, Canada, and western Europe upon arrival. Long-term visitors can either apply for renewal or head to Nicaragua or Panama for 72 hours and be issued a new tourist card upon reentry.

Money

Costa Rica's currency is the **colón** (¢), which locals may also call pesos. Bills come in denominations of ¢1,000 (referred to as a *rojo*), ¢2,000 (referred to as *dos rojos*), ¢5,000 (called a *tucán*), and ¢10,000 (called a *jaguar*). At the time of this writing, US$1 was equal to ¢493.

U.S. dollars are accepted by most businesses, which is a plus since dollars can only be legally changed to colónes at the airport, at a bank, or at a hotel cash desk. It can be hard to get change, so traveling with small bills is advisable. It can be even harder to change travelers checks, but there is at least one 24-hour ATM in every large town.

COSTA RICA

Health

Costa Rica's excellent health care means that there are fewer concerns here than in nearby countries. Vaccinations are not required to enter Costa Rica, although some might be recommended—check with your doctor or local clinic. Epidemic diseases have mostly been eradicated, but malaria and dengue exist in limited cases.

Safety

Crime rates are also *much* lower here than in other Central American countries, but passport theft is a problem. Maintain your street smarts when in San José, and no matter where you are in the country, be careful with your belongings and avoid flashing valuables.

PANAMA

Famously divided by its canal, Panama's tropical location has long beguiled everyone from tourists to volunteers, adventurers to retirees. Sandwiched between the Atlantic-Caribbean Ocean (to the north) and the Pacific Ocean (to the south), Panama connects North and South America, with Costa Rica providing the western border and Colombia the eastern. With long golden coastlines, the country's obvious attraction is its beaches, but it has much more to offer. A varied ecology of rainforests, cloud forests, mangroves, and swamps provides homes for myriad wildlife— from jaguars to sea turtles—and 1,200 types of orchids. The historic district of its capital, Panama City, is the soul of this glitzy, modern metropolis.

Thanks to enormous revenue generated by the canal, Panama is a relatively wealthy country, with a gross national income per capital of US$7,910 (2010 World Bank figure). Its economy is one of the fastest growing and most competitive in Latin America. All that prosperity is unevenly divided, however; one-third of the country's 3.6 million people live below the national poverty line.

Volunteering is not as developed in Panama as in the rest of Central America, but there are certainly opportunities for those who want to travel here. Orchid lovers can help conserve native species at a nursery and conservation center. Surfers (or volunteers who dream of becoming one) can support efforts to better equip local communities to receive tourists. Volunteers enticed by sea turtles can head to the beaches July-mid-January to

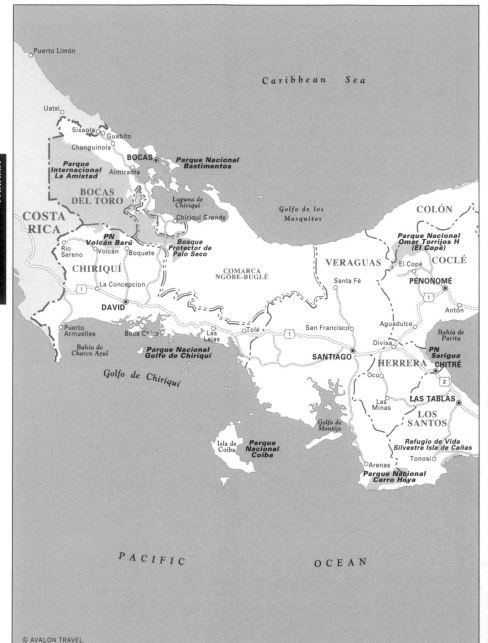

Puerto Limón

Caribbean   Sea

Uatsi

Sixaola   Guabito

Changuinola

BOCAS   Parque Nacional
Bastimentos

Parque
Internacional   Almirante
La Amistad

BOCAS   Laguna de
DEL TORO   Chiriquí

COSTA   Chiriquí Grande   Golfo de los   COLÓN
RICA   Mosquitos

PN   Bosque   Parque Nacional
Río   Volcán Barú   Protector de   Omar Torrijos H
Sereno   Volcán   Boquete   Palo Seco   (El Copé)   COCLÉ

CHIRIQUÍ   VERAGUAS   El Copé   PENONOMÉ

COMARCA   Santa Fé
La Concepción   NGÖBE-BUGLÉ   1

DAVID   Antón

Puerto   Las   Tolé   San Francisco   Aguadulce   Bahía de
Armuelles   Boca Chica   Lajas   1   Parita

Bahía de   Parque Nacional   Divisa   PN
Charco Azul   Golfo de Chiriquí   SANTIAGO   HERRERA   Sarigua
CHITRÉ

Golfo de Chiriquí   Ocú   2

Las   LAS TABLAS
Minas   LOS
SANTOS

Isla de   Parque   Golfo de   Refugio de Vida
Coiba   Nacional   Montijo   Silvestre Isla de Cañas
Coiba   Tonosí

Arenas   Parque Nacional
Cerro Hoya

PACIFIC   OCEAN

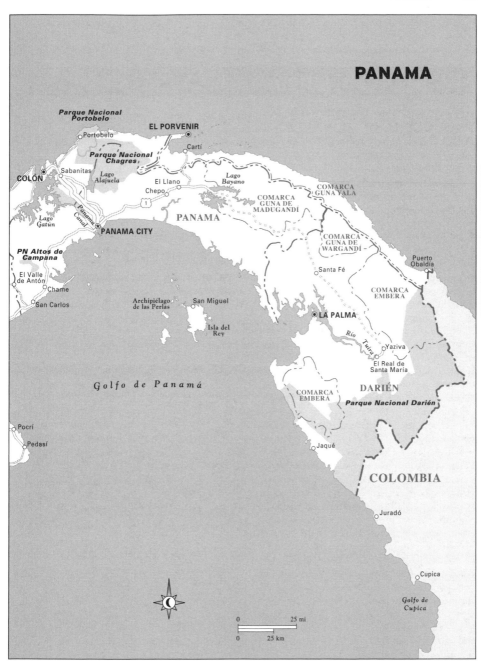

PANAMA

Parque Nacional
Portobelo

EL PORVENIR

Portobelo

Cartí

Parque Nacional
Chagres

Sabanitas

COLÓN

Lago
Alajuela

El Llano

Lago
Bayano

Chepo

COMARCA GUNA YALA

Lago
Gatún

Panama Canal

COMARCA
GUNA DE
MADUGANDÍ

PANAMA

PANAMA CITY

COMARCA
GUNA DE
WARGANDÍ

Puerto
Obaldía

PN Altos de
Campana

Santa Fé

El Valle
de Antón

COMARCA
EMBERÁ

Chame

San Carlos

Archipiélago
de las Perlas

San Miguel

LA PALMA

Isla del
Rey

Río Tuira

Yaziva

El Real de
Santa María

Golfo de Panamá

COMARCA
EMBERÁ

DARIÉN

Parque Nacional Darién

Pocrí

Pedasí

Jaqué

COLOMBIA

Juradó

Cupica

Golfo de
Cupica

0   25 mi
0   25 km

PANAMA

monitor nesting sites and protect hatchlings. Meanwhile, Spanish schools connect students and nonstudents alike with a variety of placements: working with children, the elderly, sea turtles, or on recycling projects, just to name a few.

Local Organizations

ASSOCIATION OF ORCHID PRODUCERS OF EL VALLE AND CABUYA (APROVACA)

Valle de Anton, tel. 507/983-6472, www.aprovaca.org

TYPE OF WORK: environment

APROVACA is small grassroots association "dedicated to the conservation of native Panamanian orchid species in danger of extinction." In addition to running an orchid nursery (with more than 100 native species of orchid) and conservation center, APROVACA also has a program to reintroduce orchids to the wild. Volunteers are expected to work about 30 hours per week and responsibilities include: taking care of orchids and other plants; helping maintain the gardens; designing projects of orchid conservation and ecotourism; promoting APROVACA as a tourist spot; updating, improving, and promoting their website; seeking out fundraising opportunities; taking photographs; or working in their café and hostel. Volunteers with botanical or gardening knowledge and/or computer skills, such as HTML and social media marketing, are especially needed.

APROVACA is about two hours by car from Panama City, in the town of El Valle de Anton, which is located in the crater of an extinct volcano. At nearly 2,000 feet (600 m) above sea level, El Valle has a temperate climate. Volunteers have plenty of activities to choose from in their free time, such as hiking and horseback riding, visiting an artisan market, or searching for the endangered golden frog.

Application Process: To apply, send an email with your résumé and a cover letter. Volunteers must be age 18 or older.

Cost: None. Accommodations and a weekday lunch are provided.

Placement Length: There is a minimum placement of one month.

Language Requirements: Basic (i.e., "good") Spanish skills are required.

Housing: Volunteers are given a bunk in the organization's hostel, which also offers hot showers, wireless Internet, and a fully equipped kitchen.

Operating Since: 2001

Number of Volunteers: unavailable

GIVE AND SURF

Bocas del Toro, tel. 507/6943-5807, www.giveandsurf.org

TYPE OF WORK: children and youth, community development, education, environment

A U.S.-registered 501(c)3 organization, Give and Surf's mission is to empower the indigenous Ngobe people of Bahía Hondo through education and community development

going to preschool

VOLUNTEER PERSPECTIVE

Antonia Rothschild (age 20) is from Sweden. She traveled to Panama in 2012 to work at **Give and Surf** (Bocas del Toro, tel. 507/6943-5807, www.giveandsurf.org).

I went as an independent volunteer to Give and Surf. My work included bringing the smallest children to the Bahía Hondo community to preschool by boat, and taking part in and even leading the preschool sessions (this was Mondays, Wednesdays, and Fridays). On Tuesdays and Thursdays we had after-school activities with older children, which included anything from English lessons to drama classes led by a volunteer that worked in acting, and dance classes led by me. The highlight of this experience must have been when I finally felt that I had won the children's trust and we could connect on a deeper level. I still write them letters, and they write back (in Spanish, of course, which I had studied in school but learnt almost fluently when in Panama)! There is so much I took home from this experience, too much to even sum up.

I chose Give and Surf because there seemed to be a balance between work and free time. I never felt obligated to do anything, which actually triggered my own will to do everything. I cannot tell you that this experience is for everyone, but it sure was right for me. I met so many wonderful, open-minded people that will stay with me for the rest of my life. Of course it was hard at times, but I was never alone in my struggles.

When I came home I organized a fundraiser through Facebook, announcing that I would stay silent for every raised dollar, and ended up being quiet for 15 hours straight! I then donated the 900 [US] dollars I raised to Give and Surf because I had seen for myself what the money does, and that it's in good hands for a good cause.

PANAMA

projects. Bahía Hondo is a traditional village whose 225 or so residents live in thatched huts and travel by dugout canoe.

Volunteers interested in education can help out at the preschool established by Give and Surf by reading to the children, playing games, painting, drawing, and chaperoning field trips; lend a hand at the after-school or summer-school program, which offers lessons, sports, music, movies, games, and more to elementary school-aged children; or teach English to teens and adults. Environmental and sustainability programs include a sustainable chicken project, water tank installations, and beach cleanups.

Give and Surf hosts many volunteer groups, who can get involved in large-scale construction projects. Past projects have included building or repairing a playground, water catchment systems, a new roof, a dining hall, a community garden, a library, and bathroom/septic tank installations.

As might be guessed from the name, Give and Surf was founded by passionate surfers, and volunteers can take free lessons, or if they are already experienced, simply borrow a board and watch for the next big wave. It is not at all necessary, however, to have an interest in surfing in order to volunteer with Give and Surf. Besides surfing and swimming, volunteers can spend their free time snorkeling, hiking, spelunking, zip-lining, kayaking, and more. Spanish lessons are also available, for no charge (!).

Application Process: Send an email. Volunteers under the age of 18 must be accompanied by a chaperone, and it is a great family volunteer opportunity.

Cost: US$500/week for stays of less than a month. Long-term volunteers pay US$400/week. Accommodations, weekday lunches, use of surfing equipment, surf lessons, Spanish lessons, and most local boat transportation are included with the fees, and half of the fees go directly to the project.

Placement Length: No minimum.

Language Requirements: None.

Housing: Accommodations are on Isla Bastimiento, "steps from the ocean and a short boat ride from the volunteer site in Bahía Hondo." There is a volunteer guesthouse, but community homestays can also be arranged if preferred. Lunch is provided to volunteers. Groups can have all meals provided for an additional US$75 per week per person.

Operating Since: November 2010, with the first volunteers arriving in March 2011

Number of Volunteers: 50 in 2012; anticipating at least 120 in 2013

HABLA YA PANAMA

Boquete and Bocas del Toro, tel. 507/730-8344, U.S. tel. 315/254-2331, www.hablayapanama.com

TYPE OF WORK: children and youth, community development, education, environment, health, wildlife protection

Habla Ya means "speak already," and as the name suggests, it is a Spanish school with two campuses: in Boquete, in Panama's western mountains, and in Bocas del Toro, a beach town on an archipelago a 30-minute boat ride away. Accredited by the Cervantes Institute from Spain, Habla Ya offers both high-quality language lessons along with volunteer opportunities. It is also possible to volunteer with Habla Ya without signing up for Spanish lessons, although the placement and daily fees are then higher.

Habla Ya partners with several NGOs (nongovernmental organizations) that work with children and youth, and depending on the volunteer's skills and interests, tasks can include "working in orphanages assisting with daily activities such as laundry duties or cooking meals, and child care duties such as feeding or bathing the children; working with teenage mothers and their newborn children; helping kids from public schools with their homework; running sports lessons, giving computer instruction, and music, dance and singing classes; helping to prepare meals and secure funding for schools' dining rooms; playing with children during their breaks; assisting health professionals to take care of ill children; teaching English or other subjects in a classroom; or being a mentor for a group of children once per week."

There are volunteer opportunities in many other areas as well: helping protect sea turtles, their eggs, and hatchlings; working with the disabled or the elderly; assisting animal and wildlife programs; supporting floating doctors and mobile clinics; and participating in community recycling. Some types of volunteer placements have limited spots, so signing up in advance will help volunteers get the type of work they prefer.

Free-time activities depend on the campus chosen. Both offer Latin dancing sessions and movie nights for free; excursions and activities such as hiking, caving, wildlife and botanical expeditions, white-water rafting, surfing, horseback riding, scuba diving, snorkeling, bike and boat tours, and visits to indigenous villages and coffee plantations can all be arranged.

Application Process: There is an online registration form, and an online volunteer "interview." Families are welcome, and children who volunteer with their parents do not pay the volunteering fee.

Cost: For volunteers who also take Spanish lessons, the placement fee is US$50, and there is a daily fee of US$5. For volunteering only, the fees are US$75 and US$15 respectively. No fee to teach English. Volunteers are responsible for their own expenses.

Placement Length: Five days minimum for most programs; three-week minimum for teaching English.

Language Requirements: Varies according to the opportunity; no Spanish required for several, while others require intermediate to advanced.

Housing: Accommodation choices include family homestays (which include meal options), a range of hostels and hotels (ranging US$10-300 per night), or apartment and other vacation rentals.

Operating Since: 2005 in Boquete, and 2011 in Bocas del Toro

Number of Volunteers: about 110 in Boquete and 40 in Bocas del Toro in 2012

PLAYA MALENA CONSERVATION ASSOCIATION

Playa Malena, www.playamalena.org, tanagertourism@gmail.com

TYPE OF WORK: community development, environment, wildlife protection

Playa Malena is a nonprofit group of community volunteers dedicated to the protection of the beach and its wildlife; in particular, the sea turtles that nest and hatch on its shores July-mid-January. Volunteer tasks include participating in night patrols on the beach (by foot or in a boat) to keep away poachers, recording turtles laying eggs, transporting eggs to protective cages, releasing hatchlings to the ocean, keeping records of turtle activities, and performing beach cleanups. Volunteers with skills in carpentry, building, and conservation are especially welcome. Volunteers are not accepted outside of turtle season; the best months are September and October.

Located on the southern coast of Panama, roughly five hours from Panama City, Malena is on the Azuero Peninsula. Despite the far-flung location, volunteers will find plenty to do in their free time: swimming in the ocean, walking to local waterfalls, horseback riding along the beach, or looking for whales and dolphins in the Pacific. Hiking and snorkeling tours can also be arranged. Visitors are welcomed by the local community (population 140) and quickly integrate into Panamanian culture.

It's worth noting that there is a fledgling organization doing similar work in Quebro, 18 kilometers (11 mi) away, where there is a larger beach, mangroves, and poison dart frogs. To contact the **Centro Educativo de Preservación de la Flora y Fauna** in Quebro, call Secundino "Castro" Peralta at 507/6101-5973 (Spanish only) or email Tanager Tourism at tanagertourism@gmail.com.

Application Process: Send an email to Tanager Tourism (a local business that supports the project) at tanagertourism@gmail.com in the best Spanish you have (or in English if you have no Spanish), including your age, gender, and place of study or work. Include any background or interests relevant to the volunteer work. Alternatively, applicants can call Ana Gonzalez (507/6865-8908) or Choli "Florentina" Fuentes (507/6865-8924), community members involved with the project (Spanish speaking only). Individual volunteers must be 18 or older; families are welcome.

Cost: US$200/week, including homestay and meals.

Placement Length: Minimum of 5-7 days.

Language Requirements: Basic Spanish is helpful.

PANAMA

INTERNATIONAL ORGANIZATIONS

The following international organizations support volunteer efforts in Panama:

Spanish at Locations (toll-free U.S. tel. 877/268-3730, www.spanishatlocations.com), page 208.
Type of Work: agriculture, children and youth, community development, education, environment, health, wildlife protection

TECHO (U.S. tel. 305/860-4090, www.techo.org), page 209.
Type of Work: community development

Housing: Homestays, including meals, are provided for volunteers. Other simple accommodations can be arranged upon request and will cost a bit more.

Operating Since: 2002
Number of Volunteers: two in 2012

Essentials

BACKGROUND
Geography and Climate
Measuring just 75,500 square kilometers (29,160 sq. mi), tiny Panama packs a punch of ecological, biological, and ethnic diversity into an area just smaller than the state of South Carolina. Thanks to geography that includes cloud-tipped mountains, damp rainforests, sunny beaches, rivers, and islands, Panama varied ecology is home to more than 10,000 species of plants and over 1,000 species of birds.

The weather in Panama is uniformly warm, with temperatures of 24-30°C (75-86°F) in the capital, with weather often a few degrees cooler on the Pacific side of the isthmus and up in the mountains. High season is dry season, which lasts mid-December-April, at least on the Pacific side. North of the mountains, on the Caribbean side, the drier months are February, March, September, and October, although they can still be pretty rainy. May is the wettest month of the year.

Ethnically, close to 70 percent of the population is *mestizo*, or of mixed Amerindian and European descent, the remainder black, white, Asian, and Amerindian. The Amerindians are composed of seven indigenous peoples in Panama: the Ngäbe, Kuna (Guna), Emberá, Buglé, Wounaan, Naso Tjerdi (Teribe), and Bri Bri. However, while indigenous people make up a mere 9 percent of the population, they accounted for 26 percent of the poor and 47 percent of the extreme poor in 2010, according to the World Bank.

History and Economy
Prior to the arrival of the Spaniards in the early 1500s, Panama was widely settled by Chibchan, Chocoan, and Cueva peoples. Quickly recognized to be the shortest route between the Atlantic and Pacific Oceans, Panama was colonized by Spain in 1538, and it remained part of the empire until it broke from Spain in 1821, in order to join Colombia. Panama remained a department of Colombia for 80 years, until the United States switched allegiances in support of Panama's separatist movement (a successful play to gain control over the isthmus for the development of a canal). With U.S. support, Panama was able to secede from Colombia in 1903, and in exchange, Panama granted the United States the concession for the creation of the 48-mile-long canal, which was completed in 1904. At noon on December 31, 1999, the United States returned the canal (and the surrounding Canal Zone) to Panamanian control. The canal itself remains a neutral international waterway, and even in times of war, any vessel is guaranteed safe passage, with a joint U.S.-Panamanian task force for its defense.

Revenue from canal tolls continues to represent a significant portion of Panama's gross domestic product (GDP), and an expansion project promises that its importance will grow. Other important economic sectors include banking, commerce, trade, and tourism, with the latter accounting for around 10 percent of the GDP. Bananas are the country's leading export, followed by shrimp, sugar, coffee, and clothing.

PREPARATION
Transportation
Tocumen International Airport (PTY, www.tocumenpanama.aero) in Panama City will be the point of arrival for most travelers. American, Delta, and United Airlines service Tocumen, as well as several domestic, regional, and European airlines. Tocumen is also the hub for Copa Airlines, a spinoff of the now-defunct Continental, which offers flights all

© DANIELHO/ISTOCKPHOTO

Panama City is a modern seaside capital.

over the Americas. There is a US$45 departure tax at the Tocumen Airport, usually included in the airplane ticket.

Good bus service covers most of Panama, and roads are well maintained. Domestic flights can take visitors to the most remote locations.

Passports and Visas

Most European and North American visitors need only a valid passport to enter Panama and will be issued a 30- or 90-day stamp on their passport. Passports must be valid for at least six months beyond the date of arrival.

Money

While the official Panamanian currency is the **balboa** (B/.), it is a dollarized economy: U.S. dollars are the only currency in circulation (and the terms *dólar* and *balboa* are used interchangeably), while the coinage is balboas.

ATMs are widely found and are the easiest way to get access to cash. Credit cards are not universally accepted, so check before showing up somewhere remote without enough cash to get you through your stay. Travelers checks can be hard to change outside of banks.

Health

Health conditions and medical care in Panama are both good. Travelers won't have to worry about many of the illnesses found elsewhere in Central and South America, such as malaria or yellow fever. The tropical climate does promise plenty of bugs, however, so do bring insect repellent–just look for an environmentally friendly one.

Safety

Panama is a fairly safe country, although as anywhere, it is always recommended to be aware of your surroundings and to avoid flashing valuables. In Panama City, be careful on the side streets of the historic district (the *Casco Viejo*) and walking around at night.

COLOMBIA

Located at the northern tip of South America, Colombia is bordered by Venezuela and Brazil to the east, Peru and Ecuador to the south, and its western edge is lined by the sea, with Panama dividing its Caribbean coastline from its Pacific coast. Colombia is dotted by cosmopolitan cities, such as its capital, Bogotá, home to the posh Zona Rosa, with its sophisticated restaurants and shops, and the centuries-old district of La Candelaria, with its first-rate museums and colonial architecture. Cartagena is another city that enchants, with cobblestone streets and evocative architecture, while those who prefer to get away from urban areas may be tempted by a mud bath at Volcán Totumo, a hike in the jungles of Tayrona National Park, or horseback riding and a cup of freshly brewed coffee at a plantation in the Eje Cafetero, or Coffee-Growing Axis.

With 47 million people, Colombia is the third most populous country in Latin America (after Brazil and Mexico). More than half the population is *mestizo* (of mixed European and indigenous ancestry), while 20 percent is of European-only descent and 15 percent claim a mix of European and African ancestry. Only 1 percent of the population is indigenous only, but there are 500,000 people that speak indigenous languages, mainly Quecha.

With a gross national income per capita of US$6,110 (2011 World Bank figures), Colombia's people are wealthier on average than neighboring Peru and Ecuador. But they also face greater income inequality, with 37 percent of the population living below the

national poverty line. As security in the country increases, however, Colombia is seeing business (and tourism) grow, and poverty rates are slowly dropping.

While volunteering is a nascent business in Colombia, the opportunities that exist tend to be highly regarded. Volunteers might work with a center for disadvantaged children, teach English to locals in order to better prepare them for the burgeoning tourism industry, work in an orchid nursery or botanical garden, help protect sea turtles or endemic birds, or assist park rangers to maintain national parks.

Local Organizations

CASA DE CULTURA DE LA BOQUILLA
Cartagena, tel. 57/318-237-9574, www.facebook.com/CasaCulturadelaBoquilla, ronymonsalve@gmail.com

TYPE OF WORK: children and youth, education

La Boquilla is a small town 15 minutes outside the beautiful colonial city of Cartagena. Its Casa de Cultura (cultural center) seeks volunteers to teach English to locals working in tourism or related fields. The Casa de Cultura's mission is to "enhance cultural and educational knowledge within our community," and it offers English classes (2:30pm-4pm Monday-Friday) to children and adults. Volunteers are encouraged to bring their ideas for children's arts and crafts projects to the Casa de Cultura. There are sometimes other activities related to the center's programs to which volunteers can lend a hand. Training is usually provided by previous volunteers.

Beaches and mangrove forests are just a short walk from the Casa de Cultura. There is frequent and cheap bus service between La Boquilla and Cartagena, Colombia's fifth-largest city and a UNESCO World Heritage Site, with stunning colonial architecture that includes ornate government buildings and colorful cobblestone streets.

La Boquilla is a poor community, but it's very safe, and volunteers can move around freely, even at night.

Application Process: Send an email to apply. Individual volunteers must be 18 or older and should have finished high school. Families with children may be considered.

Cost: None. Volunteers are responsible for their own expenses.

Placement Length: There is a minimum placement of two weeks.

Language Requirements: Basic Spanish is required.

Housing: Casa de Cultura de La Boquilla encourages homestays(US$14/night), which provide the volunteer with greater contact with the local community and the community with an additional source of income. Hotels and furnished apartments (US$30-35/night per person) can also be arranged.

Operating Since: December 2012

Number of Volunteers: three in December 2012 and three in January 2013

CENTRO DE INVESTIGACION PARA EL MANEJO AMBIENTAL Y DESARROLLO (CIMAD)
Guapi, Gorgona, tel. 57/2-519-1341, www.cimad.org

TYPE OF WORK: environment, wildlife protection

The Research Center for Environmental Management and Development (known as CIMAD for its Spanish initials) is dedicated to "the promotion, dissemination and exchange of knowledge through the development of scientific and technological research aimed at natural resource management with social participation." Based in the town of Guapi on the Pacific coast, CIMAD offers year-round volunteer opportunities in programs dedicated to the conservation of marine turtles. Projects include: rescue and veterinary care of sea turtles; monitoring turtles on beaches (Oct.- Feb.); open-water monitoring (all year);

COLOMBIA

COLOMBIA

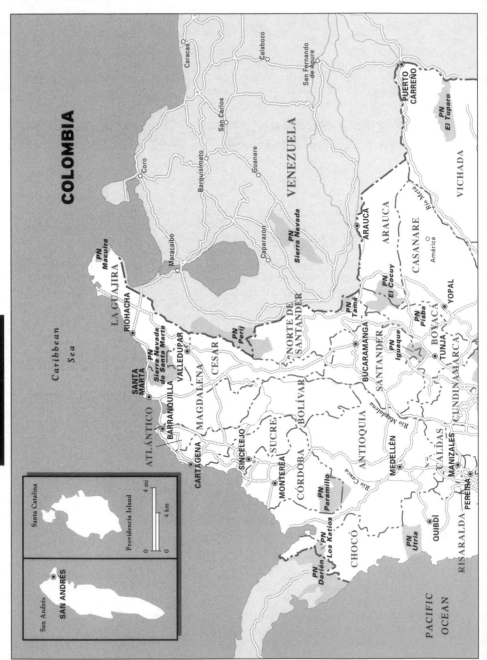

COLOMBIA

Caribbean Sea

VENEZUELA

Caracas

Calabozo

San Fernando de Apure

Coro

Barquisimeto

San Carlos

Guanare

Maracaibo

Caparazon

PN Sierra Nevada

PUERTO CARREÑO

PN El Tuparo

VICHADA

PN Macuira

LA GUAJIRA

RIOHACHA

ARAUCA

ARAUCA

CASANARE

América

Río Meta

PN Perijá

PN El Cocuy

YOPAL

SANTA MARTA

PN Sierra Nevada de Santa Marta

VALLEDUPAR

NORTE DE SANTANDER

PN Tamá

PN Pisba

BOYACÁ

BARRANQUILLA

MAGDALENA

CESAR

BUCARAMANGA

SANTANDER

PN Iguaque

TUNJA

ATLÁNTICO

ICA

CARTAGENA

SINCELEJO

SUCRE

BOLÍVAR

Río Magdalena

CUNDINAMARCA

MONTERÍA

CÓRDOBA

ANTIOQUIA

MEDELLÍN

CALDAS

MANIZALES

PN Paramillo

Río Cauca

QUIBDÓ

PERÉIRA

PN Utría

RISARALDA

CHOCÓ

PN Los Katíos

PN Darién

PACIFIC OCEAN

Santa Catalina

Providencia Island

4 mi

4 km

0

0

San Andrés

SAN ANDRÉS

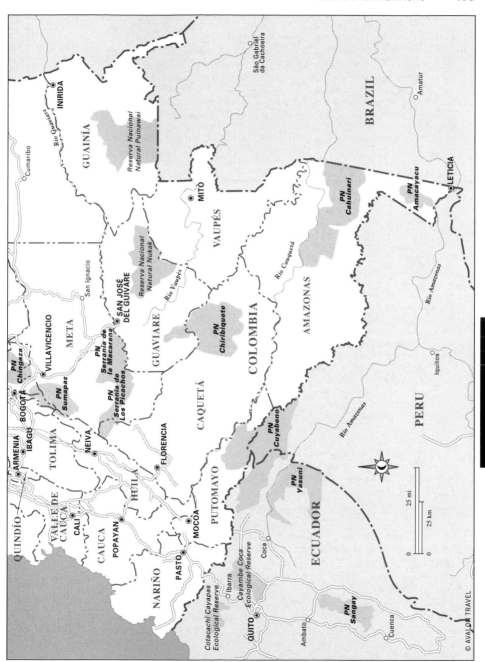

COLOMBIA

VOLUNTEER PERSPECTIVE

Serena Star-Leonard (age 33) is passionate about making a difference. When I caught up with her, she and her husband, John, were near the end of a year traveling in Latin America, filming stories about people who make a difference in their communities, for a variety of different sized charitable organizations including World Vision, and making their own difference along he way. During the year they volunteered with Fundación Mariposas Amarillas (Santa Marta, tel. 57/311-638-1609, U.S. tel. 720/253-2155, www.fmacolombia.weebly. com), Casa Guatemala (Las Brisas, Guatemala, Río Dulce, tel. 502/2331-9408, www.casa-guatemala.org, www.viajescasaguatemala.org), and the Endangered Wildlife Trust (Pacuare Nature Reserve, Costa Rica, tel. 506/2234-5890, www.turtleprotection.org).

What made you think that your travels needed "purpose"?

We were going to travel anyway but felt that we wanted something more than the usual tourist experience. I have always had this feeling that I wanted to make a difference in the world and have been part of different projects and charities, but volunteering overseas takes it to a whole new level. As well as a sense of satisfaction from the work, I feel like a different person; more happy, grateful, and brave.

We have found the most memorable and exciting bits of our travel are all related to these experiences. We have shared events and intimate moments that many people will never get to experience.

For many, Colombia has a scary reputation. What made you choose to travel there?

I had heard that Colombia was a very special place, and we were excited to visit. We have been to several cities that are considered "extremely dangerous" in Venezuela, Mexico, and Honduras, and in those places we limit our risk, carry less cash or cards, be more aware of our surroundings, take taxis when we have all our gear on us, don't be flashy with camera equipment, etc.

Overall we have found Latin America to be a safe, friendly, and welcoming place and have had zero problems so far.

What made you choose Fundación Mariposas Amarillas (FMA)?

First, I had a good feeling about the organization from reading their website. I emailed them, we had a conversation about what it entailed, and they sent teaching tips in their welcome pack. This made me feel a little better as I had no experience with teaching. I liked that the experienced teachers would lead a class and the inexperienced teachers would assist.

Secondly, they only had a one-off donation of US$50 to join the program. Some organizations require you to pay large fees for every day or week you volunteer, which sustains the program. We wanted to be at an organization that was genuinely looking for people to contribute, rather than people to contribute their money.

We also liked the fact that they seemed less structured and more authentic than some other places we looked at.

---

environmental education; and fisheries biology. Volunteers usually work 8am-6pm, with a two-hour break for lunch. Volunteers are occasionally asked to help with evening activities, such as movies in the town park.

The island of Gorgona is about 50 km off Colombia's Pacific coast and is a national park noted for a large number of endemic species. The launching point to get there is the town of Guapi (a not-especially-nice place).

Thankfully, there is lodging and a restaurant on the island, so volunteers can minimize their time in Guapi. Free time can be spent exploring the island (with a guide, and watch out for venomous snakes!), swimming, snorkeling or diving, or watching for humpback whales that pass by its shores (Aug.-Oct.).

Application Process: A downloadable application form is available online. Volunteers must be age 18 or older.

© SERENA STAR LEONARD, WWW.FIVEPOINTFIVE.ORG

COLOMBIA

What did you take away from your experience there?

My experience at FMA showed me how it doesn't take much to make a big difference. Oscar, the founder, was a street kid himself and is living proof that you can start with nothing and empower a whole community. One school is in a slum where some taxis are afraid to enter, but you get there and the kids all come running out to meet you. They are funny, naughty, cute, and rowdy and come from the worst backgrounds you can imagine, yet they are so keen to learn and dream like kids anywhere in the world. What I will take away is that there is hope for every single child; when you are sitting in your office wondering if your time or money can make a difference, I know that it does.

Serena is the author of *How to Retire in 12 Months*. Her website, www.FivePointFive.org, shares stories, videos, and inspiration for volunteer travel.

Cost: Volunteers are responsible for their own expenses.

Placement Length: There is a minimum placement of two weeks.

Language Requirements: Functional Spanish is required.

Housing: Volunteers stay in local homes or simple hotels (US$17-26).

Operating Since: 2002

Number of Volunteers: one in 2012

FUNDACIÓN MARIPOSAS AMARILLAS (FMA)

Santa Marta, tel. 57/311-638-1609,
U.S. tel. 720/253-2155, www.fmacolombia.weebly.com

TYPE OF WORK: children and youth, community development, education, women's empowerment

Based in the beachside city of Santa Marta, FMA (Yellow Butterflies Foundation in English) is a grassroots organization that seeks to fight poverty and social injustice through the provision of services (education, workshops, recreation); supplies and information on nutrition; and child care to disadvantaged children and families. Responsibilities depend on the interests, skills, time commitment, and language abilities of the volunteer. According to FMA, "we welcome people with any skill, or none!"

FMA has a variety of projects that volunteers can support. Those who want to work with children can assist or teach in the after-school program for kids age 4-14. Others go to homes for one-on-one literacy classes with young mothers and fathers. Group English lessons are taught to adults in the evenings in marginalized areas of the city. Workshops are taught in social work, sexual health, nutrition, and parenting. There is occasionally construction work to be done on existing buildings, and FMA is working on raising funds to build a new school or community center. Volunteers are also needed to help out with administration, fundraising, and publicity (in particular, writing, photographing, blogging, tweeting, and social networking).

In their free time, volunteers can study Spanish or learn how to scuba dive, explore the city or the nearby Tayrona National Park, or just laze around on the beach. FMA can arrange both Spanish classes and salsa dancing lessons.

Application Process: There is a downloadable application form on their website. Families are welcome, and many have volunteered with them in the past.

Cost: There is a US$50 fee. Volunteers are responsible for their own expenses, and they are expected to contribute to the purchase of classroom supplies (FMA suggests allocating US$20 per week for this).

Placement Length: One-week minimum for classroom assistants; classroom teachers must make a commitment of at least three weeks.

Language Requirements: Basic Spanish is required, but FMA can arrange lessons from local teachers at discounted prices.

Housing: Volunteers are responsible for their own accommodations and meals, but FMA can help find homestays for US$15/night, including meals, laundry, and Internet. Hostels are US$5-10 per night, and there are lots of hotels, some of which offer discounts for volunteers. It is also possible to rent a house in one of the neighborhoods where FMA works, for US$70/month, but this is only recommended for men or couples, for safety reasons. If not in a homestay, FMA recommends budgeting US$150-200/month for food, and another US$20/month for transportation.

Operating Since: 2007; first international volunteers in 2009

Number of Volunteers: 110 in 2012

FUNDACIÓN POR LA MADRE

Minca, tel. 57/320-318-8186,
www.fundacionporlamadre.org

TYPE OF WORK: children and youth, education, environment

Fundación Por La Madre (FPLM) is a nonprofit organization that was created to work on environmental issues, education, and sustainable local development in vulnerable communities. Located in a region that was once torn by civil war, FPLM's goal is "to create sustainable educational programs in which people of different communities join to our projects and thus promote tolerance, family and youth integration and encourage social reconstruction."

They have projects in small towns and rural communities along the Sierra Nevada mountain, which include Kogui, Wiwa, Arhuaco, and Wayuu indigenous populations. The focus is on strengthening local education for children ages 7-16, with English, culture (such as music), ecology and conservation, as well as self-sustaining projects in education.

Volunteers are asked to work daily, and the school day runs 7am-noon (during which English lessons are taught). There is an after-school program 2pm-5:30pm, in which English lessons are reinforced using teaching based on artistic expressions, as well as cultural lessons and activities. Each class is about one hour, and volunteer schedules are flexible and vary according to the classes taught. Volunteers are welcome to lead lessons in areas besides

© SERENA STAR LEONARD, WWW.FIVEPOINTFIVE.ORG

There are volunteer opportunities in the beachfront city of Santa Marta, as well as in the surrounding hills.

English, depending on their own skills and interests—there is a special need for classes in culture, environment, and artistic expression, as these are not part of the regular curriculum. While the foundation can provide support and advice, volunteers must develop their own lesson plans.

Minca is a hillside town a little over half an hour by car from the beachside city of Santa Marta. In their free time, volunteers can take Spanish lessons or explore the surrounding area—home to waterfalls and a huge variety of birds and plants. Heading farther afield, volunteers can travel between snow-capped mountains and the desert of La Guajira, or to national parks such as Tayrona. Note that school holidays are December-mid-February, so volunteers are not accepted during that time. **Application Process:** There is a downloadable application form to complete, along with a code of conduct that all volunteers must sign and return. Individual volunteers must be between the ages of 18 and 68. Families are also welcome.

Cost: There is a US$50 registration fee, and housing is US$180 for two weeks, US$350 for a month.
Placement Length: Minimum of two weeks.
Language Requirements: At least basic Spanish is required.
Housing: FPLM provides accommodations in a volunteer guesthouse, as well as three (organic!) meals a day Monday-Friday. There is wireless Internet, and workshops on topics such as organic coffee, chocolate, and yoga are included.
Operating Since: 2008
Number of Volunteers: typically 30-45 per year

PARQUES NACIONALES NATURALES DE COLOMBIA
head office in Bogotá, tel. 57/1-353-2400, ext. 308, www.parquesnacionales.gov.co
TYPE OF WORK: environment
The national park service of Colombia is a subsidiary of the country's Ministry of Environment, and its mission is to "conserve

COLOMBIA

in situ the biological and ecosystemic diversity of the country, providing and maintaining environmental goods and services, protecting the cultural heritage and the natural habitat where the traditional cultures develop as part of the National Heritage, and contribute to Sustainable Human Development; under the principles of transparency, solidarity, equity, participation, and respect for the cultural diversity."

The park service accepts volunteer park rangers (national and international), whom they place in one of 13 national parks across the country. Volunteers may be placed in the Andes or Amazon, Pacific coast or Caribbean, or even on an island. Volunteer activities include: management, guidance, and environmental interpretation for visitors; maintenance and repair of park infrastructure, including trails; data collection from meteorological stations; radio communication support; park patrols; surveillance and protection of endangered fauna; prevention and support in the control of forest fires; creation of teaching materials and audiovisual aids for community work; design, formulation, and execution of projects; administrative and operating tasks; support of park ecotourism.

Application Process: There are two calls for volunteers per year: In 2013, the first, in March, was for volunteers interested in serving between May and September, and the second, in August, was for those interested in working sometime between October 2013 and April 2014. A downloadable application form, and a detailed list of required documents for applying, is on the website, along with five addresses in Colombia where the documents can be sent or turned in.

Cost: None. Volunteers are responsible for their transportation to the park where they will work, and for their own meals.

Placement Length: Minimum of one month.

Language Requirements: Intermediate Spanish. The application and work are entirely in Spanish.

Housing: The park service offers accommodations to volunteers, but they are responsible for their own meals.

Operating Since: 1987

Number of Volunteers: 230 in 2102 (225 Colombians and 5 foreigners)

INTERNATIONAL ORGANIZATIONS

The following international organizations support volunteer efforts in Colombia:

A Broader View (U.S. tel. 215/780-1845, toll-free U.S. tel. 866/423-3258, www.abroaderview.org), page 193.
Type of Work: agriculture, children and youth, community development, education, environment, health, wildlife protection, women's empowerment

Global Communities: Partners for Good (U.S. tel. 301/587-4700, www.globalcommunities.org), page 200.
Type of Work: children and youth, community development, education, environment, women's empowerment

International Volunteer HQ (IVHQ) (toll-free U.S. tel. 877/342-6588, www.volunteerhq.org), page 203.
Type of Work: agriculture, children and youth, community development, education, environment, health, wildlife protection

Intern Latin America (ILA) (U.S. tel. 718/878-6393, www.internlatinamerica.com), page 205.
Type of Work: children and youth, community development, education, environment, health, wildlife protection, women's empowerment

TECHO (U.S. tel. 305/860-4090, www.techo.org), page 209.
Type of Work: community development

Essentials

BACKGROUND
Geography and Climate

Colombia is the fifth-largest country in Latin America, with an area of 1,138,903 square kilometers (439,733 sq. mi), making it as large as Texas, New Mexico, and Arkansas (or the United Kingdom, France, and Germany) combined. Its coastline stretches from the Caribbean Sea to the north Pacific Ocean, for a total of 3,207 kilometers (1,993 mi). Its ecology is diverse, from the Andean mountains, to the savanna of the *llanos,* to the tropical jungles of the Amazon, to the golden sands of the coast.

Weather can vary considerably according to the region, and temperatures change more with the altitude than the season. In the Colombian Andes, there are two dry seasons—December-March and July-August—while the plains are dry only during the first *verano* (December-March), and the Amazon is rainy year-round. However, the Pacific coast area has one of the highest rainfalls in the world, so if that's your destination, bring your umbrella no matter what month it is.

Below 900 meters (2,953 ft) in elevation is the *tierra caliente* (hot land), where temperatures range 24-38°C (75-100°F). The *tierra templada* (temperate land) is between 900 and 1,980 meters (2,950-6,500 ft), and it's the country's most productive land, as well as where the majority of the population resides.

History and Economy

The eponymous explorer Christopher Columbus arrived in Colombia in 1502, and it became a Spanish colony in 1525–a status that was maintained until Colombia declared its independence in 1810. Its republican history was peppered by violence due to internal political and territorial divisions, culminating in the assassination of a populist presidential candidate in 1948. Repercussions became increasingly violent, including U.S.-backed military attacks on peasant villages, and in response, armed guerrilla groups, such as the Revolutionary Armed Forces of Colombia (better known as FARC), were formed. The de facto civil war raged for decades, in tandem with increasing violence from Colombia's infamous drug cartels.

Colombia finally saw a turn in its fortunes in 2002, with the presidential election of Alvaro Uribe, whose (somewhat controversial) pressure on FARC and other paramilitary organizations resulted in a sharp decrease in homicides and kidnappings, and a significant improvement in overall security.

Tourism is on the rise, with a reported 1.4 million visitors in 2010, and business is improving with the creation of a stock market, increasing oil exports and soaring investments. Other important exports include coal, coffee, gold, emeralds, and cut flowers.

PREPARATION
Transportation

Most visitors to Colombia will arrive at **El Dorado International Airport** (BOG, www.elnuevodorado.com) in Bogotá. Air Canada, American Airlines, Delta, JetBlue, Spirit, and United all have frequent flights to Colombia, as well as several regional and European airlines. The U.S. State department recommends internal travel via air rather than by road, and distances can be long while internal flights are often cheap. There is an exit tax of US$38 (C$68,000) (cash only, payable in Colombian pesos or U.S. dollars but not a combination of the two) for visitors whose stay has exceeded two months.

As in all of Latin America, inexpensive buses crisscross the country. Safety can vary by route and region, so it is best to discuss transportation with the volunteer organization and follow their recommendations.

Passports and Visas

Passports must be valid for at least 90 days after your arrival date, but it is recommended that

COLOMBIA

they be valid for at least six months. A visa is not required for Americans, Canadians, Brits, Aussies, or EU passport holders. Colombians with dual citizenship, including anyone born in Colombia who might not have completed paperwork for a passport, must present a Colombian passport to enter the country.

Money

The currency of Colombia is the **peso** ($ or Col$). Bills are printed in denominations of $1,000, $2,000, $5,000, $10,000, $20,000, and $50,000. At the time of this writing, US$1 was equivalent to $1,815 Colombian pesos. Travelers checks can be a challenge to exchange, and rates for U.S. dollars are not always favorable. Bring credit and debit cards that you can use overseas and get pesos while in Colombia.

Health

Yellow fever vaccine is required for visitors to the national parks along the Caribbean coast and is recommended for travelers elsewhere. Visitors should be up-to-date on other vaccinations, especially typhoid (to keep "traveler's tummy" at bay).

Malaria and dengue are both found in the low-lying areas of Colombia. Unless you'll be staying in the mountains, be sure to bring plenty of insect repellent.

Safety

While Colombia was at one time notorious for the violence of its drug cartels and guerrilla groups, government military pressure (supported by U.S. aid) has led to a significant reduction in homicides, kidnappings, and other violence since 2002. Remote rural and jungle areas can still be dangerous, but volunteers who follow the safety guidelines outlined by their volunteer organization shouldn't encounter problems.

While crime rates have lowered dramatically in recent years, visitors should still be careful at all times. Theft is the most likely problem, so minimize temptation by keeping valuables out of sight. Withdraw cash only from indoor ATMs and do so only during the day. Keep a small bundle of cash (equivalent to US$5-10) handy to quickly hand over in the event of a mugging, and keep the rest stashed carefully away.

Unfortunately, the drug trade remains rampant. Cocaine and marijuana are easily available in Colombia, but sales are often setups. Police shakedowns can be costly at best (fines range US$300-3,000) and may land you in the slammer at worst.

ECUADOR

Located in northwest South America, Ecuador is bordered by Colombia, Peru, and the Pacific Ocean. The country is home to four distinct regions: the mountainous Sierra, with its chain of volcanoes and a vibrant indigenous culture; the Oriente, home to the flora and fauna of the Amazon jungle; the golden sands and laid-back culture of the coast; and the renowned Galapagos Islands, 600 miles offshore.

Ecuador is home to more than 13 million people. The country boasts significant ethnic and racial diversity; although counts vary, *mestizos* (persons of mixed European and Central American Indian ancestry) are certainly the largest ethnic group, followed by indigenous peoples, who make up roughly 25 percent of the population. More than 30 percent of the population lives below the national poverty line, and poverty rates are much higher for Ecuador's indigenous people. (The gross national income per capita is US$4,140, per World Bank 2011 figures.)

As a "megadiverse" country, Ecuador boasts more than 20,000 exotic animal and plant species, including orchids, ocelots, hummingbirds, howler monkeys, and, of course, the famed Galapagos tortoise, making it an ideal place for environmentally focused volunteering. Volunteers might rehabilitate animals for release into the Amazonian jungle or replant native flora species on the Galapagos Islands in order to preserve its unique ecosystem. There are sustainable farms all across the country where volunteers can both lend a hand and engage with the local community through environmental education or teaching English.

© AMY E. ROBERTSON

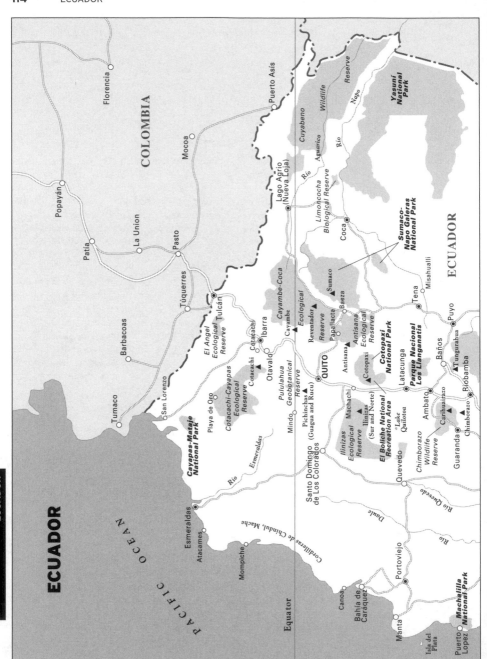

ECUADOR

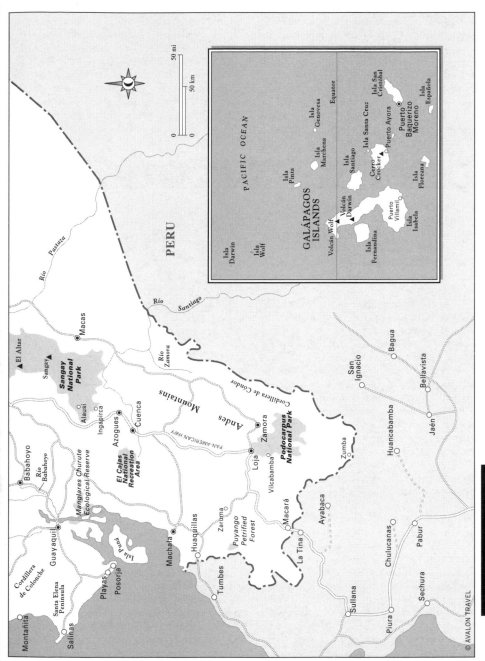

ECUADOR

PACIFIC OCEAN

GALÁPAGOS ISLANDS

Equator

Isla San Cristóbal
Isla Española
Puerto Baquerizo Moreno
Isla Santa Cruz
Puerto Ayora
Isla Genovesa
Isla Marchena
Isla Santiago
Cerro Crocker
Isla Floreana
Isla Pinta
Volcán Darwin
Volcán Wolf
Puerto Villamil
Isla Isabela
Isla Fernandina
Isla Darwin
Isla Wolf

PERU

Río Pastaza
Río Santiago
Río Zamora

Macas
El Altar
Sangay
Sangay National Park
Alausí
Ingapirca
Azogues
Cuenca
Andes Mountains
PAN-AMERICAN HWY
Cordillera de Cóndor
Loja
Zamora
Vilcabamba
Podocarpus National Park
Zumba
Macará
Ayabaca
La Tina
Bagua
Bellavista
San Ignacio
Jaén
Huancabamba
Chulucanas
Pabur
Sullana
Sechura
Piura

Bábahoyo
Río Babahoyo
Manglares Churute Ecological Reserve
El Cajas National Recreation Area
Guayaquil
Isla Puná
Posorja
Playas
Santa Elena Peninsula
Cordillera de Colonche
Montañita
Salinas
Machala
Huaquillas
Zaruma
Puyango Petrified Forest
Tumbes

0   50 mi
0   50 km

In fact, there are opportunities to teach English in all regions of the country, from remote mountain villages to coastal towns like Puerto Lopez. Puerto Lopez serves as a jumping-off point for trips to Isla de la Plata, where visitors pass humpback whales during the boat ride to see the island's red-breasted frigate birds and blue-footed boobies. In the capital city of Quito, volunteers often work to support disadvantaged communities—such as street children, homeless elderly, or children with disabilities—and study Spanish in the afternoons.

When considering costs, note that there is a US$100 entrance fee to Galapagos National Park. Some organizations can arrange the paperwork to have this fee waived for their volunteers, but not all have the ability to do this. It normally takes six weeks for the paperwork to be completed, so volunteers must plan in advance.

Local Organizations

ECUADOR VOLUNTEER FOUNDATION

Quito, tel. 593/2255-7749, U.S. tel. 212/461-0428, www.ecuadorvolunteer.org

TYPE OF WORK: agriculture, children and youth, community development, education, environment, wildlife protection

The Ecuador Volunteer Foundation (EVF) aims to serve as a bridge between would-be volunteers and projects in Ecuador that can utilize their efforts. Their mission is "to help develop programs for the well-being of mankind and the environment and to improve the quality of life of the people who need it most by generating transparent and direct-impact activities that work towards the transformation of a more sustainable world." Short-term volunteers pay higher fees than long-term as meals and accommodations are subsidized for the latter, but it is all very reasonable. There are also one-week "alternative spring break" packages available.

Volunteers on the coast might work along local beaches to monitor animal species, clean up and maintain the beaches, and assist with tourist activities and environmental education in the nearby communities, and have the chance to visit nearby Isla de la Plata, an island also known as the "poor man's Galapagos" thanks to its diversity of fauna and affordability. In the Amazon, volunteers might work with an animal rescue and rehabilitation center, assisting in animal care and feeding; cleaning, repairing, and constructing cages; and

maintaining the center's trails and facilities. They'll also have the chance to learn about making pottery or chocolate in the afternoons. Those in Quito might spend their mornings lending a hand at a day care center and their afternoons exploring museums and the historic center or taking Spanish lessons. Volunteers on the Galapagos Islands might help replant native plant species, help install a community water supply, or teach local children about how to take care of the environment.

While EVF strives to select the best projects in terms of both effectiveness and organization, it does not take responsibility for the volunteer's experience within the project. If volunteers are not happy with the tasks assigned to them within a project, they need to take it up with the project coordinator themselves; however, if volunteers are not satisfied and want to change projects, EVF will try to help them find an alternative placement. At the end of the placement period, EVF asks all volunteers to return to Quito to complete an evaluation and receive a certificate.

Application Process: At least one month before your proposed dates, send an email to start the application process. The minimum age for individual volunteers is 16, but there is no minimum for those traveling with parents, and families are welcome.

Cost: There is a one-time registration fee of US$150, as well as a "support fee," covering administration costs, which is US$200 for up to six weeks in short-term projects (or the first

© AMY E. ROBERTSON

El San Francisco is one of many colonial churches in Quito's historic center.

three months in long-term projects). For longer stays, volunteers pay US$50/month after the initial period covered by the support fee. For short-term projects, there is an additional daily fee for meals and housing. (So the fee for stays of 1-6 weeks is US$350, plus the cost of meals and housing.) Long-term volunteers are encouraged to make an additional (but optional) donation in exchange for hosting them for little to no additional cost, which volunteers may use to buy project materials, books, or educational materials. Alternative spring break trips include all the fees, plus food and lodging (but not sightseeing excursions or transportation within Quito), and run US$700-800.

Placement Length: Varies by project, but there are ecological, community, and social projects with one-week minimums. Teaching requires a minimum one-month commitment.

Language Requirements: Varies according to project, but there are opportunities available for those with no or only basic Spanish skills; one- to two-week intensive Spanish classes are available through their partner Spanish school in Quito.

Housing: Accommodations vary according to the project. Some projects utilize hostels or hotels, while others have a volunteer guesthouse, and still others offer homestays (in that case, volunteers usually get a private room, but not always).

Operating Since: 2003
Number of Volunteers: 130 in 2012

ECUAEXPLORA

based in Quito, with placements around the country, tel. 593/8186-7006, toll-free U.S. tel. 877/909-ECEX, www.ecuaexplora.org

TYPE OF WORK: children and youth, community development, education, environment, health, wildlife protection

EcuaExplora coordinates volunteer opportunities with nonprofit organizations throughout Ecuador. Most placements are located in Quito or Guayaquil, but there are also placements available in the Amazon jungle and a couple scattered in smaller towns. The majority of the offerings center around humanitarian work, such as volunteering with children who live and work as scavengers at Quito's city dump, although there are some environmental and sustainability projects available as well, such as working with a conservation, training, and research center on the outskirts of the Amazon. Volunteers placed in one of the more remote sites will be accompanied to the site by an EcuaExplora representative, and may not have access to cell phone and Internet service.

Homestay housing is usually part of the placement, and breakfast and lunch are included Monday-Friday in most programs; some include three meals a day, seven days a week. Some work sites have the possibility of language instruction at an additional cost.

EcuaExplora organizes cultural and sightseeing excursions that volunteers can opt into for an addition cost: trips to other cities, towns, and regions; trips to indigenous markets, cloud forests, and wildlife reserves; and visits to the beach and to the Amazon jungle, just to name some of the possibilities.

ECUADOR

VOLUNTEER PERSPECTIVE

Shannon MacAdams (age 23) is from the United States. Through **Ecuador Volunteer Foundation** (Quito, tel. 593/2255-7749, U.S. tel. 212/461-0428, www.ecuadorvolunteer.org), Shannon spent eight days working in an animal rescue center in Ecuador's Amazonian jungle.

In one word, my experience was incredible!

The director of Ecuador Volunteer met me at the Quito airport and briefed me the following day on the project before sending me on the bus to Puyo. Five hours later, I was in the jungle! I got started the following day gathering food for the animals: monkeys, peccaries, turtles, parrots, and more. The hopeful endpoint of the animals' stay at the organization is reentry into the wild, so most of these animals are about a 15-minute hike into the forest. Feeding the animals was an incredible experience. We fed them twice a day, and in the off times, we would do things to improve the grounds, such as chop branches off fallen trees with machetes to make pathways and build cages. We spent time with the family who runs the grounds. The mother, Marcia, makes pottery for a living and sells it in Puyo. She took us volunteers under her wing, and we all made different kinds of pottery.

The time with others is intense – working, harvesting, sharing these incredible experiences. We were together from the time we got up to the time we went to bed – but once you leave you have no real way of contacting the family ever again. It's a very different experience than it would be visiting another state in the United States and then going back home to resume regular life and continuing contact via email.

Part of the experience was being a tourist in the nearby town of Baños, which is between Puyo and Quito. I went with five other volunteers to Baños for a day of canyoning down multiple waterfalls, rafting down the Amazon among the piranhas. We enjoyed the night-

Application Process: There is an online application form, and a US$150 application fee is required (refundable if you are not accepted or if the project is unavailable for your dates). Families are welcome.

Cost: For projects in Quito, the standard cost is US$950 for two weeks, and US$250 for each additional week. Outside of Quito, the standard cost is US$1,050 for two weeks, US$200 each week thereafter. Programs in the Galapagos have surcharges.

Placement Length: Most are two weeks to four months, although there are a couple of six month and one year teaching positions available.

Language Requirements: Depends on the project, but some, including most of the conservation and reforestation, animal rescue, and orphanage projects, can accept volunteers with little to no Spanish. Five hours of Spanish classes per week are included in the program fee for Quito-based volunteers, and those based elsewhere can get a week of intensive Spanish in Quito before setting off to their site for US$125.

Housing: Typically with a host family; sometimes in volunteer dorms at the project site. Meals are included.

Operating Since: 2008 (known until 2010 as EcuaExperiencia)

Number of Volunteers: 50 through groups and 40 individuals in 2011, double that in *life that evening, and the next day, after some more sightseeing and shopping, we went our separate ways.*

In Quito, I had the whole next day to see so many places. I went with two other volunteers to see a crater that housed an entire community. We ate authentic food and saw some amazing places. There is no place like Quito. Even the clouds are different, I swear! Sadly, the day after was the day we all had to go home.

What was a highlight of the experience?
The sense of companionship and bonding experience was once in a lifetime. I can go back to the jungle to the same place but never will be able to re-create the people and situations we all experienced together.

What did you take away from the experience?
Things were so different – the culture was a complete 180. One of the random things I realized is that we use the refrigerator by default here in the United States, when most of the time it really isn't necessary, especially if you're eating fresh, local food. I also realized how wasteful we are as a culture in the United States. My habits and perspective have changed. Before Ecuador, I was a regular non-diet restricted, nonrecycling, wasteful person. Since the trip, I now avoid most dairy and all meat but fish (really, it's cheaper/simpler). I re-

cycle everything I possibly can and avoid using plastic as much as possible. I try to live as simply as possible, which can be difficult when you literally have everything you ever need/want at your fingertips. In the jungle, the nearest store was an hour away by bus, and you could only purchase what you could personally carry and bring back home.

Was there a downside to your experience?
The only downside was leaving! I really would love to do an extended volunteer stay at Ecuador Volunteer if I can raise the capital and make it work with my schedule.

Were you able to share the experience once you got home?
Definitely! I like to talk to future volunteers and answer any questions they may have. I would recommend it to anyone, especially those who love animals!

2012, and the numbers are expected to double again in 2013

EQUILIBRIO AZUL

Puerto Lopez, tel. 593/2243-1097 in Quito, www.equilibrioazul.org

TYPE OF WORK: children and youth, education, environment, wildlife protection

Equilibrio Azul (EA) is a nonprofit dedicated to the conservation of Ecuador's marine ecosystems and resources. Volunteers may participate in EA's turtle project, which researches and protects hawksbill, green, and olive ridley sea turtles. Work might be on one of the beaches in the Machalilla National Park or at the sea turtle hatchery on La Plata island, a

short boat ride from Puerto Lopez (volunteers are expected to stay on La Plata for one week per month). Responsibilities may include diurnal and nocturnal patrols of beaches, measurement and tagging of turtles, egg counting and nest tagging, egg transfers to a hatchery, installation of transmitters on turtle shells, or telemetry activities onboard a boat. Volunteers may also help out with EA's regular censuses of marine birds on La Plata island, and responsibilities include collecting data; monitoring bird nests; identifying by GPS the location of nests; capturing, measuring, and tagging marine birds; or capturing and releasing sea turtles. Volunteers can also get involved with EA's community outreach, which includes an

ECUADOR

"ecoclub" for local youth, beach cleanups, and outreach at local schools. There are occasional opportunities for certified divers to conduct underwater marine surveys. All volunteers must help with the maintenance and cleaning of the volunteer house, as well as of EA's field equipment, for a typical minimum of three hours per week.

Volunteers usually work about six hours per day. During turtle nesting season (November-April), volunteers may be asked to work Saturday and Sunday as well. Besides hanging out on the beach or studying Spanish in Puerto Lopez, volunteers can go fishing, snorkeling, hiking, arrange for horseback riding, or take a tour to see humpback whales. It is also possible to scuba dive and to earn PADI diving certification in Puerto Lopez.

Application Process: There is an online application, and volunteers must also email a cover letter. Volunteers must be 20 or older.

Cost: US$400/month, which includes accommodations in the volunteer guesthouse and project-related local transportation

Placement Length: There is a minimum placement of one month.

Language Requirements: Basic Spanish required.

Housing: The volunteer guesthouse in Puerto Lopez has shared dorm rooms, and volunteers may be expected to share a room with the opposite gender. It also has hot water, a kitchen, and wireless Internet. The guesthouse on La Plata island, operated by the Ministry of Environment, has limited water and electricity (volunteers cannot take daily showers). Volunteers are responsible for their own meals.

Operating Since: 2004

Number of Volunteers: 46 in 2012

ESCUELA KATITAWA

Salasaca (Sierra), tel. 593/9846-2212,
www.katitawa.blogspot.com

TYPE OF WORK: agriculture, children and youth, community development, education

The motto at Katitawa School is "Sumai Kawsay Yachay," meaning Beautiful, Life, Education in Kichwa, the language of the indigenous people of Salasaca. (It is also the name of the foundation behind the school.) This Montessori-style school teaches children ages 4-11 with a highly individualized approach. Uniquely, it is a trilingual school, teaching English, Spanish, and Kichwa, as well as core subjects such as math, art, history, and geography, as well as electives including computers, sports, and dance. At the time of this writing, there were 35 students and four teachers.

Volunteers stay in a guesthouse that is about a 40-minute walk (downhill) from the school. The large, beautiful house, overlooking the Andes and Chimborazo, has five bathrooms and a fully equipped kitchen. It hosts up to 20 people in shared or private rooms. Volunteers work at the school 8am-1pm on weekdays and take a 3pm-8pm shift at the library once per week. Other afternoons may be filled teaching English to adults in the community, or volunteers can just relax. On weekends, volunteers typically head out to explore, visiting Baños and its thermal baths, half an hour away, or heading farther afield to colonial Quito or to hike the Chimborazo or Cotopaxi volcanoes.

Sometimes there are 1 or 2 volunteers at the school, while other times there are 20. Tasks depend on the interests, skills, and time commitment of the volunteer, and include helping in a classroom, working in the garden/farm, or working on construction projects. Besides teaching English or other core subjects, volunteers may teach a music lesson or an arts and crafts project. The school is run on donations and resources are limited, so volunteers should bring with them any supplies they think they might want to use in the classroom.

Application Process: There is a simple online form.

Cost: US$10 per week

Placement Length: A few days to a few months, depending on the volunteer.

Language Requirements: None.

Housing: Accommodations, breakfast, and lunch are provided. Dinner is prepared communally, and volunteers take turns cooking and paying for ingredients, usually spending another US$5 per week. Meals are all vegetarian.

Operating Since: 1997

Number of Volunteers: more than 250 between 2006 and 2012 (65 in 2012)

FOUNDATION BOLIVAR EDUCATION

based in Quito, with placements around the country, tel. 593/2223-4708, www.ecuadorvolunteers.org

TYPE OF WORK: children and youth, community development, education, environment, health, wildlife protection, women's empowerment

Foundation Bolivar Education (FBE, Ecuador Volunteers) is a Quito-based organization that facilitates volunteer opportunities all across Ecuador. Placements include working with children, the elderly, or women facing domestic violence in Quito; rescuing abused domestic pets, or assisting nurses and patients at a public hospital, in Cuenca; supporting a community association's efforts to provide agricultural and tourism training to local families in a small town in central Ecuador; rehabilitating injured and trafficked wild animals in the Sierra or Amazon; and helping with reforestation and habitat preservation on the Galapagos Islands.

A 10 percent discount at the organization's affiliated Spanish school (in Quito) is offered to volunteers who stay and study for two weeks or more. Volunteers in Cuenca can also look for a local Spanish school. Other placements may be more remote, and formal lessons may not be available nearby. Likewise, free time activities vary widely according to the placement, ranging from exploring colonial cities and indigenous villages to hiking in the jungle or cloud forest and swimming in the sea.

FBE markets itself, and a selection of its volunteer opportunities, as particularly senior friendly.

Application Process: There is an online application form, and a US$25 application fee is required when your application is accepted.

Cost: None, other than the application fee; volunteers pay for their own housing and food.

Placement Length: Anything from one week

© AMY E. ROBERTSON

There are 13 different indigenous groups in multicultural Ecuador.

ECUADOR

to one year, depending on the volunteer's interests and availability.

Language Requirements: Most volunteer opportunities through FBE require Spanish, but the organization is affiliated with a Spanish school in Quito. (They recommend six weeks' study prior to volunteering for beginners.) There are a few opportunities volunteering with kids in day care centers and teaching English that do not require Spanish.

Housing: A homestay, hostels, hotels, or even apartments are available for volunteers who stay a month or more.

Operating Since: 2008
Number of Volunteers: 482 in 2012

FUNDACIÓN ARTE DEL MUNDO (FAM)

Baños (Sierra), tel. 593/3274-2244,
www.artedelmundoecuador.com

TYPE OF WORK: children and youth, education

FAM is a program that seeks to "encourage literacy, creativity and a love of the arts" by providing a free after-school program for children (ages 6-12), English programs for children and adults, and theatrical entertainment in Baños. FAM also operates a library (3:30pm-6pm Monday-Friday) where they provide services to the community. The after-school program changes weekly based on volunteer skills and interests; programs have included arts and crafts, dance, archaeology, music, theater, chess, photography, sports, yoga, martial arts, and puppetry. There is a daily meeting to plan the activity of the day, and one volunteer might lead an activity in origami or guitar or modern dance while other volunteers lend a hand. English classes are offered to children in the afternoons and to teenagers and adults in the early evenings. FAM also serves as the town's only cinema, organizing a weekly open-air movie and a monthly children's movie.

The number of volunteers at any one time varies but averages about six. Mornings are free to study Spanish, get a massage, take a hike, or participate in any of the adventure sports that Baños is famous for, such as canyoning and rafting.

Application Process: There is an online form, and two personal references must be provided. Volunteers must be age 18 or older unless accompanied by an adult.

Cost: US$180-280/month for a dorm room to a double room with private half bath

Placement Length: The average placement length is one month, but a shorter visit might be considered.

Language Requirements: Spanish is helpful, but it is not required as long as the volunteer has the desire to learn it.

Housing: Volunteers stay in a guesthouse with dorms and private rooms. They are responsible for their own meals, but there is a kitchen in the guesthouse. Wireless Internet, a shared computer with Internet, and the use of a washing machine are available.

Operating Since: 2008
Number of Volunteers: 65 in 2012

GALAPAGOS ICE

Galapagos, tel. 593/5301-5108,
www.galapagosice.org

TYPE OF WORK: children and youth, community development, education, environment, health, wildlife protection

The mission of Galapagos Immerse-Connect-Evolve (Galapagos ICE) is to "improve the educational and medical systems in the Galapagos Islands, and to encourage ecological efforts that recognize the local population as integral participants in the conservation of this unique natural habitat." It was founded by American Emily Pozo after she visited the islands, based on her belief that a local population that has "greater access to healthcare, education, and economic opportunities can serve as a strong bulwark against ecological deterioration." While Galapagos ICE is a registered 501(c)3 organization in the United States, its main office is on the Galapagos, where Pozo lives year-round.

Galapagos ICE personalizes its placements in accordance with the volunteer's skills and interests. Doctors, nurses, dentists, and nutritionists have worked in local hospitals and clinics, and visiting teachers have led after-school programs as well as teacher training workshops; placements have also been found for eco-architects, yoga teachers, artists, university professors, and more. Ongoing projects include community outreach and education related to nutrition, exercise, hypertension, and diabetes; medical assistance; support to English teachers; and after-school programming in sports and fine arts. Groups are welcome for medical brigades, and for building projects such as playground restoration or library construction. Galapagos ICE also needs volunteers to help with administration and fundraising.

While there are plenty of opportunities to practice your Spanish, there are no formal language programs for foreigners on the island, so it's best to brush up on your language skills prior to arrival.

Application Process: To apply, send a completed application form via email with a copy of your résumé, two letters of recommendation. There is a US$50 application fee, which can be paid online. Families are welcome.

Cost: US$250 for stays of up to two weeks, US$300 for stays up to four weeks, and US$100 for every two weeks thereafter. If volunteers choose a homestay, the costs are US$100 every two weeks without meals; with meals the cost is US$200 every two weeks. While volunteers can stay for an odd number of weeks, the cost cannot be prorated for a partial fortnight. Family discounts are available.

Placement Length: There is a minimum placement of two weeks.

Language Requirements: Basic Spanish is required for some projects, while intermediate to advanced Spanish is required for others.

Housing: Volunteers can choose between homestays through Galapagos ICE or making their own housing arrangements. The homestays have private bedrooms, and volunteers can choose whether to have meals included or not. Most homestays have cold-water showers.

Operating Since: 2006

Number of Volunteers: approximately 100 in 2011

INTAGTOUR

Cuellaje, Sierra, tel. 593/6-301-7543,
www.intagtour.com, www.cloudforestadventure.com

TYPE OF WORK: agriculture, children and youth, community development, education, environment

Founded by British expat Ned Cresswell, IntagTour (IT) offers tourism and volunteer work in one of Ecuador's least-known and most beautiful areas, Intag–a cloud forest region located in the Imbabura province of northern Ecuador, on the western slopes of the Andes. IT's goal is to slow degradation of the cloud forest by providing sustainable alternative sources of income for locals, while offering first-rate ecotourist experiences for visitors.

IntagTour places volunteers in several village schools, where they can help teach English, sports, music, arts, mathematics and dance. Volunteers who teach crafts are also welcome, but they will need to bring their own supplies. The school in Cuellaje, the largest town in the area, has 270 children ages 5-16, and volunteers are especially needed to teach English geared toward tourism. Adult-education teachers are needed in the areas of English, as well as those with skills such as craftwork, cooking, mechanics, agriculture, health care, and sports. (Almost any skill or interest that volunteers may care to share would be welcome.) Farming volunteers have no shortage of responsibilities, which may include milking and cheesemaking; caring for poultry; preparing soil, sowing, participating in aftercare, and harvesting; caring for cattle; maintaining pastures; performing simple veterinary skills; or building and repairing fences. IT also connects volunteers with an interest in the environment to park rangers at the Cotachachi-Cayapas Reserve, where they might carry out GPS surveys and map local forest areas; speak to the communities on environmental issues; accompany the reserve rangers on daily visits; carry out inventories of the plants and animals of the area; or teach English to the rangers. Volunteers in this area should have biological or ecological qualification and experience with GPS and mapmaking. Volunteers interested in their own scientific research and field work, on anything

ECUADOR

from bromeliads to the Andean bear, are also very welcome.

Volunteer work here is flexible: You won't receive an hour-by-hour schedule, or even a day-by-day one. But as the local communities love having volunteer help and there is always work to be done, self-starters will find plenty to stay busy. Volunteers will need to find their own entertainment for free time, but there is plenty to explore on nature walks, including waterfalls, cloud forest, and jungle. IT offers help with Spanish-language learning, and horseback-riding lessons are free of charge for volunteers. Volunteers will need to be willing to adapt to a rural lifestyle in which homestay families will be rising early and heading to bed around 8pm. Volunteers can request to be placed in a home in or near Cuellaje, if they prefer to be less remote.

Application Process: Volunteers can email to reserve a spot ahead of time, but it is also possible to just show up and stay for a day or two at the community guesthouse before deciding to volunteer and arrange placement. While there is no minimum age required, individual volunteers under the age of 18 should have parental permission. Families are always very welcome.

Cost: US$42/week for teaching; US$49/week for ecological or farm work. Housing is included, and all money is paid directly to the host family.

Placement Length: There is a minimum placement of one week. Volunteer placements and host families are arranged by Ned Cresswell and his wife, Patricia, a native of the Intag region.

Language Requirements: Basic Spanish or the willingness to learn.

Housing: Volunteers are usually placed in homestays, often after an introductory stay in the community guesthouse (US$10/night and US$2/meal). All meals in the homestay are included. Volunteers have private rooms but may only have cold water. The closest Internet connection may be in the next town. It is also possible to stay in one of the rustic guesthouses for the duration of a visit.

Operating Since: 2007

Number of Volunteers: around 30 in 2012

JATUN SACHA

main office in Quito (Sierra), tel. 593/2243-2240, www.jatunsacha.org

TYPE OF WORK: children and youth, community development, environment, health, wildlife protection

Jatun Sacha (JS) is a self-sustaining nonprofit organization that owns and maintains five private nature reserves across Ecuador. Its mission is to "promote the conservation of Ecuador's biodiversity, through technical training, scientific research, environmental education programs at national and international level, community development, sustainable management of natural resources, and the training of leaders with greater ethnic and gender participation to improve the quality of life of the communities." Each reserve works carefully with the local community.

Volunteers work eight-hour days and can choose from sites in the Amazonian or Coastal rainforest, Andean forest, or on the Galapagos Islands. Volunteers should be interested in the areas of biodiversity, conservation, ecology, and nature, and may work on reforestation, removal of invasive species, trail maintenance, or infrastructure repair. However, placements are not limited to scientific research. As JS works closely with local communities to deepen support of its efforts, volunteers can also choose to work in a local clinic or preschool, help plant a community garden or consult on microenterprise training, teach English, or lead a campaign on sexual health or environmental protection. JS has a document that it can email to interested persons that has details about the different volunteer tasks and free-time activities, best seasons to visit, and accommodations at the different reserves.

Activities for after-work hours depend on the duty station but can include Spanish lessons or dance practice, hiking, swimming, and, of course, nature observation.

Application Process: There is a simple online form to complete (it requires your passport number). Families are welcome. If youth under age 18 are travelling without their parents, they must have parental authorization.

Cost: There is one set of prices for volunteering

on the mainland and a second (higher) set for volunteering on the Galapagos. On the mainland, rates start at US$310 for one week and increase by US$100-130 for each additional week. In the Galapgaos, one week is US$541, and it is roughly US$240 for each additional week. In addition, there is an application fee of US$47 for mainland programs and US$67 to work in the Galapagos. Volunteers should bring about US$20 per week for incidentals.
Placement Length: Minimum of two weeks.
Language Requirements: None.
Housing: There are volunteer houses with electricity at each of the reserves. Accommodations and meals are included with the program fees.
Operating Since: 1985
Number of Volunteers: close to 1,000 in 2012

LAS TOLAS COMMUNITY

Las Tolas (Sierra), www.lastolas.org
TYPE OF WORK: agriculture, children and youth, community development, education

Las Tolas is a small community in Ecuador's mountain highlands, 76 kilometers (48 mi) from Quito. In a rather unique arrangement, the community has developed a tourism and volunteering setup aimed at grassroots environmental conservation and community development.

Volunteers stay with local families and participate in community life, which may include learning sustainable organic farming practices, helping with infrastructure development and farm work, creating crafts in the artisan shop, developing ecotourism infrastructure, helping in the school, and teaching English. Volunteers typically work 5-6 hours per day.

When not working, volunteers may hike to waterfalls, go bird-watching, or take a horseback ride, and they are always warmly welcomed at community events, which range from a weekly soccer match to local weddings. It's possible to visit a cultural museum and some indigenous ruins in the town of Tulipe, 20 minutes away, or take longer day trips to Mindo and its cloud forest or Quito and its historical city center.

The modest fee goes entirely to the community, and in addition to covering the cost of the homestay, it includes experienced guides for local activities and learning opportunities, and a donation toward a grassroots reforestation initiative. There is also a qualified Spanish teacher in the community for those who would like help in brushing up their language skills.
Application Process: Send an email. All ages are welcome.
Cost: US$16 per day up to one month; US$15 per day for stays of longer than a month. This covers accommodations and meals, and goes directly to the host family.
Placement Length: Minimum of one week.
Language Requirements: None, although local families speak only Spanish, so volunteers should have a strong interest in learning Spanish if they don't have a basic knowledge already.
Housing: Volunteers stay with local families and are provided private rooms. The homes have electricity, and bathrooms are typically in a freestanding separate room behind the house with running water, a sink, toilet, and shower (often cold) or bathing area. Laundry is done by hand. Meals are included.
Operating Since: 2007
Number of Volunteers: 22 in 2012

MERAZONIA

Mera (Amazon), tel. 593/9842-13789, www.merazonia.org
TYPE OF WORK: wildlife protection

According to their website, "Merazonia is a dynamic rescue and rehabilitation center for trafficked and abused Amazonian animals, located on 250 acres of rainforest." Volunteers will usually find monkeys, kinkajous, felines, other mammals, macaws, and parrots at Merazonia—but because of the focus on rehabilitation for release into the wild, there is a strict "no interaction" policy, so there's not a bunch of petting the rainforest animals. Instead, volunteers are around the animals during feedings, cleanings, or medical checks, but the rest of the time volunteers will be busy with tasks such as filling bags with sand and

ECUADOR

hauling them to a project site, building enclosures and trails, or performing general upkeep of the property. Animals not fit to be released are maintained by Merazonia.

Merazonia is located 15 minutes outside of the town of Mera, at the edge of the rainforest not far from Puyo. As one could expect, it rains a heck of a lot, so bring a rain poncho and quick-drying clothes.

Application Process: Send an email. Volunteers must be at least 18 years old.

Cost: US$240 for the first two weeks; $100 per week thereafter.

Placement Length: Minimum of two weeks, with preference given to those who can commit to at least four weeks.

Language Requirements: None.

Housing: Volunteers stay in a dorm-style guesthouse. Bathroom facilities are next to the guesthouse and do include hot showers. Meals are included in the fees; volunteers make their own breakfast and lunch, while dinner is a communal effort where people take turns cooking and cleaning. Shopping is done twice a week, on which days there is usually a meat option for dinner; the other days the food is vegetarian. There is no electricity on the site, although there is a generator that is run twice per week, and volunteers can charge any electronic gadgets at that time.

Operating Since: 2004

Number of Volunteers: On average Merazonia has 6-11 volunteers at a time, staying 3-4 weeks.

RÍO MUCHACHO

Canoa (Coast), tel. 593/5258-8184,
www.riomuchacho.com

TYPE OF WORK: agriculture, community development

Río Muchacho is an 11-hectare (27-acre) organic farm located 17 kilometers (11 mi) from the beach town of Canoa, in the province of Manabí. The farm strives to support the local community with income-generating initiatives, including a beekeeping project, training in the creation of handicrafts, and a fair-trade store, in addition to outreach on health and environment issues. In addition, in 1992 they founded the Río Muchacho Community Environmental School, which serves 35-45 students in preschool-grade 6, providing a government-accredited elementary education with a strong emphasis on environment and conservation.

A typical day on the farm begins with farm chores at 6am, which could be harvesting, irrigation, helping prepare breakfast, or feeding and cleaning animals, and breakfast is at 7:30am. The rest of the morning is spent working in the garden or at the school. At the school, volunteers who have appropriate skills can help in their area of expertise, such as art, music, sports, creative writing, English, reading, yoga, martial arts, maintenance, or construction. On the farm, volunteers will have the chance to learn about planting and transplanting, weeding and organic weed control, harvesting, pest control, composting, fertilizers, the principles of organic farming, permaculture, recycling organic waste, and composting toilets. After lunch, volunteers work on individual projects until 4pm, which may include painting, doing carpentry and other construction work; translating, organizing information, and artwork (e.g., murals and information boards); performing community outreach; participating in infrastructure development (e.g., bridges, water pipelines) and maintaining paths, gardens, trails, and so on; making and jarring sauces, pickles, or marmalades with the farm's produce; and much more, depending upon the volunteer's skills and what is currently needed. Movies, presentations, or cultural activities are offered in the evenings.

There is a 14-day language and volunteering program available for groups of seven or more that includes language study, organic farming, and a visit to the school; there are also one- to three-day tours available.

Spanish lessons can be arranged upon request, but for a minimum of a 40-hour week of study—it's easier and cheaper to study Spanish upon arrival to Ecuador in Quito or Guayaquil.

Because of its remote location, there is no

Internet and limited cell phone service at the farm. There is a shortwave radio for emergency use.

Application Process: Send an email with skills, interests, and proposed dates. Families are welcome.

Cost: US$365 for four weeks for individual volunteers; additional time is at a lower rate. The 14-day group program is US$430 per person.

Placement Length: Usually four weeks, although they will consider shorter or longer stays.

Language Requirements: None, although Spanish skills will always improve the experience and allow for a wider variety of volunteer responsibilities.

Housing: There are private rooms (for couples), and dorm-style rooms that sleep 2-6. The farm has both electricity and running water. Food on the farm is mainly vegetarian, although some fish, shrimp, and white meats are served.

Operating Since: The farm was purchased by its current owners in 1987, the school was founded in 1993, and volunteers were first accepted in 1998.

Number of Volunteers: about 150 in 2012, both individuals and groups

INTERNATIONAL ORGANIZATIONS

The following international organizations support volunteer efforts in Ecuador:

A Broader View (U.S. tel. 215/780-1845, toll-free U.S. tel. 866/423-3258, www.abroaderview.org), page 193.
Type of Work: agriculture, children and youth, community development, education, environment, health, wildlife protection, women's empowerment

Earthwatch (U.S. tel. 978/461-0081, toll-free U.S. tel. 800/776-0188, www.earthwatch.org), page 196.
Type of Work: environment, wildlife protection

Global Volunteers (toll-free U.S. tel. 800/487-1074, www.globalvolunteers.org), page 200.
Type of Work: children and youth, community development, education

International Volunteer HQ (IVHQ) (toll-free U.S. tel. 877/342-6588, www.volunteerhq.org), page 203.
Type of Work: agriculture, children and youth, community development, education, environment, health, wildlife protection

ProWorld (toll-free U.S. tel. 877/429-6753, www.proworldvolunteers.org), page 207.
Type of Work: children and youth, community development, education, environment, health, wildlife protection, women's empowerment

TECHO (U.S. tel. 305/860-4090, www.techo.org), page 209.
Type of Work: community development

UBELONG (U.S. tel. 202/250-3706, www.ubelong.org), page 210.
Type of Work: agriculture, children and youth, community development, education, environment, health, wildlife protection, women's empowerment

VOFAIR (www.vofair.org), page 211.
Type of Work: agriculture, children and youth, community development, education, environment, health, wildlife protection, women's empowerment

ECUADOR

Essentials

BACKGROUND
Geography and Climate
The country measures 283,560 square kilometers (109,483 sq. mi), making it slightly smaller than the state of Nevada. While most folks are aware of the exceptional flora and fauna of the Galapagos Islands, many forget that the islands are part of Ecuador, a country whose mainland is pretty darn exceptional as well, with its diversity of geography and climate, and its rich indigenous culture.

With an altitude that varies from sea level to 2,800 meters (9,850 ft) in Quito, and even higher in some towns, Ecuador has a varied climate and countless microclimates.

In the Sierra, the dry season (summer) runs June-September, and the wet season (winter) is October-May. It's pleasantly warm in the summer, but never hot; a light jacket is good for the evenings, even during the warmest months. Sweaters are needed during the rainy season; April is the wettest month. In the Amazon, the dry season is brief, from October-December, and temperatures tend to hover in the mid-20s C (mid-70s F). Temperatures are similar along the coast, but the dry season is longer, from June to November. *Invierno* (winter) in the Galapagos Islands is May-December, when it is cooler and drier, but the weather is warm year-round (ranging 22-32°C or 70-90°F).

History and Economy
Ecuador has a long pre-Columbian history, with traces of cultures dating as far back as 9000 BC. The Incan invasion from Peru in the late 15th century was met with fierce resistance by local tribes, but the Incans managed to prevail and left their mark with Ingapirca, a set of Incan ruins easily visited as a day trip from Cuenca. Spanish conquistadores followed soon thereafter, arriving in 1531 and ruling until their defeat in 1822.

There are 13 indigenous nationalities, concentrated in the Sierra and the Oriente,

and there is a notable population of Afro-Ecuadorians, primarily located in the northwest coastal region. Depending on who's counting, there are roughly a dozen languages spoken in Ecuador, including eight or nine dialects of Quichua, but Spanish is the country's official language, spoken by more than 90 percent of the people.

Although modern political history in Ecuador is one of oligarchies and coups, it is also a largely peaceful one, with effective leaders dotted among the less-successful ones. Current president Rafael Correa was elected in 2006 (taking office at the beginning of 2007) on a populist platform of "Citizen Power." Reelected in 2009, he was the first president in 30 years to win a second term; he was then reelected for a third term in early 2013, with more than 50 percent of the vote.

The Ecuadorian economy has two main prongs: exports, of bananas, shrimp, oil, gold, and other primary products; and remittances—money transfers sent home by nearly a million Ecuadorian emigrants working abroad—which totaled over US$2.3 billion in 2010.

PREPARATION
Transportation
Ecuador has two international airports. The **Mariscal Sucre International Airport** (UIO, www.aeropuertoquito.aero) lies 11 miles (18 km) outside of the capital city of Quito. It is serviced by American Airlines, Delta, and United, as well as domestic, regional, and European airlines. **José Joaquín de Olmedo** (GYE, www.tagsa.aero) is in Guayaquil, the country's business capital on the coast. American is the only North American airline to fly to Guayaquil. Most flights to the Galapagos go through Guayaquil, although it is also possible to travel by direct flight to the Galapagos from Quito. Departure taxes in both Quito and Guayquil are included in the ticket price.

Bus service is safe and cheap, and can take you just about anywhere. Small towns and villages often only see one bus per day, however, so it pays to find out schedules ahead of time. Avoid traveling on the cheapest buses, if possible, as they tend to break down more and have the most reckless drivers.

Passports and Visas

The expiration date on your passport must be at least six months after the date your trip begins or you will not be able to enter the country (or even board your plane). Immigration officials may ask to see proof of return or onward travel (such as an airline ticket). Travelers who enter Ecuador for tourism purposes do not require visas (with the exception of Chinese citizens) and are automatically granted a 90-day stay.

Money

Ecuador's official currency is the **U.S. dollar**. Bring plenty of small bills, especially if you're planning to spend time outside of the cities and major tourist destinations, as it can be a challenge to get change for anything larger than a US$5 bill in villages or rural areas.

Health

If spending time in the Sierra, be prepared to take a couple of days to adjust to the altitude. Most people simply feel more tired than usual the first couple of days, while an unfortunate few may find themselves nauseated and needing serious rest. To minimize the impact of altitude change, stay hydrated and manage your sun exposure. How your body reacts to the altitude does not seem to depend on fitness level, and young children seem to adjust more easily than adults. Should your symptoms prove serious, local doctors may treat them with extra oxygen.

Yellow fever vaccinations are recommended for travel to certain parts of the Ecuadorian Amazon and must be applied 10 days before travel. Malaria is not present in the Galapagos Islands, Guayaquil, Quito, or most of the Sierra (it is not present over an altitude of 1,500 m/5,000 ft).

Because of Ecuador's proximity to the equator, the sun's rays are powerful year-round, so be sure to bring sunscreen, and slather it on even on cloudy days.

Safety

Crime has been on the increase in Quito and Guayaquil. Be aware of your surroundings at all times; avoid deserted areas, and spring for a taxi at night. In Quito, book your taxi with one of the services inside the airport. In Guayaquil, use a taxi service rather than hailing one on the street. Always check with your host organization for the latest on safety recommendations in the place you will stay and work.

ECUADOR

PERU

Famed for Machu Picchu and its Incan history, Peru lies bordered by Ecuador and Colombia to the north, Brazil and Bolivia to the east, Chile to the south, and the Pacific Ocean to the west.

While the breathtaking ruins of Machu Picchu draw 2,500 visitors per day, there are countless places meriting a visit of their own: the ruins of Chan Chan, the capital of the Chimú Empire; the mysterious 1,500-year-old geoglyphs known as the Nazca Lines; the Incan ruins and living indigenous villages of the Sacred Valley; the crafts market and Spanish colonial center of the Arequipa.

The colonial city of Cusco makes an ideal base for trips to the Sacred Valley, including Ollantaytambo and Machu Picchu.

In addition, the fourth-largest Latin American country (by area) boasts Amazonian rainforests teeming with flora and fauna, and world-class surfing along its golden coastline.

Statistics testify to the need for volunteers: Peru has a gross national income per capita of US$4,700 (2011 World Bank figures), and more than 30 percent of the country's population lives below the national poverty line. Fittingly, many of the opportunities in Peru relate to education and community development, such as replacing fire pits in homes with stoves, working with special-needs children, or supporting microenterprises. There is also conservation work—restoring natural habitats and rehabilitating wild animals, for example.

© LUCA RENDA

Local Organizations

ALDEA YANAPAY

Cusco, tel. 51/8423-5870,

www.aldeayanapay.org

TYPE OF WORK: children and youth, community development, education

Yanapay is a Quechua word that means "to help," and that encapsulates the philosophy behind this organization. Founded in 2004 by an idealist from Cusco, Aldea Yanapay provides alternative education to underserved children. The founder's goal is to create sustainable development projects, including one day a hospital, a garden, and an orphanage, all funded by profitable sister business projects. Currently, a hostel and its restaurant/café provide the funding for two schools, one with students ages 4-8, the other with students ages 9-11, as well as a cultural center that serves youth 12-16.

The schools have class 3pm-7pm Monday-Friday, and on Saturday mornings there are school excursions to the park or countryside for sports and games. Volunteers do a little bit of everything, from teaching to sweeping or cleaning. There are standard courses that are taught, such as English and social studies, but there is also space for volunteers to create their own activities and lesson plans based on their interests (but bring your own materials!).

There is plenty to explore in Cusco and in the surrounding Sacred Valley, from museums to Incan ruins. Volunteers with Yanapay can receive a 5 percent discount on Spanish classes at Excel Spanish school.

Application Process: To apply, send an email. There is no minimum age to volunteer and families are welcome.

Cost: There is no fee to volunteer with Aldea Yanapay.

Placement Length: Minimum of one week.

Language Requirements: None.

Housing: Volunteers are responsible for their own accommodations and meals. Yanapay operates a tourist hostel, with rooms US$9-13.50 per person. They also have a homestay (US$13.50 per person per day with breakfast included, or US$17.50 per person per day with all three meals), a guesthouse (perfect for families or small groups), and can arrange for an apartment. There are weekly and monthly rates as well.

Operating Since: 2004

Number of Volunteers: There are typically more than 20 volunteers working each week, of whom 2 or 3 are new each week.

ANDEAN ALLIANCE

Huaraz, tel. 51/9437-89330,

www.andeanalliance.org

TYPE OF WORK: children and youth, community development, education, women's empowerment

Andean Alliance (AA) is a nonprofit run by the Canadian owners of the mountain lodge Lazy Dog Inn, located 6 miles (10 km) outside of Huaraz. It is a grassroots organization whose goals are to: "strengthen the economic income base of Andean communities and foster their inclusion into the formal economy via skills training and small business development while conserving Andean cultural traditions; strengthen the social capital of Andean communities by implementing educational, sports and youth development programs; and support improved natural resource management and conservation practices among the Andean people."

Volunteer opportunities vary with current needs, and AA tries to match your skills and availability with suitable projects. Past projects have included assisting with infrastructure improvements to a local elementary school; supporting improvements to community roads; and purchasing and distributing hand radios to improve neighborhood

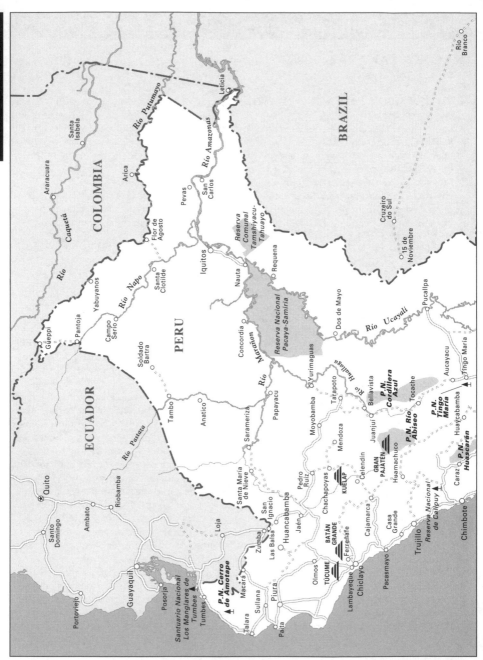

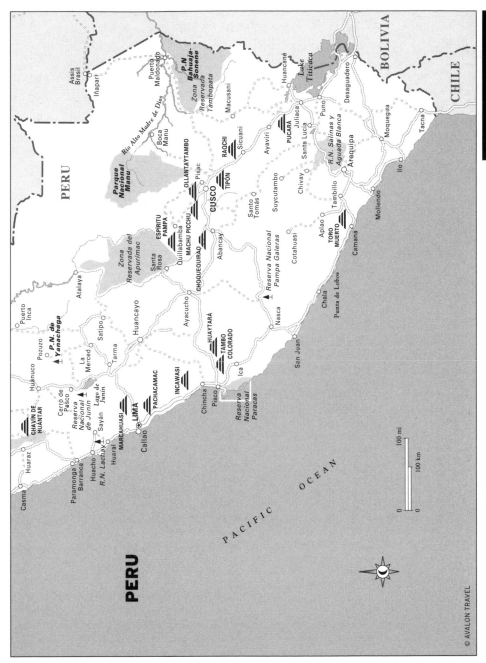

PERU

© AVALON TRAVEL

© JOËLLE BADMAN

Canadian youth visit the Yurac Yacu Development Center supported by Andean Alliance.

security. Volunteers have helped revamp AA's website and worked in community greenhouses. At the time of this writing, AA had a need for short-term volunteers to assist at Yurac Yacu Centro de Desarollo, a community center project supported by AA that directly works with aspects of education, encompassing preschool, computer classes, help with homework, as well as youth development in the form of leadership and outdoor education. In addition, volunteers are needed to assist the small business coordinator in efforts to train local women for running a café, developing guiding and tourist services, and organizing a new library or computer center; and to support the organization of annual soccer and volleyball tournaments in the local community. Volunteers taking their meals at the inn may also be asked to help out with tasks such as preparing dinner and setting the table. Long-term volunteer placements are also available. If lodge guests want to spend just a few days volunteering, it may be possible, but it should be arranged in advance.

In their free time, volunteers can go hiking in the surrounding mountains or go bird-watching, go horseback riding or rock climbing, visit archaeological ruins of the pre-Columbian Recuay and Wari cultures, go mountain biking, or snuggle up with a book in front of the fireplace at Lazy Dog Inn. Spanish lessons can be arranged with an experienced teacher for US$12-15/hour, or conversation practice with a local youth for cheaper.

Application Process: There is an easy online application form. Individual volunteers should be 21 or older.

Cost: US$8/day, which covers accommodations and meals.

Placement Length: Ideally a minimum of three weeks, although there may be flexibility depending on the volunteer's skills and the organization's needs.

Language Requirements: The ability to communicate with at least basic Spanish required.

Housing: Volunteers are given a room in a small cabin with a shared bath and a small kitchen. Of course, if volunteers would like to splurge on a room at the well-appointed inn, they are welcome to do so. Volunteers receive the same meals as guests, unless there are no guests, in which case volunteers will need to cook for themselves.

Operating Since: 2003

Number of Volunteers: three individuals, one couple, and one family in 2012

AWAMAKI

Ollantaytambo, tel. 51/8420-4149,
U.S. tel. 570/850-5260, www.awamaki.org

TYPE OF WORK: children and youth, community development, women's empowerment

Awamaki is an organization working to promote sustainable development in and around the village of Ollantaytambo, in Peru's Sacred Valley, not far from Cusco and Machu Picchu. Its focus is on economic empowerment of disadvantaged Quechua women, and its efforts are a three-pronged approach: women's cooperatives, sustainable tourism, and community education. Awamaki has been instrumental in recovering ancient weaving techniques in the area and in assisting weavers to market their products both at local crafts markets and internationally.

Volunteers might teach English or computer skills, support a workshop that teaches household financial management or tourism hospitality skills, help out at the Awamaki Fair Trade shop, or even lead a hike through Incan ruins. Those interested in working with children can lend a hand at the local preschool. Awamaki's program is a well-thought-out combination of volunteering, learning, and cultural immersion, with six hours per week of Spanish-language instruction, group discussions on relevant topics of culture and development, and instruction in basket weaving, Andean cookery, and backstrap weaving. While fees are not cheap, a significant portion goes into the project work.

Named a UNESCO World Heritage Site and described as a "living Incan city," Ollantaytambo is home to a fascinating mix of Incan ruins and indigenous Andean culture. Thanks to its thriving tourism industry,

there are plenty of restaurants and cafés, and endless possibilities for weekend explorations. Excursions to Cusco, Machu Picchu, and around the Sacred Valley are available for an additional fee.

Application Process: Send an email or call, and Awamaki will send information and an application form. There is no minimum age to volunteer, and families are welcome. Awamaki has even helped enroll visiting children in the local school.

Cost: US$1,250 for three weeks, US$200 each additional week

Placement Length: Three weeks minimum.

Language Requirements: None. Language instruction is part of the program.

Housing: Awamaki offers a homestay program with middle-class families in Ollantaytambo. Volunteers have their own rooms and a private bathroom, and meals are provided by the family—coffee and tea with toast (and sometimes eggs) for breakfast; soup, chicken or beef, and rice or potatoes for lunch; and a smaller portion of the same for dinner.

Operating Since: 2009

Number of Volunteers: around 50 in 2012

ESPERANZA VERDE

outside of Curimana (Amazon),
www.esperanzaverdeperu.com

TYPE OF WORK: environment, wildlife protection

Founded in 2010 by a Dutch couple who have experience with a similar center in Ecuador, Esperanza Verde is a wildlife rescue and rehabilitation center located in the central Peruvian Amazon. Their aim is to work with the local community on sustainable management of the forest and to provide rehabilitation for animals that have been confiscated from illegal traders.

At the time of this writing, volunteer work was focused on preparations: construction of cages and enclosures, building a volunteer guesthouse, creating and maintaining trails, planting seeds and seedlings in the tree nursery, planting fruit trees to support the future animals, mapping the area, and setting up a water system. While they were not yet "officially" open, they have already accepted hurt animals and abandoned baby animals that have been brought to them, and by the beginning of 2013 had already taken in a tayra, a young tapir, a squirrel monkey, a baby sloth, a Spix's guan, a tortoise, an otter, and several monkeys (two capuchin, a squirrel, and a tamarin), and volunteers are already involved in their care, with tasks such as feeding the animals and cleaning their cages.

Volunteers who can commit to longer stays (three months or more) can also get involved in an inventory of fauna and/or flora on the land or lend a hand at the local primary or secondary school, teaching English, environmental classes, sports, or assisting generally.

Regardless of their tasks, volunteers generally work five or six days per week, 7:30am-5pm (with a lunch break), and take turns helping prepare dinner. Evenings are free, but entertainment is up to the volunteer—reading by candlelight, listening to music (as long as your player is battery operated), or just relaxing.

Application Process: Send an email. Volunteers must be 18 or older.

Cost: US$75 per week, including housing

Placement Length: Minimum of three weeks.

Language Requirements: None, although intermediate Spanish will make it easier to communicate with the locals.

Housing: There is a volunteer guesthouse (with shared rooms), and meals are provided. There is no hot water, nor electricity, but there are a few solar lights and a gas stove (although most cooking is by wood fire).

Operating Since: 2010

Number of Volunteers: between 40 and 50 in 2012

FAIRPLAY

Cusco, tel. 51/98478-9252, www.fairplay-peru.org

TYPE OF WORK: children and youth, education, women's empowerment

FairPlay is an organization based in Cusco that seeks to create work opportunities for families and, in particular, single mothers, so that the cycle of poverty can be broken and both standards of living and futures can be improved.

As nearly three-quarters of Peruvians living in extreme poverty are in single-mother households, the focus on single mothers is well aimed. Capitalizing on its location in touristic Cusco, FairPlay trains single mothers to teach Spanish, offering a fair wage and reasonable hours in return. It also runs a homestay program with 22 families in Cusco, salsa lessons taught by disadvantaged youth that have been trained by FairPlay, and WaaW, an after-school project that serves 25 children between the ages of 5 and 11.

Volunteer opportunities are available at WaaW. The project focuses on three main areas: education, nutrition, and hygiene. Tutoring is given to the children at the program, along with classes along thematic units, sports, a meal, and weekly excursions. Those committing to just one month can work with the children at WaaW as general "mentors," while those with more time can become program coordinators or even an operations manager.

In addition to Spanish and salsa lessons through FairPlay, volunteers can endlessly explore Cusco's colonial history and the region's Incan past.

Application Process: There is a very simple online form for making the first contact. Families are accepted as long as they can make the four-week-minimum commitment.

Cost: US$25 per week

Placement Length: There is a minimum placement of four weeks.

Language Requirements: Basic Spanish or better, at a minimum.

Housing: Volunteers are responsible for their own accommodations and food. They have the option of a homestay for US$85-95 per week (without meals), or FairPlay can help reserve a hostel.

Operating Since: 2006

Number of Volunteers: more than 100 in 2012

KIYA SURVIVORS

Urubamba, tel. 51/8420-1239, U.K. tel. 44/1273-721092, www.kiyasurvivors.org

TYPE OF WORK: children and youth, education

Kiya Survivors is based in Urubamba, an indigenous village in the valley of the same name near Cusco, perhaps better known as the Sacred Valley. Kiya is dedicated to children and youth with special needs, which include speech or visual/hearing problems, autism, Down syndrome, cerebral palsy, or abuse survivors, through rehabilitation, free physiotherapy, social work, and psychological services. Working with parents and the local community is also an important part of Kiya's work. Their Rainbow Centre has classrooms and therapy rooms, a cafeteria, a farm, and soccer field, and Kiya also operates the Rainbow House, a home for special-needs children who have been orphaned, abandoned, or abused. In 2008, Kiya helped open a second children's home in northern Peru, where they also operate an early-education center. At the time of this writing, some 200 children and families were being served by Kiya.

Responsibilities are tailored to the interests and skills of the volunteer. Those interested in helping in the Rainbow Centre might work as teacher's assistants, leading sports or drama activities, chaperoning an excursion, or helping to make bread, pizza, jewelry, or crafts, all of which are sold in the Rainbow Centre shop. Volunteers might teach English to local children and families, or to Kiya staff, or lend a hand with other practical skills such as building, decorating, woodworking, gardening, and performing administrative tasks. Interested volunteers can also have the chance to work alongside Kiya's team of physiotherapists, speech therapists, and psychologists in individual or family therapy, or in house visits. Volunteers receive a two-day training (either in the United Kingdom or upon arrival in Peru) before they begin their work. The workday at the center runs 8:45am-2pm, and volunteers are expected to spend at least one afternoon per week at the Rainbow House.

Besides exploring the Incan ruins and indigenous villages of Peru's Sacred Valley, volunteers can also arrange for Spanish lessons and participate in endless outdoor activities such as hiking, camping, mountain biking, and even paragliding.

Application Process: Contact Kiya for the "booking form." After that has been completed and a nonrefundable deposit (£200 or US$300) has been made, volunteers must provide references and, if 18 or older, a background check. Applying at least two months prior to your intended departure is recommended. Individual volunteers must be 18 or older; youth ages 14-18 are welcome as groups. Families are welcome, as long as it is understood that parents are responsible for their children.

Cost: US$1,375 for the "Basic" one-month package. "Standard" is US$2,535 and includes hotels and tours in Lima and Cusco, as well as the flight between the two cities, while "Full" is $3,420 and includes meals as well. All variations include a donation to the program. The two-week youth group programs are customized, so the price varies, but as a ballpark figure, a 14-day all-inclusive trip for 12 youth and two chaperones could be about US$3,200 per person (excluding international flights).

Placement Length: One-month minimum (two weeks for groups).

Language Requirements: None.

Housing: Kiya has a volunteer house but can also arrange for a homestay for an additional cost. Meals are only included in the "Full" program.

Operating Since: 2001

Number of Volunteers: 27 individuals and three youth groups in 2012

THE LIGHT AND LEADERSHIP INITIATIVE

Huaycan (Lima), U.S. tel. 708/459-8803, www.lightandleadership.org

TYPE OF WORK: children and youth, education, women's empowerment

The Light and Leadership Initiative was founded by a young American woman who visited Peru while she was in college, then returned the next year after graduating to found an initiative to support development in Huaycan, a marginalized suburb of Lima. Their mission is to is to "respond to the needs of the women in the Ate-Vitarte district of Lima, Peru in their struggle out of poverty by improving the availability and quality of education offered to women and children." The Light and Leadership Initiative offers workshops and classes for women, on everything from nutrition and hygiene to dealing with domestic violence and developing artisan skills. They also offer literacy (in Spanish), English, and computer skills training for women. The children's program seeks to support their schooling, with classes and tutoring in English, French, math, sports, art, music, and dance, as well as chess games. While there are specific start dates for long-term volunteers, short-term volunteers are welcome year-round, depending on availability. (Volunteers may not be accepted mid-December-mid-January, due to the local school break.)

Volunteers work 20-40 hours per week and always have Wednesday and Thursday off. In their free time, volunteers might play soccer or eat at a local restaurant, and they usually use their days off to explore Lima or head elsewhere in Peru, such as Cusco and Machu Picchu. The Light and Leadership Initiative is not able to accommodate large groups at this time but welcomes smaller groups of 4-6 people.

Application Process: There is an application form available online. Volunteers must be age 18 or older and will need to provide two references. Apply early for visits during June-August, as these are the busiest months at the guesthouse. There are no placements mid-December-mid-January.

Cost: US$200 registration fee. The program fee is US$150 for the first week and US$80-100 per week thereafter. Fees include housing, airport pickup, meals, and a cell phone.

Placement Length: There is minimum placement of one week.

Language Requirements: Requirements vary according to placement. No Spanish is required to teach English, PE, or art. Advanced Spanish is required to lead women's empowerment programs.

Housing: Volunteers stay in a guesthouse with shared bedrooms, a kitchen, computer, and Internet access. The house is cleaned six days a week, and there is a security guard outside the premises overnight. There are typically around a dozen volunteers staying at the house at a time, including a resident volunteer house manager.

Operating Since: 2008
Number of Volunteers: average 50 per year

OTRA COSA NETWORK

Huanchaco (north coast of Peru), tel. 51/4446-1302, U.K. tel. 44/1926-730-029, www.otracosa.org

TYPE OF WORK: agriculture, children and youth, community development, education, environment, health, women's empowerment

Otra Cosa Network (OCN) seeks to connect community-led projects with capable volunteers. Located in the beach town of Huanchaco, just north of Trujillo, OCN works with a network of more than 20 organizations across northern Peru.

Because of its extensive network of partners, there is a wide variety of volunteer work available, and OCN has a search engine on its website to help would-be volunteers narrow down placements by type of work, language skills required, and the minimum time commitment. They also include helpful comments about how structured the volunteer placement is and tips from former volunteers about what to bring.

Opportunities range from teaching at the local music conservatory and helping to organize a concert, to working at a community health clinic or on a fair-trade coffee farm, to teaching skateboarding to disadvantaged kids. Volunteers with special skills are always welcome to suggest additional ideas as well.

Huanchaco is renowned for its surfing, and it is also close to the World Heritage ruins of Chan Chan. Spanish lessons can be arranged, and OCN can often help arrange a free conversational language exchange for interested volunteers.

Application Process: There is an online application form. For individual volunteers the minimum age is 18-25, depending on the project, but families are also welcome.

Cost: The minimum donation depends on the

length of volunteer commitment; a two-week placement is US$233. Placements away from the Huanchaco/Truillo area may include accommodations and food, but most projects do not.

Placement Length: Varies by project. Most have a minimum of one month or more, but there are one or two opportunities for those of two weeks.

Language Requirements: Varies by project.

Housing: Varies by project, but for most in the towns of Huanchaco and Trujillo, the volunteer makes his or her own arrangements. In Huanchaco, OCN runs a volunteer guesthouse, with rooms for US$4-8 per night, as well as a homestay program (rates are roughly US$30-70 per week). A few projects in smaller towns may include accommodations for the volunteer.

Operating Since: 2007

Number of Volunteers: about 120 in 2012

RESPONS SUSTAINABLE TOURISM CENTER

Huaraz, tel. 51/4342-7949; Cusco, tel. 51/8423-3903; Lima, tel. 51/1446-3228; www.respons.org

TYPE OF WORK: children and youth, community development, education, environment

Respons is a multiservice organization whose mission is "to offer, develop, stimulate and broaden sustainable tourism in Central and Northern Peru." They offer tours and accommodations compatible with responsible tourism, as well as volunteer opportunities in the village of Vicos, located on the western flank of the Cordillera Blanca in the Peruvian Andes. The organization has offices in the larger town of Huaraz, about 45 minutes away, as well as in Lima and Cusco.

Respons volunteer projects fall within three categories—education, construction, and environment—but exact projects vary according to community needs. At the time of this writing, those with just a couple of days could volunteer with the *Cocinas Mejoradas* (improved kitchens) project, assisting local families to improve their kitchens by replacing open fire pits with enclosed adobe ovens that utilize a steel plate

griddle, reducing the use of firewood and keeping smoke out of the house. The volunteer(s) cover the cost of the steel plate, while oven recipients contribute the adobe bricks. Other kinds of construction projects are welcome, but volunteers must raise their own funds for materials.

Volunteers available for two weeks or more may teach English, working 8am-1pm. Shorter-term volunteers are asked to work five days per week, but those staying a month or more may work only three days per week if preferred. In addition to teaching in the schools, volunteers may also teach English to community members who deal with tourists, such as host families and members of the tourism committee. Volunteers interested in environmental projects or work in other areas can contact Respons for possibilities—the widest variety of volunteer work is available in the Cusco office, and the director will work to find an opportunity that matches the volunteer's skills and interests.

Because Respons also operates as a sustainable tour company, they can make arrangements for transportation from Lima, for private translators, and for additional activities, such as tours to the nearby Chavín de Huantar ruins or farther afield to the Inca Trail and the Pacaya-Samiria National Reserve in the Amazon.

Application Process: To apply, send an email indicating possible dates, the length of your stay, the amenities you are looking for, and if applicable, the number of volunteers in your group. There are no age restrictions; families are welcome.

Cost: The cost varies according to the project. For a fee, Respons can help arrange additional transportation, accommodations, and meals.

- The cost for the improved kitchens project ranges from US$172 (two days for a solo traveler) to US$62 per person with a group of four people. The fee includes accommodations, food, transportation, a contribution to the community tourism fund of the local community, as well as the cost of materials for the new stove for the family.

VOLUNTEER PERSPECTIVE

Ross Anderson (age 17) is from Edmonton, Canada. Ross went to Peru for two weeks on a trip organized by the Alberta Council for Global Cooperation (www.acga.ca). Part of his time was spent with the **Respons Sustainable Tourism Center** (www.respons.org) in Vicos.

What was a highlight of the experience?
As part of our homestay in Vicos with Respons, we helped build stoves with our host families. In North America, there is a disconnect between the products we use every day and the actual creation of those products. The time, effort, and knowledge that goes into building a stove, especially with the materials at hand, is one that cannot be understated.

Also, in Vicos I noticed the lack of lighting and electricity – there was one single light bulb, and it was in the kitchen. The positive effect of this one light bulb was enormous: allowing a family to accomplish meaningful tasks after dark is a powerful impact.

What did you take away from the experience?
In Vicos, I realized that culture and tradition are things that are extremely precious and valuable but also easily lost. It forced me to think about what is happening in my own country, and about why culture is important: It reminds us where we came from and who we are. It brings us together, makes us family, and gives us purpose as a community.

Was there a downside to your experience?
Every part of the experience in Vicos was valuable– the good and the bad. Nothing is without a negative, but when it is seen as an experience to learn from, there is no real negative.

Were you able to share the experience once you got home?
I went to Vicos with four other youths from Alberta with the Alberta Council for Global Cooperation. While we were there, we filmed a documentary (http://www.youtube.com/watch?v=cFcYFT3x75k) to show our story and share our experiences. We also went on a speaking tour to about 20 or 30 schools during the fall of 2012. We showed the video, spoke about our experiences, and had the chance to talk to kids of all ages. It was a valuable experience for us to share our stories and show other youths how they can make a meaningful impact in their lives, their communities, and around the world.

© JOËLLE BADMAN

Sharing in the construction of a stone oven was a highlight of Anderson's trip.

• The cost for teaching English ranges from US$25 per day (individual) to US$14 per person for a group of four people. The fee includes accommodations and meals, as well as the contribution to the local community development fund.

Placement Length: There is a minimum placement of two days to a maximum of six months.

Language Requirements: Depends on project, but Spanish skills are not necessary.

Housing: Volunteer accommodations are in guesthouses located next door to host families, granting a bit more privacy than the typical homestay. There are composting toilets and running water, and hot water is provided in the mornings for washing; not all guesthouses have electricity. Meals invariably include one of the many varieties of potatoes available in Peru and may even include guinea pig, a local delicacy.

Operating Since: 2009

Number of Volunteers: 20 for the *Cocinas Mejoradas* project in 2012

SANTA MARTHA FOUNDATION / VILLA MARTHA HOME FOR CHILDREN

Lima, tel. 51/1231-1323,
www.fundacionsantamartha.org

TYPE OF WORK: children and youth, education

Located in the Pachacamac district of Lima, Villa Martha is a Christian orphanage dedicated to giving physically and emotionally abandoned children "education, protection, love, and moral and spiritual formation." Children are given both basic education and technical trade training (baking, carpentry, welding, shoemaking and repair, and arts and crafts), and those who demonstrate exceptional academic abilities are encouraged to continue on to university. The goal for all children is that they become self-sustaining, and the orphanage teaches them how to dress themselves, work in the fields, breed animals, harvest crops, and learn trade skills so that they may "live a healthy and dignified life without need for begging." Villa Martha is home to just over 100 children, living on a property measuring nearly 4 hectares (10 acres).

Volunteers help with the overall care of the children and can participate in every area of the home (cooking, cleaning, teaching, leading workshops), based on the volunteer's skills/talents and the needs of the home.

In their free time, volunteers can take advantage of all that Lima has to offer, from restaurants to museums, bars to salsa clubs. There are archaeological sites in the area as well, such as the ruins of Pachacamac, located 30 minutes from the orphanage.

Application Process: To apply, send an email with a photo, letter of recommendation, and résumé/cv. Volunteers must be 21 or older.

Cost: None.

Placement Length: One-month minimum.

Language Requirements: None, although Spanish skills are certainly helpful.

Housing: Volunteers receive accommodations and meals at Villa Martha.

Operating Since: 1997

Number of Volunteers: more than 10 in 2012

TAMBOPATA MACAW PROJECT

near Puerto Maldonado, Amazon,
www.macawproject.org

TYPE OF WORK: wildlife protection

The Tambopata Macaw Project (TMP) is a long-term research project on the ecology and conservation of macaws and parrots in the lowlands of southeastern Peru, operating under the direction of Dr. Donald Brightsmith, of the Schubot Exotic Bird Health Center at Texas A&M University. The surrounding forest has the highest concentration of avian clay licks in the world (and the largest known macaw clay lick in the Amazon is just 500 yards1,500 ft away), and hundreds of macaws flock to the licks to feed. The project is run out of the Tambopata Research Center, which also houses an 18-bedroom luxury lodge.

Short-term volunteers are trained to identify all the local parrots by sight and become experts at clay lick monitoring and macaw nest observation with video camera systems

(November-March). They also assist with data entry. Due to the short length of stay, volunteers will have only minimal involvement in activities requiring higher training levels, like parrot censuses and tree climbing. Weather is hot year-round, and November-March is the wet season. Although volunteers come to work on the macaw project, they also have good chances of spotting five kinds of monkeys, capybaras, caimans, agoutis, peccaries, and, if they are very lucky, perhaps a jaguar, tapir, or harpy eagle.

Ten- to twelve-hour workdays are common. The daily work schedule often starts early with 4am trips to monitor the parrots at the clay lick or 5am walks to look for foraging parrots. Breakfast is at 7:30am, followed by more activities 9am-1:30pm. After lunch, around 3pm, volunteers are usually back out in the forest, conducting parrot counts, climbing nests, looking for foraging parrots, and so on. On rainy days volunteers work on data entry, or clean and maintain gear at the house.

Conducting research in a protected area in Peru requires a research permit from the office of Servicion Nacional de Areas Naturales Protegidas (SERNANP) in Puerto Maldonado. TMP applies for this permit once per year, and volunteer information is submitted at that time. TMP can add up to three appendices per year with additional volunteer names, but because of the complicated process, volunteers should apply as far in advance of their travel dates as possible (four months out at a minimum).

Application Process: To apply, volunteers must send an email with a letter of interest, their résumé/cv, email addresses for at least three references, and a date range of availability. Volunteers should be age 18 or older.

Cost: US$30 placement fee, plus a US$40 daily fee. Housing is included, as is transportation to the lodge from Puerto Maldonado.

Placement Length: 12-30 days for short-term volunteers

Language Requirements: None, although Spanish is always helpful.

Housing: Accommodations are in the rustic researcher area, in shared rooms. There are running water and flush toilets, but showers are cold water only. Meals are with lodge staff; lunch and dinner are typically Peruvian fare, such as chicken and rice. There is limited electricity and Internet.

Operating Since: 1989
Number of Volunteers: 33 in 2012

TRAVELLER NOT TOURIST

Arequipa, tel. 51/98676-6794,
www.travellernottourist.com

TYPE OF WORK: children and youth, education

Arequipa is the capital of a province by the same name in southern Peru. With close to a million residents, it is Peru's second-largest city. It is also one of its most beautiful—in 2000 its historical center was deemed a UNESCO World Heritage Site for its ornamental architecture and unique combination of European and indigenous building techniques. But the aesthetic beauty of the city is marred by the poverty of its residents, and Traveller Not Tourist (TNT) wants to do something about it.

TNT's mission is to "give foreigners visiting Peru the opportunity to be involved in the true Peruvian reality and Peruvians the chance to lift themselves out of poverty and believe in the chance of a better world, and then create it." Their foremost focus is the needs of the beneficiaries, but TNT also works hard to ensure positive and effective experiences for its volunteers. TNT supports education through its Yachayhuasi Learning Centre, which offers free classes and workshops geared to youth, in English, life skills, and vocational skills. Volunteers with the learning center may prepare and give English lessons, prepare and run conversation/revision classes, give and grade tests, and/or help students with additional needs. There are also opportunities to run courses in other subjects.

TNT also supports the Casa Hogar Luz Alba Orphanage, and volunteers here help with the day-to-day running of the orphanage, which can include cleaning, cooking, ironing, washing clothes, helping children with their homework, and general child care. Volunteers may also help with enrichment activities for the children, such as teaching English, arts, crafts, music, dance, and drama, or just playing games. Volunteers who want to commit to anything between one day and two weeks will participate in the "volunteer for a day" program, where work depends not only on the needs of the organization at the time, but also on the skills, experience, and interests of the volunteer. Past volunteers have helped out with construction, cleaning, administration, marketing, repairs, decorating, and trips. Placements are finalized upon the volunteer's arrival, and TNT does not guarantee placement at your first-choice project.

In addition to its volunteer program, TNT operates a travel agency, selling airline tickets, bus tickets, and tours, and 50 percent of their profits go back into their project work. Besides exploring Arequipa's colonial history, visitors can hike through the Incan terraces in the hills outside of town and take Spanish lessons, which can be arranged through TNT for an additional cost.

Note: There have been numerous reports in Arequipa of taxi drivers assaulting passengers. Check with locals for current conditions, and use a taxi dispatch service whenever possible.
Application Process: To volunteer for a day, visitors can drop by the day before to make arrangements or call or email in advance. Note: A personal reference is required, which can be brought along, or it can be emailed to them. For longer volunteer placements, there is a volunteer application form online. Volunteers must be 18 (families cannot be accommodated at this time).
Cost: US$15 per day if less than one week; US$100 for placements of one week or longer.
Placement Length: As little as one day; two weeks minimum at the learning center, and one month minimum at the orphanage.
Language Requirements: None.
Housing: Volunteers have the option of staying in a shared room in the TNT guesthouse for US$8 per night or US$230 per month, and they must make their own arrangements for meals. Space is limited in the guesthouse, so

making a reservation is recommended. There is a kitchen in the guesthouse, and meals at inexpensive restaurants in Arequipa run US$3-6.
Operating Since: 2007
Number of Volunteers: average of 30 per year

WAVES FOR DEVELOPMENT

Lobitos (northern Pacific coast),
www.wavesfordevelopment.org
TYPE OF WORK: children and youth, community development, education, environment
WAVES stands for Water Adventure Voluntourism Education Sustainability, and its mission is to create "life-enriching experiences in coastal communities through Educational Surf programs." Their community-based programs are built on five pillars: cultural exchange and understanding, environmental conservation, life skills or healthy living, social entrepreneurship, and sustainable tourism.

Lobitos is a village of 1,500 located about 65 kilometers (40 mi) south of the city of Mancora, famed for its surfing. Lobitos's economy revolves around fishing, but the local government has identified surf tourism as a key area of development, and WAVES's volunteer programs are designed to equip local youth for a future in it. The program "begins and ends" in Talara, a 30-minute drive from Lobitos— Talara is a 2-hour drive from the nearest airport in Piura or a 17-hour bus ride from Lima.

Volunteers typically work six hours per day and have helped offer swimming, surf, English, and environmental education classes to youth (ages 8-25); helped build the capacity of the teachers at the local school and assisted in their classes; taught photography and/or taken and compiled photos and video as part of a film and photography program; helped coordinate sports activities for the kids during and after school hours; and taught both English and social entrepreneurship to interested community members and organizations such as the fisherman's union. WAVES is also interested in other skills that volunteers might bring to the project.

Those who want to learn to surf or brush up on their skills can participate in the weekly

INTERNATIONAL ORGANIZATIONS

The following international organizations support volunteer efforts in Peru:

A Broader View (U.S. tel. 215/780-1845, toll-free U.S. tel. 866/423-3258, www.abroaderview.org), page 193.
Type of Work: agriculture, children and youth, community development, education, environment, health, wildlife protection, women's empowerment

Biosphere Expeditions (toll-free U.S. tel. 800/407-5761, www.biosphere-expeditions.org), page 195.
Type of Work: environment, wildlife protection

Cross-Cultural Solutions (toll-free U.S. tel. 800/380-4777, www.crossculturalsolutions.org), page 195.
Type of Work: children and youth, community development, education, health, women's empowerment

Earthwatch (U.S. tel. 978/461-0081, toll-free U.S. tel. 800/776-0188, www.earthwatch.org), page 196.
Type of Work: environment, wildlife protection

Elevate Destinations (U.S. tel. 617/661-0203, www.elevatedestinations.com), page 199.
Type of Work: children and youth, community development, education, environment, wildlife protection

Global Communities: Partners for Good (U.S. tel. 301/587-4700, www.globalcommunities.org), page 200.

Type of Work: children and youth, community development, education, environment, women's empowerment

Global Volunteers (toll-free U.S. tel. 800/487-1074, www.globalvolunteers.org), page 200.
Type of Work: children and youth, community development, education

International Volunteer HQ (IVHQ) (toll-free U.S. tel. 877/342-6588, www.volunteerhq.org), page 203.
Type of Work: agriculture, children and youth, community development, education, environment, health, wildlife protection

ProWorld (toll-free U.S. tel. 877/429-6753, www.proworldvolunteers.org), page 207.
Type of Work: children and youth, community development, education, environment, health, wildlife protection, women's empowerment

REI Adventures (toll-free U.S. tel. 800/622-2236, www.rei.com), page 208.
Type of Work: environment, wildlife protection

UBELONG (U.S. tel. 202/250-3706, www.ubelong.org), page 210.
Type of Work: agriculture, children and youth, community development, education, environment, health, wildlife protection, women's empowerment

VOFAIR (www.vofair.org), page 211.
Type of Work: agriculture, children and youth, community development, education, environment, health, wildlife protection, women's empowerment

---

lessons for free or arrange for private instruction for a small additional fee. Other activities include Spanish lessons and biweekly cultural activities, such as visiting local caves, fishing with local fishermen, learning to cook Peruvian cuisine with a local family, and viewing the seals at the oil platforms.

Application Process: There is an online application form that will take about 30 minutes to complete; it requires emergency contact information. Upon acceptance, a US$200 deposit is required to confirm placment. Individual volunteers should be 18 or older, although exceptions have been made for

mature minors with signed parental consent forms. Families are welcome.
Cost: Volunteer contribution of US$495 minimum, plus US$295 per week, which includes accommodations and use of surfboards.
Placement Length: Minimum of two weeks, starting the first and third Saturday of each month.
Language Requirements: None.

Housing: Volunteers stay in shared rooms in a local home, together with other volunteers as well as the volunteer coordinator. Three meals a day are included, which volunteers take turns preparing. There is a community center with Internet on-site.
Operating Since: 2008
Number of Volunteers: 68 in 2012 and 225 in total since WAVES's inception

Essentials

BACKGROUND
Geography and Climate

Covering about 1.3 million square kilometers (more than 500,000 sq. mi), Peru is about twice the size of Texas but has only about 15 percent more people (total population: 29 million). Spanish and Quechua, an indigenous language, are the two official languages of the country; the latter is spoken by about 4.5 million people in Peru. Thanks to its varied terrain, Peru is one of 10 countries described as "megadiverse," boasting 25,000 plant species, 2,000 fish species, over 1,700 bird species, 330 amphibian species, 460 mammal species, and 365 reptile species, many of them endemic.

Temperatures and rainfall vary widely according to the region. In the Andean mountains and highlands, June-August are the driest months. Peru's *verano* (dry season) is December-April, when it is drier in Lima but rainier in Cusco and the mountain highlands. Winter can be cool at night. Temperatures can be warm during the day (and the sun punishing due to the high altitudes—bring sunblock even for overcast days!), but average nightly temperatures drop to 10°C (50°F), so plan on buying an alpaca sweater.

Rain falls year-round in the Amazon, but never for more than a few hours at a time. The driest months are June-September. Along the arid coast, it's hot and dry December-March, while fog often closes in on coastal cities like Lima April-November.

History and Economy

Evidence of humans in Peru date back as far as 9000 BC, and complex societies date as far back as 3000 BC. with the Norte Chico civilization, followed by other famed empires including the Nazca, Chimú, and Inca. The Spanish conquistadores arrived in the mid-1500s, squeezing labor from the Peru's Amerindians and silver from Peruvian mines until its independence from Spain in 1821.

Services, namely Peru's thriving tourism sector, account for over half of the country's GDP. Extractive industries (iron, gold, silver, and copper mainly) are an important part of the local economy, as is manufacturing.

PREPARATION
Transportation

The **Jorge Chávez** airport (LIM, www.lap.com.pe) at the capital city of Lima is the only one in Peru that receives international flights. It is serviced by American Airlines, Delta, US Air, and United, as well as many regional and European airlines. There are domestic airports all over the country, including Cusco, Arequipa, and Iquitos. If you've got the money, domestic flights can save hours and hours in travel time. If purchasing a domestic ticket when already in Peru, be forewarned that some airlines run specials for residents only, so non-resident foreigners could be subject to hefty surcharges at the airport—read the fine print of any deal carefully. There is a US$31 departure tax when leaving the country, payable in dollars or Peruvian New Soles.

PERU

As in all of Latin America, buses crisscross the country and are a cheap way to travel. It is usually worth spending a few *soles* more for "luxury" lines when possible, as the ride is more comfortable and the bus is less likely to break down.

Passports and Visas

Passports must be valid for at least six months beyond your departure date. Travelers usually receive 90-day visas in their passports upon arrival; if you are given less time but need more, explain this to the immigration official at the border.

Money

The national currency is the Peruvian **new sol** (plural: *soles;* currency symbol: S/), which comes in notes of S/10, S/20, S/50, S/100, and S/200. U.S. dollars are the second currency, dispensed at ATMs (along with soles), and widely accepted in tourist areas. Counterfeit notes are common, so check for the watermark if receiving a significant amount of cash, and use ATMs affiliated with banks rather than freestanding ones if possible. No one will accept bills if they are overly worn or have any type of tear, so don't accept them either. Travelers checks are a challenge to change, as are large bills.

Health

Unless you decide to skip Machu Picchu, Cusco, and the Sacred Valley altogether, altitude sickness is the affliction that you're most likely to run into during your stay in Peru. Machu Picchu is at nearly 2,400 meters (7,800 ft), towns in the Sacred Valley at 2,700-3,000 meters (9,100-9,700 ft), and Cusco is at a staggering 3,400 meters (11,150 ft). Take local advice to sip a *mate* (tea) and take it easy on your first day in the clouds. Should you experience severe nausea or other worrisome symptoms, your hotel should be able to call a doctor, who will most likely hook you up with an oxygen tank to help you transition. *Be sure to use sunscreen in the Andean highlands* also, even on cloudy days, as the risk of sunburn is much greater.

In the Amazon, malaria is rare, but many travelers choose to take a prophylaxis to be on the safe side. Check with your local travel clinic. **A yellow fever vaccination is recommended** for entering the Peruvian Amazon and must be administered at least 10 days prior to arrival.

Safety

Travel in Peru is generally safe. The exception is Lima, which has high rates of petty crime. Be smart at the airport, in particular—keep a close eye on your passport and other belongings at all times and make arrangements for a taxi from inside the airport if you are not being met. In the Amazon, there have been cases of river assaults, so be smart about where you keep your valuables. In the Andes, it is recommended to travel in groups when hiking the Incan Trail. If hiking elsewhere in the Sacred Valley, always check first with locals before heading off solo.

BOLIVIA

With six major cities located at altitudes of 2,574-4,150 meters (8,445-13,615 ft), Bolivia is a country that can, quite literally, take your breath away. Staggering Andean mountains, cities rich in colonial architecture and indigenous culture, a steaming Amazonian jungle in the lowlands teeming with wildlife—this is a country of superlatives. It is also South America's only landlocked country. Bolivia shares a border with Peru to the west, Chile to the southwest, Brazil to the north and east, Paraguay to the southeast, and Argentina to the south.

More than half of Bolivia's 10 million people are indigenous, the largest groups being Aymara and Quechua. While Bolivia's main language is Spanish, there are 37 official indigenous languages as well, and roughly 10 percent of the population does not speak Spanish.

Bolivia ties with Honduras for the largest percentage (60 percent) of population living below the national poverty line in mainland Latin America. The gross national income per capita is a meager US$2,040 (2011 World Bank figures), and, as might be expected, there is a wealth of opportunities to support the country and its people.

Volunteer opportunities might include working at an orphanage, teaching English, doing construction work, working in a health clinic, offering support to drug addicts or women and children suffering from abuse, working side by side with locals in an indigenous village, or helping to rehabilitate pumas or monkeys that have been rescued from illegal trade.

© CARLOS LAGUNA-DRISCOLL

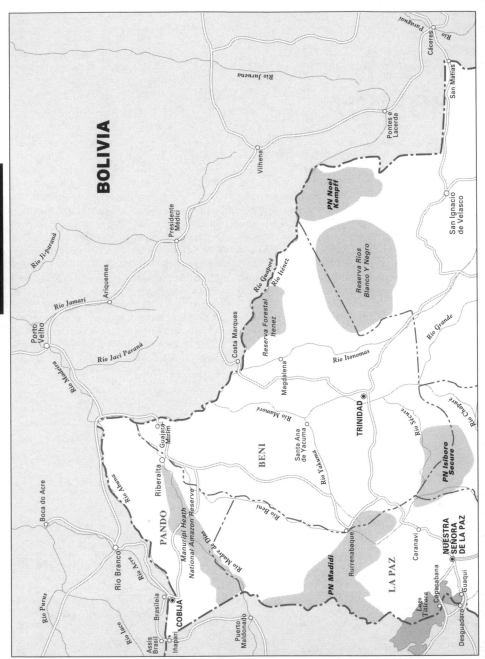

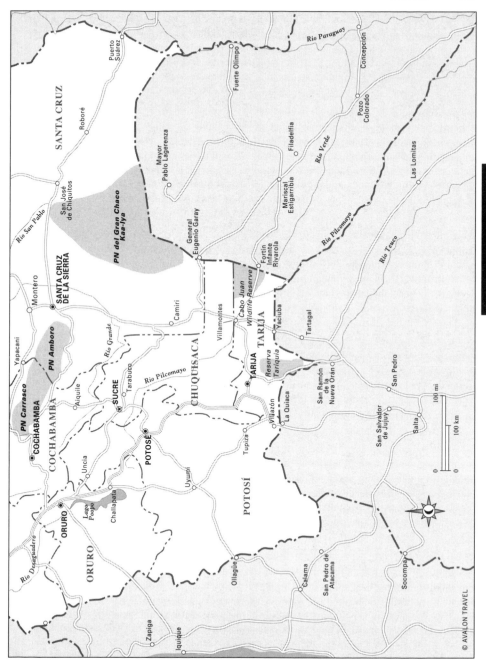

Local Organizations

COMUNIDAD INTI WARA YASSI

Chapare, Cochabamba, tel. 591/44-136-572, www.intiwarayassi.org

TYPE OF WORK: wildlife protection

Comunidad Inti Wara Yassi (CIWY) runs three animal refuges, which rescue and rehabilitate wild animals that have been illegally traded on black markets, kept as pets, or kept in zoos and circuses. Parque Machía is outside of Villa Tunari in the region of Cochabamba and was the first animal refuge in Bolivia, created in 1996. It houses over 700 animals of more than 30 species. Parque Ambue Ari was created in 2002 and is a large, remote park in the Bolivian Amazon that cares for felines in particular and is also home to howler monkeys, birds, coatis, a tapir, and a deer. Parque Jacj Cuisi (north of La Paz) is the newest of the parks and is still in construction stages, although it does have volunteer accommodations with showers and a kitchen, and is home to four pumas.

CIWY encourages volunteers to select the volunteer site they feel fits them best. Machía has the most comfortable accommodations (electricity, hot showers, etc.) and a wide variety of animals to work with; the work at Ambue Ari focuses on felines, with additional responsibilities with house animals, construction (of a veterinary clinic), and camp chores; while volunteers are needed at Jacj Cuisi to help with construction and caring for the four pumas. If working with a feline, the volunteer spends the duration of his or her stay working with that animal; if working with monkeys, birds, reptiles, or small mammals, the volunteer will be assigned to one area and will stay there for the duration (CIWY tries to honor preferences but cannot guarantee all requests to work with a specific type of animal will be met). CIWY hosts many volunteers at peak times of the year; they rarely are full at all three parks, but it can happen at one. They try to keep their website current with where volunteers are most needed.

Volunteers start their workday at 7am and generally work through the afternoon (and sometimes into the early evening). In their free time, volunteers might visit the local villages, practice Spanish, explore nature trails, do photography, bathe in the local rivers, or carry out art projects.

Application Process: No application is necessary; volunteers are invited to just show up. Volunteers must be 18 or older.

Cost: US$200 for 15 nights, US$350 for 30 nights, and US$7 each night thereafter (payable only in Bolivianos).

Placement Length: Minimum 15 days; minimum 30 days if working with a feline.

Language Requirements: Basic Spanish recommended but not required.

Housing: Volunteers sleep in guesthouses but must bring their own sleeping bags. Volunteers receive meals at the Jacj Cuisi and Ambue Ari parks but are responsible for their own food at Machía.

Operating Since: 1992

Number of Volunteers: CIWY doesn't keep exact numbers but estimates between 600 and 800 in 2012.

CONDOR TREKKERS

Sucre, tel. 591/728-91740, www.condortrekkers.org

TYPE OF WORK: children and youth, community development, education, environment, health

Condor Trekkers (CT) is a nonprofit organization whose mission is to provide financial support to projects in and around Sucre. Their revenue comes from the one- to four-day guided hikes they offer in the mountains near Sucre, as well as their guided city tours. The money raised supports a myriad of projects and organizations in and around Sucre, including partially funding Fundación Guía, a job placement program for adolescents, and Ñanta, which helps street children in Sucre. They also support a day care center just outside of Sucre with both monetary contributions and volunteer assistance, and in the areas where they trek, they support around 10 schools through the purchase of books and school supplies.

Volunteers can help in a variety of areas. In the office, volunteers do promotional work and graphic design, help prepare for treks, collect tourist information about Sucre for CT's website, teach the guides English or another language, or help translate (if they already speak Spanish). Volunteers staying for a month or more can also help on the treks themselves; help develop fundraising strategies; research and develop informational brochures about local flora and fauna, the area's natural history, and the indigenous culture and history of the area; or develop CT's web presence. There are also special projects that CT would love for volunteers to help develop: cultivation of mushrooms, reforestation, composting, volunteering at the day care CT supports, leading a hygiene or environmental workshop at a local school, or providing support and advice for the opening of CT's new café.

CT is based in the UNESCO World Heritage city of Sucre, renowned for its well-preserved colonial architecture, and it's a starting point for explorations of nearby indigenous villages and low mountains nearby.

Application Process: Send an email explaining why you'd like to be part of CT and what you'd like to do.

Cost: None. Volunteers are responsible for their own expenses. Volunteers pay for their first multiday trek, the cost of which is refundable after two months' volunteering.

Placement Length: No minimum, but the longer you can stay the better. There is a two month minimum to volunteer as a trek guide.

Language Requirements: Depends on the volunteer work. No Spanish is requried for many tasks; basic Spanish is required to volunteer as a trek guide; intermediate Spanish is required to teach hygiene or environmental workshops in local schools.

Housing: Long-term volunteers can stay in the volunteer house for free. Short-term volunteers must make their own arrangements;

homestays can be arranged through a local Spanish school. Hostels start at US$6/night and a room in a shared house starts at around US$90/month. Groceries are inexpensive, and meals in restaurants are US$2-5.

Operating Since: February 2010
Number of Volunteers: around 40 in 2012

LA SENDA VERDE

Yungas, near Coroico, tel. 591/747-22825, www.sendaverde.com

TYPE OF WORK: wildlife protection

La Senda Verde (LSV) (in English it means the Green Path) is a privately run ecotourism retreat/resort that is also home to an animal refuge. Its goal is to provide "the best care possible to animals rescued from illegal traffic in a natural environment under technical and scientific conditions." The resort helps to fund the animal refuge.

Volunteers work 8am-6pm and spend most of their time feeding the animals and cleaning their areas. When not working with the animals, volunteers help maintain the existing animal facilities, build new ones as new animals arrive, and help prepare the quarantine area for new arrivals. Evenings are spent watching movies or just hanging out. Volunteers are welcome to use the resort swimming pool, or they can take a dip in the river or a hike in the jungle. No specific skills are needed, but volunteers with special skills such as veterinary, IT, or carpentry are always especially welcome.

In addition to the usual volunteer program, LSV has a "Care Bears" program, where volunteers who can commit to at least four weeks spend one week as a general volunteer, then three weeks working with Andean bears. There is also a two-month foster program for baby monkeys where, after the first week, volunteers spend their time acting as a surrogate parent to a baby monkey (including sleeping with the monkey in the nursery!).

LSV is located at 1,200 meters (4,000 ft) and enjoys sunny and warm weather, with temperatures usually around 25-30°C (75-85°F). (Although nights can get cool, so bring

BOLIVIA

a jacket.) November-March is the wet season; April-October dry.

Application Process: There is a very simple online form. The minimum age is 18.

Cost: US$150 per week, including accommodations and meals. There is a discount after the second week.

Placement Length: There is a minimum placement of two weeks.

Language Requirements: Spanish is not required, but it it highly recommended to learn at least some Spanish.

Housing: There is a volunteer house with hot showers, sheets and towels, and laundry facilities, but volunteers will likely want to bring a sleeping bag. Three meals a day are provided.

Operating Since: 2003

Number of Volunteers: 170 in 2012

MANO A MANO INTERNACIONAL

Cochabamba, tel. 591/4-452-0297,

www.manoamano.org

TYPE OF WORK: agriculture, community development, health

Mano a Mano (MaM) was founded by a Bolivian who resides in the United States, together with his wife, a former Peace Corps volunteer in Bolivia. They began by bringing medical supplies to Bolivia, and as support grew, they started constructing health clinics. In 2003, MaM expanded and now also offers continuing education for health care providers and scholarships for low-income students, as well as continues to construct schools, housing for teachers and health care workers, airstrips, and more. The organization now encompasses five organizations: Mano a Mano International, the U.S.-based promotional, fundraising, and reporting division; Mano a Mano Bolivia, the health and education division; Mano a Mano Nuevo Mundo, the economic development division; Mano a Mano Apoyo Aereo, the emergency response aviation program; and Mano a Mano Internacional, the travel support and training center.

Volunteer responsibilities depend on skills and interests, but in the past volunteers have: researched foundations and other funding sources, worked as a medical professional in a MaM health clinic, designed and updated MaM's web presence, made stretchers and desks in MaM's workshop, supported the educational outreach program in the communities where MaM works, collected data and prepared reports about MaM's work, assisted with construction work, and edited videos or computer presentations that share the work of MaM. One of MaM's latest projects is a garden and demonstration center in Cochabamba for training rural farmers in crop management and nutrition, perfect for volunteers with a green thumb. Volunteer initiatives are welcome as well. Clinic workers tend to spend most of their time in the rural areas that MaM serves, while administrative volunteers tend to spend most of their time in the office at Cochabamba, but MaM makes sure that each volunteer has the opportunity to visit a rural community to see the impact of the work.

Cochabamba is considered by many to be the culinary capital of Bolivia. Fresh fruit and vegetables are available year-round, thanks to its moderate climate, and typical foods are soups, rice, potatoes, meat, and eggs (vegetarians, be forewarned that you might not find a wide choice of food). There are plenty of restaurants, as well as Spanish schools for those who are interested in brushing up on their language skills, and it's centrally located, making it a good departure point for explorations of the country. It tends to be fairly rainy November-March, so it's a good idea to bring a waterproof jacket.

Application Process: Send an email with your résumé/cv, availability, and volunteer interests.

Cost: None. Volunteers are responsible for their own expenses. MaM hopes that volunteers will respond to a fundraising challenge when they return to their home country. MaM does cover the cost of travel from Cochabamba to project sites.

Placement Length: There is a minimum placement of four weeks, although longer is preferred.

© CARLOS LAGUNA-DRISCOLL

Calle Jaén, a colonial street in Bolivia's capital city

Language Requirements: Basic communication skills in Spanish are required.
Housing: Volunteers must make their own arrangements, but MaM can give recommendations. Volunteers in rural medical centers can stay in the centers.
Operating Since: 1995
Number of Volunteers: approximately 30 in 2012

REMAR BOLIVIA

La Paz, tel. 591/2-231-2106, www.remarbolivia.com
TYPE OF WORK: children and youth, education, health, women's empowerment

Founded originally in Spain in 1982 as an outreach and assistance center for drug addicts, REMAR has been in Bolivia since 1997, where it reaches out to "anyone in need": addicts, street children, women who suffer domestic abuse or whose partner has abandoned them and their children, and children and youth who suffer from physical and sexual abuse.

REMAR runs programs in six cities across Bolivia: La Paz, El Alto, Viacha, Oruro, Cochabamba, and Santa Cruz de la Sierra. They have 20 orphanages/shelters that provide some 400 children and women with clothing, food, and education, as well as shelter and protection from abuse. They provide medical and psychological assistance, run soup kitchens, and operate a rehab center. All services are provided free of charge to the beneficiaries; REMAR receives income from the sale of cleaning products, chocolates, and the output of an upholstery business, all of which are enterprises staffed by REMAR beneficiaries.

Volunteers typically work 6-8 hours per day. Tasks are flexible, depending on the volunteers' skills and interests, but might include taking care of the children and helping in the office.
Application Process: Send an email to apply. Volunteers should be age 18 or older.
Cost: None. Volunteers are responsible for their own expenses.
Placement Length: There is no minimum.
Language Requirements: Basic Spanish is required.
Housing: Volunteers make their own arrangements.
Operating Since: 1997
Number of Volunteers: Of its many volunteers in 2012, four were international.

SPIRIT OF THE ANDES

Sopacachi, La Paz, tel. 591/2-241-1660,
www.spiritoftheandes.com
TYPE OF WORK: children and youth, community development, health, women's empowerment

Spirit of the Andes is a not-for-profit organization that trains indigenous women from marginalized neighborhoods in El Alto, La Paz, and Cochabamba to knit high-quality products from Bolivian alpaca, llama, and cotton yarns. In addition to providing knitting expertise and a market for the products, Spirit of the Andes also allocates a portion of the proceeds to go to projects that seek to empower women by improving their health, knowledge of their rights, and their ability to exercise them.

Spirit of the Andes manages several projects, including identifying and training women for

BOLIVIA

BOLIVIA

© CARLOS LAGUNA-DRISCOLL

Indigenous women in Bolivia exercise their rights with a sit-in.

the knitting project, registering women and their families with the local health center, training the women who are already involved with Spirit of the Andes in health and human rights, and creating a support network for those who suffer domestic abuse. They also run a day care center for the women who are knitting.

Specific volunteer needs vary; Spirit of the Andes works with its volunteers to create a personalized schedule. English-speaking volunteers can respond to English emails and Skype calls, help identify and reach out to international markets for the organization's products, and assist with inventory management and quality control. Spanish-speaking volunteers can work with children in the day care or with women in the cooperative.

Spirit of the Andes is located in Sopacachi, a great neighborhood in La Paz, within walking distance to restaurants, gyms, and clubs. Spirit of the Andes can also arrange Spanish lessons for those who want to brush up on their skills.

Application Process: There is a contact form available online. There is no minimum age for volunteers.

Cost: There is no cost to volunteer, but estimate US$200/month for housing.

Placement Length: Volunteers are encouraged to stay at least three weeks, to allow time to adjust to the altitude and make a meaningful contribution.

Language Requirements: None, although Spanish is always helpful.

Housing: Spirit of the Andes has an apartment (US$200/month) on-site for volunteers, which includes a do-it-yourself breakfast, wireless Internet, and use of the kitchen and washing machine.

Operating Since: 1994
Number of Volunteers: four in 2012

SUSTAINABLE BOLIVIA

Cochabamba, tel. 591/4-423-3786,
U.S. tel. 415/513-5582, www.sustainablebolivia.org
TYPE OF WORK: children and youth, community development, education, environment, health, women's empowerment

Sustainable Bolivia (SB) is dedicated to the promotion of "economic and environmental sustainability while providing global educational opportunities and work experience." Their office is based in Bolivia's third-largest city, Cochabamba. They place volunteers in 32 different organizations, each of which has a detailed listing on their website. Volunteers might support medical services at a local clinic, support children who spend their days working in the local market, install solar panels and biomass kitchens in rural areas, assist with skill shares and microfinance projects for disadvantaged women, work with disabled children, or support people living with HIV/AIDS. Volunteers typically work 30-35 hours per week, although there can be some flexibility to be able to take language lessons or a long weekend. While there are many opportunities that require a one-month commitment, some of the volunteer sites do require a commitment of three months or longer.

Sustainable Bolivia runs a language school, offering Quechua, Aymara, and Guarani in addition to Spanish, and all classes are one-on-one (prices start at US$8.50/hour and drop to US$7/hour for 20 hours per week). Besides studying Spanish, volunteers can take advantage of the lectures, travel outings, film evenings, and parties that Sustainable Boliviaorganizes. Sustainable Boliviaalso runs a scholarship program for disadvantaged Bolivian students.

Unique to Sustainable Bolivia is a mini-grant program, where volunteers who stay one month or longer are given US$75 to help fund a project or purchase supplies for their volunteer site.

Application Process: There is an online application form. Individual volunteers must be age 18 or older; families are also welcome.

Cost: There is a US$50 registration fee, plus US$100-160 per week for housing, which includes an airport pickup as well.

Placement Length: Minimum placement of one month. Many of the organizations that Sustainable Bolivia works with require a commitment of at least three months; exceptions

VOLUNTEER PERSPECTIVE

Sara Roque Loureiro (age 22) is from Portugal. Here's what she had to say about her volunteer experience through **Sustainable Bolivia** (Cochabamba, tel. 591/4-423-3786, U.S. tel. 415/513-5582, www.sustainablevolivia.org).

In July 2012, I flew to Cochabamba, a city lost in a valley in the middle of the Bolivian Andes, and didn't know exactly what to expect. I arrived at CECAM, a small organization created and run by Bolivians, whose aim is to help low income populations while protecting the environment, through the production of solar stoves and efficient ovens. The owners, Freddy and Rocío, were extremely welcoming, and sat down with me and discussed both the organizational needs and my expectations as soon as I arrived. I am a business major, and it was great to have the opportunity to use my skills to help them design a business plan and rethink the organizational processes so that social impact could be increased! The family feeling inside the organization was unique; the opportunity to participate in other projects and see the surrounding countryside and have contact with the local community, and the lunchtimes together sharing experiences with the other volunteers, made me wake up every morning and go to work with a smile in my face. It was a truly rewarding and unique experience that I brought home with me! I was able not only to experience incredible Bolivia, but also to use my interests to help others while learning and discovering new things.

BOLIVIA

© CARLOS LAGUNA-DRISCOLL

La Paz lies at an elevation of 11,975 feet.

can be made if the volunteer has a high level of Spanish or a needed skill.

Language Requirements: Varies according to volunteer placement.

Housing: Sustainable Bolivia can place volunteers in homestays, which include a private room and three meals per day, for US$160/week. Or they can stay in a private or shared room in one of SB's three guesthouses, which have fully equipped kitchens, wireless Internet, and free cleaning service, for US$100-125 per week (but volunteers are responsible for their own meals when in the guesthouses).

Operating Since: 2007

Number of Volunteers: 80 in 2012

UP CLOSE BOLIVIA

La Paz, tel. 591/7-307-9008, www.upclosebolivia.org

TYPE OF WORK: children and youth, community development, education, environment

Up Close Bolivia is a family-run, community-based organization located just outside of La Paz, in a mostly indigenous Aymara community in the semirural valley of Mallasa. It operates a volunteer program based on a philosophy of reciprocity; that is to say, volunteer contributions enrich both the person giving and the person receiving equally, as the volunteer receives an authentic cultural experience while the community receives the benefit of the volunteer's efforts.

At the time of this writing, volunteers could choose between three types of placements, although there might be additional opportunities depending on community needs.

- Working at the child care center: The founders of Up Close Bolivia founded a child care center in 2004, created together with the local mothers club, providing a place for nearly 90 children between the ages of six months and four years to play and learn. Volunteers work alongside the educators in the daily running of the nursery and care of the children, which includes feeding and washing them, and preparing, serving, and cleaning up after meals for the children.

Volunteers can also help by initiating creative play and new activities. Volunteers can choose to work full- or part-time here, and lunch is included.

- Supporting the tourism sector: Volunteers work with adults and youth in the evenings, teaching "English for Tourism"; work with children, providing classroom support in the local schools during English lessons; or work with children and youth in after-school and summer school English clubs. Teaching experience is helpful but not required. Alternatively, volunteers with relevant experience and skills can provide advice to local businesses in the tourism sector, to help them improve the quality of their services (strong Spanish skills required).

- Rehabilitating recreational and green areas: Volunteers work with members of the local community, especially children and youth, on the rehabilitation of recreational and green areas, and the creation of public murals. Volunteers can help design and execute murals, plant trees, maintain public green spaces, and provide environmental education to children. The only requirements are a love of the outdoors and a willingness to get dirty, although artistic skills for the murals are always very welcome.

Volunteers have flexibility in how they want to divide their time between working on a project, traveling, and exploring La Paz. There are plenty of opportunities to learn something new in nearby La Paz, from playing a native instrument to dancing *morenada* (one of the many Bolivian national dances) or even tango or salsa. La Paz also has a rich cultural life, with markets and art galleries, music and dance events, and a lively restaurant and bar scene. Volunteers can study Spanish at the nearby Instituto Exclusivo for US$8/hour for private lessons, less for two or more people. Up Close Bolivia can also help find free language exchange partners with members of the local community.

Application Process: An application form is available for download on their website. Accepted applicants must provide two personal references. Individual volunteers are usually age 21 or older, although exceptions may be made for those 18-20. Families, youth groups, and retirees are all welcome.

Cost: US$450 per month, including accommodations. Volunteers are responsible for their meals (volunteers at the nursery will receive lunch).

Placement Length: Minimum of one month.

Language Requirements: Basic Spanish recommended.

BOLIVIA

INTERNATIONAL ORGANIZATIONS

The following international organizations support volunteer efforts in Bolivia:

Amizade Global Service Learning (U.S. tel. 412/586-4986, www.amizade.org), page 194.
Type of Work: agriculture, children and youth, community development, education, environment, health

Habitat for Humanity International (toll-free U.S. tel. 800/422-4828, www.habitat. org), page 202.

Type of Work: community development

TECHO (U.S. tel. 305/860-4090, www.techo. org), page 209.
Type of Work: community development

UBELONG (U.S. tel. 202/250-3706, www. ubelong.org), page 210.
Type of Work: agriculture, children and youth, community development, education, environment, health, wildlife protection, women's empowerment

Housing: Volunteers stay in a guesthouse, with wireless Internet, fully equipped kitchen, and hot water—not to mention a hot tub and incredible views of the mountains.

Operating Since: The founding family has been receiving volunteers since 2002, and operations were formalized into UCB in 2010.
Number of Volunteers: 40 in 2012

Essentials

BACKGROUND
Geography and Climate
Covering 1,098,580 square kilometers (424,160 sq. mi), Bolivia is roughly the size of California and Texas combined. Geographically, it is divided into three regions: the mountains, with its high plateau (known as the *cordillera* and *altiplano*, respectively); the valleys between the mountains and the lowlands; and the lowlands to the east, home to the Amazon basin.

In Bolivia, *verano* (summer) is rainy and lasts November-March, while *invierno* (winter) is drier and cooler, but weather in Bolivia is defined more by region than by season. In the *altiplano*, or Andean plateau, average daytime temperatures are mild, ranging 15-20°C (59-68°F). Nighttime temperatures descend dramatically to close to freezing, and there are often strong, cold winds. In the valleys and the Yungas region, the weather is temperate, humid, and rainy, and cooler at higher elevations. In the *Gran Chaco,* the semiarid lowland region of the River Plate basin, the climate is subtropical, with warm days and cool nights. January is especially rainy. The eastern *llanos* and their rainforests are humid and tropical, with an average daytime temperature of 30°C (85°F). The drier season begins in May.

Summer (Dec.-Mar.) is when it tends to be warm and humid in the east and warm and dry in the west. Winters (June-August) get very cold in the west, and there is snow around the mountain ranges. Fall is a dry time in the nontropical regions.

History and Economy
Officially known as the Plurinational State of Bolivia, the country is a culturally rich and multiethnic nation home to Amerindians, *mestizos,* Europeans, Asians, and Africans (more than half of the population is indigenous). There are 38 official languages, the primary being Spanish, but with a large chunk of the population speaking the indigenous languages of Aymara, Quechua, and Guarani.

Drawn by the country's mineral wealth, Spanish conquerors arrived in the mid-1500s, when Bolivia was known as "Upper Peru" and became subject to the viceroy of Lima. Potosí was founded in 1545 as a mining town, where silver was drawn from the Cerro Rico, or Rich Mountain, and it soon became the largest city in the New World, with a population of over 150,000. In 1809 Bolivia issued the first cry for freedom in Latin America, and after 16 years of fighting, it gained independence from Spain in 1825. Fighting continued, both internally and with neighbors Chile, Brazil, and Paraguay—resulting in the loss of over half of its territory.

Modern history has been marked by tumultuous rule, including rebellions and revolutions, military juntas and CIA meddling. In 2005, it became the first Latin American country to elect an indigenous president, Evo Morales, who was reelected in 2009.

Bolivia's main economic activities include agriculture, forestry, fishing, mining, and manufacturing goods such as textiles, clothing, refined metals, and refined petroleum. It is one of the world's megadiverse countries, with nearly 400 species of mammals and 1,400 species of birds (70 percent of all known birds).

PREPARATION
Transportation
Few airlines offer direct service to Bolivia, so prices are fairly high. International travelers will arrive either at the **El Alto Airport** (LPB,

www.sabsa.aero) in La Paz, or at the **Viru Viru International Airport** (VVI, www.sabsa.aero) in Santa Cruz. American is the only North American carrier with flights to Bolivia. Lan (based out of Chile) and Avianca (based out of Colombia) are two more reliable airlines that fly to Bolivia.

Bus service is comprehensive and cheap. While there aren't the highway holdups that can happen in other Latin American countries, as a matter of safety in terms of avoiding potholes and drunk drivers, it is best to travel during the day when possible. Buses are not always well heated, however, so you may want extra socks and some kind of packable throw blanket to pull out on a long winter ride.

Passports and Visas

Your passport must be valid for at least six months from the date of entry into Bolivia. With visas, Bolivia follows the "rule of reciprocity" for most countries, which means that visitors from the United States must obtain a tourist visa (US$135). While it is possible to obtain the visa ahead of time, visas can also be obtained directly at the airport or land point of entry. In addition to the fee, visitors must present a visa application form with a four-by-four-centimeter color photograph, evidence of a hotel reservation or a letter of invitation in Spanish, proof of economic solvency (credit card, cash, or a current bank statement), and a copy of your International Vaccination Certificate for yellow fever. The application form is available online at the **Bolivian Ministry of Foreign Relations** (in Spanish, www.rree.gob.bo). Any changes to visa requirements are posted there as well.

Visitors from Canada, the United Kingdom, and most EU countries do not require a visa.

Money

The Bolivian currency is **bolivianos** ($b). Bills are printed in denominations of $b10, $b20, $b50, $b100, and $b200. ATMs are available in big cities, and some dispense U.S. dollars as well. Try to obtain as much small change as possible in bigger cities, as it can be difficult to get change in small towns. Travelers checks are difficult to use, virtually impossible to change in smaller towns, and often subject to a commission.

Health

A **yellow fever vaccination is required,** and the shot must be given 10 days prior to traveling. Check with a local health clinic about other required vaccinations.

Perhaps the biggest health risk to travelers is altitude sickness. La Paz, where most visitors will arrive, is located at 3,690 meters (11,975 ft). Symptoms are typically tiredness, headaches, and nausea, although in rare cases they can be severe, causing problems with the lungs or brain. The best treatment is simply rest and trading your beer or other alcohol (which can aggravate symptoms) for a cup of coca tea. Over-the-counter pills are available to treat symptoms; altitude sickness is called *soroche* in Spanish. In more serious cases, light symptoms can often be easily alleviated with a tank or two of oxygen, while travelers should seek immediate medical assistance if they suffer any severe symptoms. Note: Altitude affects each person differently and has nothing to do with fitness levels or age—although in the author's experience, young children tend to be *less* affected by altitude than teens and adults.

Safety

Sadly, crime is on the rise in Bolivia, particularly in the city of La Paz. Tourists are sometimes targeted, so be wary of locals or tourist police (who might be fake police) who go out of their way to offer help. In La Paz, take taxis at night, particularly in the areas of El Alto, El Cemeterio, and Avenida Buenos Aires. Pay attention to your surroundings. Remember that one of the most common tricks for thieves and pickpockets is to toss something wet (ketchup, mustard, spit) on their victim as a distraction before the theft.

BOLIVIA

BRAZIL

The reasons to visit Brazil are as endless as its beaches. Brazil is South America's largest country, bordered by the Atlantic Ocean to the east and sharing its remaining borders with Uruguay, Paraguay, Argentina, Colombia, Venezuela, Guyana, Suriname, and French Guiana. Brazil's lush Amazon jungle and Atlantic Forest teem with wildlife, while its cities pulse with Afro-Brazilian beats, samba music, and Carnival. Colorful fishing villages and cosmopolitan cities line 7,491 kilometers (4,657 mi) of sandy beaches.

With 197 million residents, Brazil is the region's most populous country. More than 20 million people live either in the political capital of Rio de Janeiro or in the business capital of São Paulo. Thanks to a flourishing economy, Brazil is a relatively wealthy country, with a gross national income of US$10,790 per capita (2011 World Bank figures).

As in much of Latin America, however, there is a significant disparity in the distribution of wealth. In Brazil, one in every five person lives in poverty. Nearly 10 percent of the population is illiterate, while one in five are functionally illiterate (reading and writing skills are insufficient to manage beyond the most basic daily living and employment tasks).

Due to bureaucratic restrictions, Brazil has fewer local organizations catering to international volunteers than many of its neighbors. However, independent opportunities can still be found. Volunteers can work with disadvantaged youth in favelas (urban slums), plant trees in the Atlantic Forest,

© CAMILA VILLACIS

teach English in a tourist beach town, or even brainstorm new ideas in jewelry and fashion design at a small business association in a community center.

Brazil is Latin America's only Portuguese-speaking country. It was a Portuguese colony from 1500 until 1822, and the language remains as its legacy.

Local Organizations

IKO PORAN

Rio de Janeiro, tel. 55/21-3852-2916, www.ikoporan.org

TYPE OF WORK: agriculture, children and youth, community development, education, environment, health, women's empowerment

Iko Poran's mission is to fight against social exclusion through the implementation of development projects and international volunteer programs that "make a positive impact on local organizations, promoting intercultural exchanges and strengthening a constant and growing number of non-governmental organizations (NGOs) in Brazil." They place national and international volunteers at some 40 organizations around Rio de Janeiro in the areas of environment, education, health, the arts, culture, and science, and with a focus on children, youth, and other social groups at risk of exclusion. They will also start placing volunteers in Córdoba, Argentina, in 2013.

Volunteers can work either part- or full-time. Environmental programs include volunteering in the Tijuca Forest, the world's largest urban rainforest; brainstorming and implementing solutions to waste management and pollution reduction; planting trees as part of a reforestation project; or working in a community garden (and possibly lending a hand at the local community center) in a favela. Volunteers in the arts might teach dance, gymnastics, English, or cooking at a local ballet school that also serves as a community center; teach acting, singing, acrobatics, or set and costume design at a community arts center; support the Social Circus school with their gymnastics or circus skills; assist a community sewing business association with skills in fashion or accessories design, sewing, and jewelry or accessories

production; or support a film and photography social organization with their skills in audiovisual, animation, or other areas of film production. Volunteers can build houses or support community health care in the favelas; work at a play center established in a local hospital for its patients; teach or simply play with disadvantaged children and youth in soccer, capoeira, basketball, or even surf programs; work with children in day cares and nurseries (the ability to develop and provide supplies for arts and crafts projects especially needed); teach English (from leading a conversation group to teaching a class); or help develop the partner NGOs by writing project and funding proposals (intermediate Portuguese or fluent Spanish required). There is even a special seasonal program of preparing for Carnival in a samba school, where volunteers can help make costumes or decorate floats.

Iko Poran (IP) is a placement organization, but a nonprofit one committed to the success of their partner organizations. Fifty percent of the *net* placement fee is donated to the organization where the volunteer will be working. Placements occur year-round, but there are set arrival dates twice per month. Volunteers wishing to arrive at any other time need to check first with IP about the possibility and any additional costs.

Two weeks (20 hours) of intensive Portuguese lessons are included in the fee. IP can tailor programs for those who already have accommodations in Rio or who already speak Portuguese. IP is also developing tailored group programs that combine tourist and cultural activities with community service, ideal for youth groups or university/college groups.

When not working or studying Portuguese, volunteers have all of Rio at their doorstep, its

BRAZIL

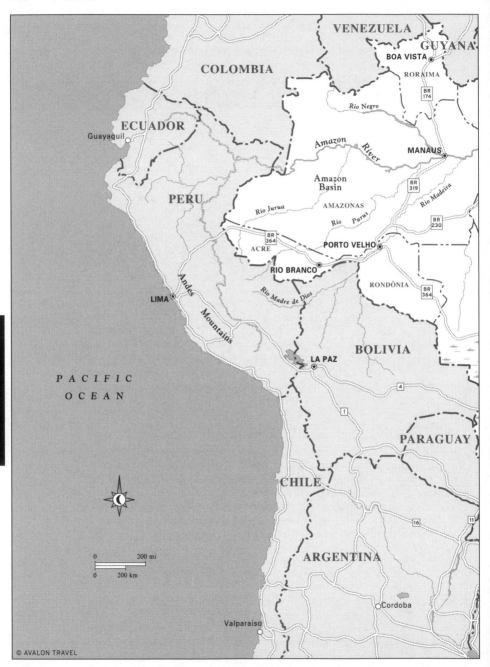

© AVALON TRAVEL

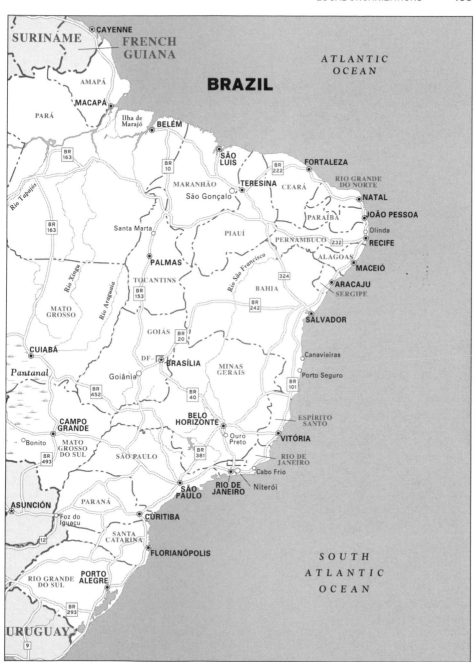

Volunteers find time to enjoy the beautiful beaches of Brazil.

beaches, cafés, restaurants, bars, cultural attractions and tourist sites.

Application Process: There is an online form that requires your physician's contact information, emergency contacts, your passport number, and a personal reference. Volunteers must be 18 or older.

Cost: US$1,100 for a four-week placement. This includes a US$190 donation to the partner organization, accommodations, two weeks of language study, and airport pickup. Volunteers are responsible for their own meals. The two-week house-building program has a US$575 fee and does not include any language classes.

Placement Length: Most are a minimum of four weeks, although house building has a two-week minimum; a few may have longer minimums.

Language Requirements: None. Portuguese lessons are included.

Housing: Volunteers stay in a guesthouse in the bohemian neighborhood of Santa Teresa in Rio. The guesthouse offers wireless Internet, a fully equipped kitchen, cleaning and laundry services. Volunteers can cook their own meals or eat out (restaurant meals can range US$3.50-15).

Operating Since: 2003

Number of Volunteers: approximately 400 in 2012

IRACAMBI

Minas Gerias, tel. 55/32-3723-1297, http://en.iracambi.com

TYPE OF WORK: wildlife protection

Iracambi works to protect the Atlantic Forest through "a program of research, education and hands-on practical actions." They are based in Minas Gerais, the second-most populous and fourth-largest state in Brazil, just inland from the Atlantic coast. Their office is in the town of Rosário da Limeira, and their research center is 12 kilometers/7 miles (30 minutes) away. It is very close to Serra do Brigadeiro State Park, part of a UN Biosphere Reserve.

VOLUNTEER PERSPECTIVE

Dani Ewert (age 26) is from Fargo, North Dakota. Here's what she had to say about her volunteer experience in Brazil's Atlantic Forest with **Iracambi** (Minas Gerias, tel. 55/32-3723-1297, http://en.iracambi.com).

How did you hear about Iracambi? What made you get involved with them?
I heard about Iracambi through Clark University. I decided to get involved because I wanted an internship that would give me a lot of freedom in my field, and Iracambi had such glowing reviews, as well as a mission that I felt strongly about.

What were your activities as a volunteer?
I mostly worked on erosion surveying and adding maps to others' projects. I also did some database organization.

What was one aspect that you especially enjoyed?
I really enjoyed the freedom. Iracambi is a very open place – I got to choose how and when to do my projects, and Robin and Binka [the founders of Iracambi] are people who know how to get the best out of their volunteers and interns. Creativity flows easily there, and it's such a rewarding, relaxing, and beautiful environment. I like knowing that I'm contributing to something that seems to actually be making a difference.

How have you continued your involvement with the cause since returning home?
I started working for them! I came back after my internship, thinking I wouldn't see Brazil again, then applied to be the volunteer coordinator. Now, I'm the GIS coordinator. I tell people about Iracambi, the Atlantic Forest, and am happy to answer questions or send people any information they might like to have.

BRAZIL

Volunteers typically join ongoing projects, and responsibilities may include monitoring forest cover and growth, water, fauna, and weather; caring for the forest nursery and planting trees; constructing new facilities for community-based tourism; helping with social media, IT, or graphics; fundraising and marketing; or creating photography and videos. If volunteers have special expertise and ideas for other ways to help, Iracambi would like to hear about that as well. Volunteers should be self-motivated and be able to work independently. The workday is 8am-5pm, with a break for lunch.

The research center is located on a working farm, with "rivers to swim in, mountains to climb, forest trails to hike, fruits to pick, and a welcoming local community to explore." Weekends offer a chance to visit nearby colonial towns.

The Atlantic Forest is different than its more famous sibling, the Amazon. It is humid, but cooler, with an average temperature range of 14-21°C (57-70°F). Winter (Apr.-Oct.) is typically dry and can get downright cold at night, while summer (November-March) is hot and wet. Iracambi is located in a drier part of the forest, which is not technically considered rainforest.

Application Process: Set up a Skype call to discuss. Volunteers must be age 18 or older.

Cost: US$625 for the first month, including accommodations in the guesthouse and meals. Staying in a semiprivate cabin is an additional US$100. There is a slight discount for subsequent months.

Placement Length: Minimum one month recommended, but exceptions may be made.

Language Requirements: None, but basic Portuguese is highly recommended. Portuguese is required for those wishing to volunteer in the community-based research work.

Housing: Volunteers stay in one of the center's six houses, in rooms shared with members of the same sex. There is 24-hour electricity, wireless Internet, and hot water. Fresh, organic meals are provided (vegetarians always have an option), and volunteers must buy their own beverages. Volunteers can also ask to move into a homestay after an initial stay at the center.

Operating Since: 1999
Number of Volunteers: 32 in 2012

SCOPE VOLUNTEER IN BRAZIL

Trancoso, tel. 55/11-3064-6574,
www.scopevolunteerinbrazil.com
TYPE OF WORK: community development, education, environment

Scope was founded in 2012 by Alexandra van Riel, a native of Trancoso, a popular beach town in the municipality of Porto Seguro, in the state of Bahia. Seeing jobs in the burgeoning tourist sector going to Brazilians from other places, Alexandra decided to create a program to bring English classes to Trancoso in order to improve tourism and business opportunities for locals. To harness volunteer interest, she then added one-week volunteer opportunities in housing construction and reforestation.

Volunteers teaching English work with both children and adults, mostly in the afternoon and evenings (4pm-9pm). The free lessons are given at a community association that seeks to provide alternatives for marginalized children and adults, and at a public high school. Experienced teachers are welcome, but teaching credentials or experience are not required; there is a qualified English teacher on staff who will give guidance to volunteers. There are specific start dates throughout the year, listed on Scope's website.

The housing construction program benefits low-income families, especially ones headed by single women. The reforestation program is about restoring parts of the Brazilian Atlantic Forest, and responsibilities vary throughout the week, including collecting seeds, cataloging native species, planting the collected seeds

at a nursery, and planting saplings in Monte Pascoal National Park.

It is suggested that volunteers enroll 1-6 months in advance. Scope can help with suggestions on how to fundraise for the program cost.

Volunteers who wish to study Portuguese can enroll for classes (US$150 for 10 hours in a week). Besides teaching and studying, the main draws are the sandy white beaches, the colorful town square, and the rich and diverse Bahian culture.

Application Process: There is a simple online application form. Individual volunteers must be 18 or older; 16- and 17-year-olds may volunteer if accompanied by a parent or guardian. Groups are welcome, and start dates can be flexible for them. Families are welcome as well.

Cost: US$1,300 for four weeks of teaching English. Accommodations, breakfast, airport pickup, and a US$150 donation to local NGOs are all included in the fee. (Note: The donation may be going to the affiliated Scope Institute to help pay the English teacher.) One week in the construction or reforestation programs is US$390 and includes a US$50 donation to Scope's work. Discounts and travel credits are available for sharing a room, photographers/filmmakers/writers who apply for the communications talents program, and for the Scope Ambassadors Program, through which current volunteers recruit new ones.

Placement Length: Minimum four weeks for teaching English. Scope is developing one-week opportunities in construction and reforestation.

Language Requirements: None.

Housing: Volunteers stay at a quaint hostel/guesthouse 5 minutes from the center of town and a 15-minute walk from the beach. There is no Internet at the guesthouse or the institute, but there are many Internet cafés in town.

Operating Since: 2012

Number of Volunteers: Scope accepted its first volunteers in August 2012 and had five between then and the end of the year; it is expecting lots of growth for 2013 and beyond.

TWO BROTHERS FOUNDATION

Rio de Janeiro, www.2bros.org

TYPE OF WORK: children and youth, community development, education

Based in the favela of Rocinha, the mission of Two Brothers Foundation (TBF) is to "promote education, community service and international exchange in low-income neighborhoods in Brazil." To achieve this, they seek to create educational communities, bring together people from diverse walks of life, and empower people to have a positive impact on the world around them, both locally and globally. Their educational communities focus on learning in languages, arts, and science.

TBF is a small-scale NGO with a bare-bones structure, so the most successful volunteers here will be those with initiative and strong self-management skills. Short-term volunteers ("voluntourists") support ongoing classes and activities by acting as assistants to full-time volunteers who are "resident" (staying for three or more months), and voluntourists can only be accepted if there are residents on-site to work with them. Voluntourists are welcome to propose programs and workshops they would like to initiate and can be responsible for. It is important that voluntourists realize they will not just be teachers at this organic school, but also learners. There are always English classes at the educational center, and "open classes" have included subjects such as personal financial management, health, physical fitness, martial arts, dance, visual arts, computer literacy, film studies, photography, and video production. Tutoring in reading, writing, math, and science is also provided.

TBF also accepts groups; in the past, they have helped out with English classes, assisted in refurbishing TBF's old building, and have offered consultation in business administration or other areas of expertise.

When volunteers are not working, they have plenty of ways to keep themselves busy: hiring a local tutor to improve their Portuguese, surfing, learning capoeira or jiujitzu, working on photography and film projects, conducting research, or exploring Rio. Some have volunteered for other organizations in Rocinha as well.

As a marginalized neighborhood, Rocinha can be dangerous. According to TBF's Volunteer Manual, "Police and members of Rocinha's drug gangs are extremely dangerous, and while it is wise to be friendly when spoken to, it is important to avoid getting involved with either." TBF will provide volunteers with guidance about staying safe.

Application Process: Volunteers should send an email and arrange for a meeting upon arrival to Brazil. Individual volunteers must be 18 or older; those younger than 18 will be considered on a case-by-case basis. Families are welcome.

Cost: None. Volunteers are responsible for their own expenses.

Placement Length: Minimum three visits for short-term volunteers.

Language Requirements: None, although if the volunteer does not have Portuguese skills, TBF asks him or her to be actively studying before and during volunteering. Local tutors can be hired by the volunteer upon arrival in Rocinha.

Housing: Volunteers must make their own arrangements, although TBF can provide a list of conveniently-located hostels (US$17-26 per night). They also work with a guesthouse that is in a local home (US$120-144 per month; shorter stays are possible, but preference is given to resident volunteers). All volunteers are responsible for their own meals.

Operating Since: 1998

Number of Volunteers: about 50 "voluntourists" and another 7 resident (long-term) volunteers in 2012

VIVA RIO

Rio de Janeiro, tel. 55/21-2555-3750, www.vivario.org.br

TYPE OF WORK: children and youth, community development, education, environment, health

Viva Rio was formed in the early 1990s in response to growing violence in Rio de Janeiro

BRAZIL

© CAMILA VILLACIS

The iconic statue of Christ the Redeemer keeps watch over Rio de Janeiro.

and is "an organization committed to research, field work, and to the formulation of public policies aimed at fostering a culture of peace and social inclusion."

Viva Rio has a wide variety of programs working toward its goal. The areas where volunteers are most likely to find an opportunity are in: family health, a program that benefits some 950,000 *cariocas* (Rio residents) through 57 community health clinics, one emergency center, and two psychological clinics; emergency response programs, such as obtaining, sorting, and distributing donations to Rio residents affected by flooding after heavy rains; and education, arts, and sports programs, which aim to counter conflict with programs that engage children and youth such as youth

apprenticeships, neighborhood gardens, after-school programs, and elementary and secondary school equivalency programs. Viva Rio also has environmental programs in the Atlantic forest and in the Cagarras Island Archipelago, and a large and multipronged violence-reduction program that includes police and municipal guard training, disarmament, and more.

While Viva Rio has long worked with Brazilian volunteers, its "Social Tourism" project, created to better work with international volunteers, was just being developed in 2012. As such, volunteers need to be fairly self-reliant and able to arrange their own accommodations and meals. Volunteers will find plenty to fill their free time in Rio, including heading to the beach; exploring cafés, restaurants, and bars; studying Portuguese or samba; and watching a soccer match.

Application Process: Email for information, and would-be volunteers will be sent a simple application form. Volunteers must be 18 or older.

Cost: Volunteers do not pay any fee, but they are expected to contribute one basic food basket for a family. A list of items is provided, and the total cost is US$30-40. Volunteers are responsible for their own expenses.

Placement Length: A *maximum* of nine hours per week, for a minimum of one month.

Language Requirements: Basic Portuguese required.

Housing: Volunteers are responsible for their own accommodations and meals.

Operating Since: 1993; the "Social Tourism" program was created in late 2012.

Number of Volunteers: Only a few as of early 2013, as the "Social Tourism" program was just being launched.

INTERNATIONAL ORGANIZATIONS

The following international organizations support volunteer efforts in Brazil:

Amizade Global Service Learning (U.S. tel. 412/586-4986, www.amizade.org), page 194.
Type of Work: agriculture, children and youth, community development, education, environment, health

Cross-Cultural Solutions (toll-free U.S. tel. 800/380-4777, www.crossculturalsolutions. org), page 195.
Type of Work: children and youth, community development, education, health, women's empowerment

Earthwatch (U.S. tel. 978/461-0081, toll-free U.S. tel. 800/776-0188, www.earthwatch.org), page 196.

Type of Work: environment, wildlife protection

International Volunteer HQ (IVHQ) (toll-free U.S. tel. 877/342-6588, www.volunteerhq. org), page 203.
Type of Work: agriculture, children and youth, community development, education, environment, health, wildlife protection

ProWorld (toll-free U.S. tel. 877/429-6753, www.proworldvolunteers.org), page 207.
Type of Work: children and youth, community development, education, environment, health, wildlife protection, women's empowerment

TECHO (U.S. tel. 305/860-4090, www.techo. org), page 209.
Type of Work: community development

Essentials

BRAZIL

BACKGROUND
Geography and Climate
Scientists estimate that Brazil's total number of species of flora and fauna might reach four million, making its ecology as diverse as its people. Complementing the famed rainforest are regions of dry forest, coastal lowlands, wetlands, and semiarid plains. Cattle ranching and agriculture, logging, mining, resettlement, oil and gas extraction, overfishing, wildlife trade, dams and infrastructure, water pollution, climate change, fire, and invasive species all present a severe threat, however, to Brazil's natural riches.

In a country as large as Brazil, climate can obviously vary, but overall it is mostly tropical. Generally speaking, the northern regions and part of the interior of the northeast region have annual medium temperatures above 25°C (77°F), while in the south and part of the southeast, average annual temperatures are below 20°C (70°F). *Invierno* (winter) is June-August, and it only really gets cool south of Rio.

History and Economy
Brazil is an enormous country, equivalent to nearly 90 percent of the area of the United States (while its population is equivalent to about 60 percent of the United States). Brazilians are heavily concentrated in the southeastern (79.8 million inhabitants) and northeastern (53.5 million inhabitants) regions, while the two most extensive regions, the center-west and the north (which together make up 64.12 percent of the Brazilian territory), have a total of just over 29 million inhabitants.

While the uncontacted peoples in Brazil have garnered much attention, less than 1 percent of the population is indigenous. From the early 1500s until the 1860s, Brazil was the largest destination in the Americas for African slaves, and roughly four million enslaved Africans were brought to Brazil during that period. Millions of immigrants arrived to Brazil in the 19th and 20th centuries, many with ancestors from Portugal, Italy, Spain, Germany, Japan, and the Middle East. Nowadays, more than 40 percent of the population self-identifies as multiracial.

After Pedro Alvares Cabral landed in Porto Seguro and claimed Brazil for Portugal, the country remained a colony for more than 300 years. This lasted until 1808, when the Portuguese royal family fled from Napoleon and established their new residence in Rio de Janeiro, and Brazil was elevated to the status of sovereign kingdom, united with Portugal (and the Algarves). Independence came a few years later in 1822, with the formation of the Empire of Brazil.

Brazil has a booming export trade, sending out aircraft, electrical equipment, automobiles, ethanol, textiles, footwear, iron ore, steel, coffee, orange juice, and soybeans. The agricultural, mining, manufacturing, and service sectors are all large and well developed.

PREPARATION
Transportation
Brazil has around 2,500 airports, the second-highest number in the world (after the United States), so getting there and traveling around by air is not a problem. Visitors are likely to arrive at the **Guarulhos International Airport** (GRU, www.gru.com.br) in São Paulo, the largest and busiest in the country, or at the **Galeão Antonio Carlos Jobim International Airport** (GIG, www.aeroportogaleao.net) in Rio. Both airports are serviced by Air Canada, American Airlines, Delta, US Air, and United, as well as many other international airlines. The Brazilian airline TAM is well regarded. Departure taxes are included in the ticket for commercial flights.

Bus service in Brazil is generally excellent, with well-maintained, punctual buses, making it a good way to get around the country (although you pay for what you get, and long-distance bus travel is a bit pricier here than elsewhere in Latin America). Roads can be less than stellar in the Amazon region, where boats plying the river and its tributaries are still an important form of travel.

Passports and Visas
Visas are required for both U.S. and Canadian citizens, which must be applied for at the consulate or embassy nearest to you, and are typically issued for 90 days. Brazilian consulates in the United States encourage travelers to apply by mail and will not grant visas the same day if applying in person. That said, the "reciprocity fee" charged is less if applying in person: US$160 versus US$180 for Americans, and US$65 versus US$85 for Canadians. Citizens of most other countries pay US$20 if applying in person, US$40 if applying by mail. Travelers under the age of 18 require additional documentation. Passports must be valid for at least six months from the date of travel. Travelers who have been to certain countries, including most Latin American countries, in the past 90 days will also need to show proof of yellow fever vaccination in order to enter.

Technically speaking, it is illegal to conduct voluntary work in a tourist visa. Obtaining a volunteer visa, however, requires an affidavit from the organization where you'll be volunteering stating that they will cover the cost of your repatriation in the event of a breach of your visa condition, several other additional documents, and a heftier fee. Unsurprisingly, and in accordance with instructions from organizations where they will volunteer, most people simply apply for a tourist visa instead. Travelers should research the matter and make their own decision about how to handle it prior to applying for a program or visa.

Money
Brazil uses the **real** (hay-OW); the plural is reais (hay-AYS) and the symbol is R$. Bills come in denominations of R$1, R$2, R$5, R$10, R$20, R$50, and R$100, and at the time of this writing, the exchange rate was R$2.05 being the equivalent of US$1.

Cash and travelers checks can be exchanged at banks and *casas de câmbio* (exchange houses), the former offering the best rates, the latter offering the most convenience. The best luck with ATMs is in cities and bigger towns;

having a four-digit PIN also makes withdrawing easier. Cash advances on a Visa card is another way to obtain funds and is usually possible even in smaller towns.

Health
Yellow fever vaccination is recommended if traveling to Iguazú Falls, and it must be administered at least 10 days before travel. Malaria, leishmaniasis, and dengue are also all present in Brazil, so bring a good bug repellent, and seek medical care if you experience a sharp fever, aching bones, or other unusual symptoms such as rashes or skin lesions. That said, the most likely illness visitors to Brazil will encounter is traveler's diarrhea; all pharmacies in Brazil sell oral rehydration salts.

Safety
According to the U.S. Department of State, "street crime remains a problem for visitors and local residents alike. Foreign tourists, including U.S. citizens, are often targets, especially in Sao Paulo, Rio de Janeiro, Salvador, and Recife." Travelers should carry a *copy* of their passport when out and about, and keep the actual passport safe in their hotel or guesthouse. Volunteers working in favelas (shantytowns) should strictly follow the recommendations of the host organization about safety. All travelers should be careful not to flash jewelry or other valuables, such as cell phones, MP3 players, or laptops. Beware of the "Good Samaritan" who offers assistance—really serving to distract you while his or her partner in crime lifts your wallet or other valuables.

BRAZIL

ARGENTINA

Argentina evokes mystery, romance, and beauty. Bordered by Chile to the west; Brazil, Uruguay, and the Atlantic Ocean to the east; and Bolivia and Paraguay to the north, this is a land of sparkling lakes, snowcapped mountains, and grassland pampas peopled with gaucho cowboys, tango dancers, and urban sophisticates. Nature lovers will be hard-pressed to choose a destination: glacial lakes carved out of mountains along the border with Chile; the Iguazú Falls bordering Brazil and Paraguay, higher than Niagara and four times as wide; or the Patagonian coast, home to seals, sea lions, and penguins. City lovers will revel in the country's baroque cafés, republican architecture, world-class steak houses, and sultry music halls.

Argentina is home to approximately 40 million people. This is an upper-middle-income country, with a gross national income per capita of US$9,740 (2011 World Bank figures). That relatively high per capita income hides the impact its roller-coaster economy (1999-2002 financial crisis, economic recovery in following years, then instability and 25 percent annual inflation by 2012) has on its most marginalized population. While the national government does not provide clear poverty figures, a recent World Bank report states that Argentina has seen the largest increase in inequality in the region over the past three decades and that there are significant pockets of rural poverty.

Few local organizations directly recruit international volunteers, but those who are looking to travel independently can find a variety of

© AMY E. ROBERTSON

opportunities, including working with disadvantaged children, sorting cans at a food bank, serving meals in a soup kitchen, or helping out at an organic farm. Many more volunteer opportunities are available through organizations that work in multiple countries (see listings in the *International Organizations* chapter).

While there are significant pockets of poverty in Argentina due to its financial struggles, overall services and traveler amenities are highly developed (tap water is potable, health care is inexpensive and good, and risks of tropical diseases are minimal), making Argentina a comfortable choice for travelers who might be apprehensive about roughing it elsewhere in Latin America.

Local Organizations

EXPANISH

Buenos Aires, tel. 54/11-5252-3040, U.S. tel. 888/EXPANISH (397-2647), www.expanish.com

TYPE OF WORK: children and youth, community development, education

Expanish is a Spanish-language school in Buenos Aires that also offers combined language study and volunteer work programs, with courses starting every Monday year-round. The school emphasizes cultural immersion along with language learning. There are several cultural activities and excursions organized each week, such as Latin American cinema club, tango and salsa lessons, and city center tours; excursions might be an outing to a traditional estancia to see the gaucho way of life, an adventure in Iguazú Falls, wine tasting in Mendoza, or a day-trip to neighboring Uruguay.

Volunteer/study packages include two weeks of language lessons followed by two weeks of volunteering. Volunteers work a minimum of 15 hours per week and can work more if desired.

Those interested in teaching English might assist a teacher or lead lessons, help with homework, or lead games and activities—depending on interest and experience. (Teaching English is not available mid-December-mid-March or during the month of July, due to school holidays.) Volunteers are also needed to provide support, companionship, time, and skills to senior citizens. Tasks include engaging in conversation, participating in the various activities that are organized by community centers, helping in the kitchen, and sharing meals. Volunteers

working with underprivileged children and youth might help children with schoolwork; oversee study sessions; participate in and/or lead playtime, sports, games, and activities; give educational workshops or basic education classes (such as on hygiene, nutrition, and safety); help prepare and serve daily snacks or meals; or simply spend quality time with the kids. Expanish also has an area they call "Volunteering for Community Development," which encompasses a variety of placements, from soup kitchens and community gardens to educational workshops and advocacy work. Responsibilities might include preparing and serving meals, participating in recreational activities, cleaning/tidying, or leading/assisting with an educational workshop, among others.

Application Process: There is a simple online application form; an emergency contact is required. Volunteers must be 18 or older.

Cost: US$350 for the volunteer placement (which includes a donation to the host organization), plus the cost of Spanish classes (US$210-495 per week, depending on the intensity of classes). Volunteers are responsible for their own living expenses.

Placement Length: Four weeks (two weeks of Spanish classes and two weeks of volunteering).

Language Requirements: None.

Housing: Expanish can arrange a variety of housing options, including homestays with breakfast and dinner daily, private rooms in shared apartments, and shared rooms in student residences. All have Internet access, and some have wireless Internet. Price varies

ARGENTINA

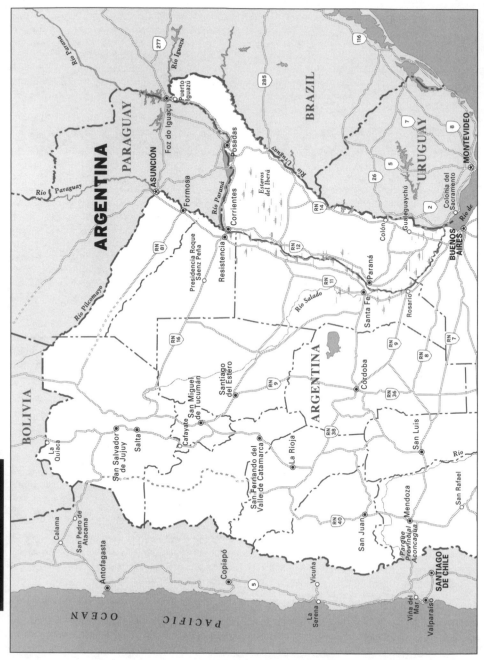

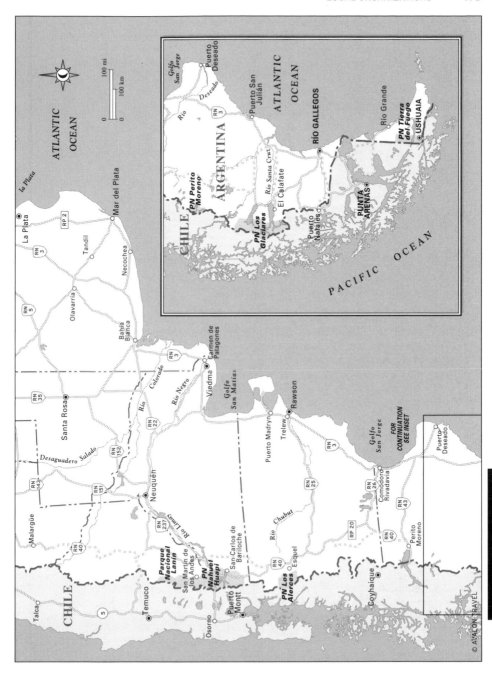

ARGENTINA

according to amenities and the distance from the school. Rates are US$175-345 per week, except for stays in an *apart-hotel* (a private apartment with hotel amenities such as maid service, gym, Internet, security, and reception) for a whopping US$875 per week.

Operating Since: 2006

Number of Volunteers: about 80 in 2012

FUNDACIÓN BANCO DE ALIMENTOS (FOOD BANK FOUNDATION)

San Martín, tel. 54/11-4724-2334,
www.bancodealimentos.org.ar,
www.volunteersouthamerica.net

TYPE OF WORK: community development

Located just outside of Buenos Aires, the Food Bank Foundation serves as a link between food-producing and food-marketing companies, and people with hunger across Greater Buenos Aires. Canned and processed foods are collected and sorted in a warehouse in the small city of San Martín (where food-production is a major industry), and volunteers help to check expiration dates, separate products, and prepare bags and boxes for delivery to food banks all around Buenos Aires.

The food bank is open 9am-6pm Monday-Friday, but volunteer hours are completely flexible, making it a good fit for anyone looking to enrich their regularly planned vacation in Buenos Aires. Free time can of course be filled with all the usual attractions of Buenos Aires—tango and cafés, flea markets and soccer.

Application Process: To apply, send an email or call. Volunteers must be age 18 or older (age 14 or older if accompanied by a responsible adult).

Cost: None. Volunteers are responsible for their own expenses.

Placement Length: No minimum.

Language Requirements: None.

Housing: None provided. Volunteers typically stay in Buenos Aires and take public transportation (about one hour each way). Volunteers who work most of a day will be provided lunch.

Operating Since: 2001

Number of Volunteers: 1,378 active volunteers in 2012

LA CASA DE MARIA DE LA ESPERANZA

Escobar, tel. 54/11-5906-0982,
www.lacasamariadelaesperanza.com

TYPE OF WORK: children and youth, education

La Casa de Maria de la Esperanza is a day care center in Escobar, a suburb of Buenos Aires 50 kilometers (30 mi) away that serves roughly 70 disadvantaged children and youth. La Casa focuses on the basic needs of the children, including food, clothing, education, hygiene, health, and assistance in social services for their families. Medical and psychological services are provided for the children as needed. Volunteers work side by side with professionals to teach reading, writing, and workshops on topics of health, hygiene, and nutrition, and the children participate in sports workshops off-site. Volunteers might also teach English or help with children's homework, and they definitely will spend time playing with the children.

The center is open 9am-4pm weekdays, but volunteers can volunteer just two or three times per week if they prefer. Volunteers also have their evenings and weekends free for exploring. Escobar itself is a small town, with beautiful parks, interesting little shops and markets, and, according to one former volunteer, very friendly people. It has a bus system that goes into the heart of Buenos Aires for approximately US$3 each way, where volunteers can visit popular tourist attractions such as the neighborhoods of Boca, Tigre, and San Telmo. Weekends can be used to reach farther-flung destinations like Iguazú Falls, or the ferry to Uruguay.

Application Process: Send an email. Volunteers must be 18 or older.

Cost: None, although volunteers are responsible for their own expenses. Alternatively, volunteers can stay in the home of the founder of La Casa for US$180 per week (minimum two weeks, includes breakfast and lunch, as well as transportation to and from the Buenos Aires airport).

A VOLUNTEER PERSPECTIVE

Here's what Karen Fowler (age 30), from Ontario, Canada, said about her volunteer experience with **La Casa de Maria de la Esperanza** (tel. 54/11-5906-0982, www.lacasamariad-elaesperanza.com) in Escobar, Argentina.

What made you choose to volunteer with La Casa Maria?

For years I have known that I wanted to help underprivileged children around the world, so after I graduated college I decided it was great time to do this. I researched various countries and projects, and when I came across La Casa Maria, I couldn't explain it, I just knew that was the place for me.

What was a highlight?

One amazing experience was I got the opportunity to take some of the teenaged boys to the zoo for a day. They spend so much of their time helping their mothers, looking after their younger siblings, and trying to be positive male role models in their families. That is a lot of pressure, so by spending the day away from all of that, they were able to have a day of just being kids.

What did you take away from the experience?

At first, I thought of all the things I could do for the kids, how much I could teach them. I never thought about how much they'd teach me. They reminded me to appreciate the little things, be grateful for what I have, and to love with all my heart.

Was there a downside?

Most of the kids that attend the center are living in extreme poverty. It's very hard to see the conditions they are forced to live in. A volunteer should just know that just by coming to help gives the kids something to look forward to, and lets them know someone loves them.

Another hard part of the trip is saying goodbye. You build friendships, you spend so much time together, and then you have to leave. The thing that helped me was knowing our lives are forever changed for the better, and that bond will never end.

Were you able to share your experience once you got home?

I have been blessed to be able to share so many stories and pictures of my experience with family and friends. My family has gotten involved, too; my mom has gone to visit twice, and we sponsor a family of four that attends La Casa Maria regularly.

Placement Length: Minimum of two weeks.
Language Requirements: Basic Spanish preferred but not required.
Housing: Volunteers can either make their own arrangements for accommodations and meals or lodge locally in a homestay in Escobar (at the home of the founder of La Casa Maria) for US$180/week, breakfast and lunch included, as well as transportation to and from the airport. Volunteers who choose to stay in Buenos Aires can travel easily, cheaply, and comfortably by bus, but it's a 60- to 75-minute ride each way.
Operating Since: 2007
Number of Volunteers: eight in 2012

LUCHEMOS PARA UNA INFANCIA FELIZ Y CON ESPERANZA (LIFE)

Buenos Aires, tel. 54/11-4806-0640,
www.lifeargentina.org
TYPE OF WORK: children and youth, community development, education, health

LIFE is an entirely volunteer-run organization that works with marginalized children and youth, "providing recreational, educational and social activities, as well as food, clothing and supplies." They work collaboratively with soup kitchens and community centers across Buenos Aires, as well as in the indigenous Guaraní village of Perutí. Their programs in Buenos Aires

© AMY E. ROBERTSON

Ornate neoclassical architecture adorns many streets of Buenos Aires.

include monthly birthday celebrations at each community center; tutoring in math, science, Spanish, and English; organized playtime; provision of school supplies and field trips; youth AIDS awareness; accompaniment and playtime with children undergoing dialysis treatment; self-help workshops for marginalized teens; and cooking classes for children who live in a particularly precarious neighborhood. Fifteen hundred kilometers (932 mi) away in Perutí, LIFE volunteers visit once a month to offer education, training, consultations, and recreational activities; much-needed supplies; and workshops on topics such as HIV/AIDS and nutrition.

Volunteers can explore Buenos Aires and study Spanish in their free time. Volunteers who head to Perutí can arrange to visit Iguazú Falls.

Application Process: There is a very simple online form. Individual volunteers must be 16 or older (16- and 17-year-olds must have written parental/guardian consent); families are also welcome.

Cost: US$40 for volunteers staying up to two weeks; US$60 for 15-29 days, and US$80 for 30 days or more. The contribution helps fund programs, projects, and activities. Volunteers are responsible for their own expenses and must also buy a LIFE T-shirt to wear while volunteering.

Placement Length: No minimum commitment.

Language Requirements: None.

Housing: LIFE offers a variety of accommodation options, including shared rooms in the office/guesthouse in the Recoleta neighborhood, a private room in a shared apartment, or a homestay. Rates are US$100-140 per person per week and do not include any meals, but all accommodations offer access to cooking facilities. Individual apartments are also available for rent.

Operating Since: 2001

Number of Volunteers: 500-600 per year, with 20-70 at any given time.

PATAGONIA VOLUNTEER

Esequel, Patagonia, tel. 54/2945-457078, www.patagoniavolunteer.org

TYPE OF WORK: agriculture, children and youth, community development, education, environment

Located on the western edge of Argentina, 2,000 kilometers (1,200 mi) from Buenos Aires, Patagonia Volunteer (PV) is a program founded by the Mapu Association, an organization that supports "projects geared towards micro-enterprise and economic solidarity, educational and cultural development, environmental education and protection and the promotion of the Mapuche language and identity" and seeks to "defend the right of the natives to occupy their ancestral lands and to promote international cooperation." As Mapu is entirely volunteer based, it has no overhead costs, and so all monies received from volunteers is used to promote, sponsor, and execute development projects in Patagonia. Volunteers in "education and culture" can choose between working with people with disabilities, assisting at a community-run radio station, helping at a day care center or local library, or tutoring children and teenagers. Volunteers interested in supporting native peoples can help digitalize audio records in the Mapuzungun language or work with the Santa Rosa Mapuche Community in their fight to raise awareness about land issues faced by the native people of Patagonia. Volunteers in "regional development" can support a micro-credit lending program, while those who wish to work in "international cooperation" can assist with the coordination, fundraising, and graphic design projects of Patagonia Volunteer and Mapu Association, or assist with website design for small local nonprofit organizations whose work supports local self-sufficiency, growth in local resources, and increased capability for positive and sustainable development.

Volunteers working in the area of "environmental care" might create computer flash games about open pit mining; develop animated movie shorts about metal mining; support community efforts in organic farming or natural building techniques; or provide administrative, logistical, and technical support to a community organization that is fighting local metal exploitation.

The volunteer fee helps support a community radio, grant microcredits, support small community projects, and support a project to revitalize and promote the Mapuzungun language (currently endangered in the Chubut province). Most volunteers work 20-25 hours per week, but it is possible to work more if desired. June and July are cold months with short days and not particularly recommended for volunteers.

There are no Spanish schools in Esquel, but PV can help arrange private lessons at a reasonable cost. Other free-time activities include joining a local swimming pool or a gym, taking dance classes or guitar lessons, climbing indoors at the local Club Andino, and more. PV will point volunteers in the right direction for these activities, as well as for weekend trips, which can include horseback riding, hiking, rock climbing, or skiing. **Application Process:** There is an online application form with which a "letter of intent" must be included. Payment is made only once a suitable placement has been confirmed. Application should be made at least eight weeks prior to your preferred start date, and payment made at least four weeks prior to arrival. Volunteers must be 18 or older. **Cost:** US$405, which covers the US$80 annual membership fee to Mapu Association and the US$325 placement fee. Volunteers are responsible for their own expenses during their stay.

Placement Length: Usual minimum is four weeks; a three-week stay might be considered, depending on the volunteer profile, availability of placements, and time of year.

Language Requirements: Intermediate Spanish or better required.

Housing: Patagonia Volunteer can arrange a homestay (US$150-240/month) and highly recommends them. Volunteers will have their own room and share a bathroom.

Operating Since: 2006

Number of Volunteers: 10-30 per year

SPANISH IN BARILOCHE

Bariloche, tel. 54/294-452-4212,
www.spanishinbariloche.com

TYPE OF WORK: agriculture, children and youth, community development, education, environment, health

Bariloche is a pleasant, busy ski resort town of 110,000 located on the shores of Lake Nahuel Huapi, in the foothills of the Andes in northern Patagonia.

The school works with several different organizations in Bariloche. The volunteer opportunity with the shortest time commitment is two weeks at an organic educational farm in the National Park Nahuel Huapi area. Volunteers will help farmers with organic farming, educate children about environmental care, and even build an ecohouse. Two-week volunteers help with feeding the animals, gardening, and maintaining the farm; those who can commit to four or more weeks and have intermediate Spanish can become involved with guiding the children who come on school excursions to learn about organic farming.

Other volunteer opportunities (which

ARGENTINA

require at least four weeks commitment, and some two or three months) include supporting a community center at a village inside the national park, teaching English and helping out at a preschool, working in both gardening and educational outreach at a native plants nursery, volunteering at a center for mentally disabled persons, working at a dental clinic (no health background required), volunteering at a community soup kitchen (men only), taking care of children at day care while their teenage parents complete high school, or working with the rangers at the national park (January and February only).

In their free time, volunteers can study Spanish (classes at Spanish in Bariloche start at US$195 for 20 hours in a week, and volunteers get a discount on that) and enjoy the restaurants, chocolate shops, and cafés of Bariloche. In the summer (December-February) volunteers can hike through the national park, while winter (June-August) visitors can ski the local slopes. Summer daytime temperatures range 18-26°C (64-79°F), but nights are still downright cold, so bring a sweater *and* a coat.

Application Process: Applicants must submit an email with a résumé and a cover letter explaining why they want to volunteer in Bariloche and the type of project they are interested in. A 100 percent commitment is needed, as the projects have minimal resources. Families are welcome (there are even specific volunteer programs for families).

Cost: There is a US$100 program fee for those also enrolled in a Spanish course; US$150 for those who come only to volunteer. A portion of the fee goes to the project. Volunteer living expenses are not included.

Placement Length: Varies by project: minimum two weeks on an organic educational farm; all other projects minimum of four or more weeks.

Language Requirements: Intermediate to advanced Spanish required for most projects; basic to intermediate acceptable for teaching English in schools.

Housing: Homestays are US$250 per week for a shared room, US$280 for a private room, and include breakfast and dinner. Hostels start at US$140 per week and include breakfast only. Volunteers can get a discount on these prices. Some projects, such as work at the organic farm or the national park, have on-site accommodations available.

Operating Since: 2002
Number of Volunteers: 15 in 2012

VOLUNTARIO GLOBAL

Buenos Aires, tel. 54/911-6206-9639,
www.voluntarioglobal.org

TYPE OF WORK: children and youth, community development, education, health, women's empowerment

Voluntario Global (VG) is a locally founded and locally run nonprofit that aims "to empower people from disadvantaged backgrounds by giving them the education, training and support needed to succeed."

Their two-week voluntourism programs include accommodations, volunteer placement at a preschool or soup kitchen, and the volunteer's choice of four tango lessons, one cycling tour, or 20 hours of Spanish lessons. Volunteers at the preschool work 9am-1pm three or four days per week, interacting with the children through games, songs, drawings, and workshops; helping to plan activities and take care of the children; and helping to cook and serve food, wash dishes, and clean up. This program is not available when the children are on break: December, January, and for two weeks in July. At the soup kitchen, volunteers work 9am-2pm three or four days per week, helping to prepare and serve food, and collecting the plates afterward. This program is unavailable in December and January.

Volunteers who can commit 4-12 weeks have many more placements available to them: teaching English; working in an orphanage; supporting health care; or doing community work, sustainable development, or journalism and PR. VG also offers longer-term volunteer placements in Patagonia, in northern

Argentina, near Iguazú Falls, and even in Bolivia.

Volunteers have all of Buenos Aires to explore in their free time, from the colorful streets of La Boca to the baroque cafés of Recoleta. Visitors in the months of February-November can watch a passionate match of soccer between rival teams River Plate and Boca Juniors. As already noted, VG can arrange both tango and Spanish lessons, which volunteers can practice while they dip into Buenos Aires's famed nightlife.

VG doesn't limit its work to connecting volunteers with projects. It also strategically and financially supports a microenterprise project, through which youth from a nearby shantytown have opened a Laundromat ("the Laundry Project"), creating financial opportunity.

Application Process: There is an online application form. Volunteers under age 18 must have written parental authorization.

Cost: US$420-650 for the two-week volun-tourism programs, and US$640 for their standard four-week program, both of which include accommodations (in a shared bedroom—a private room is US$800 for four weeks). Four-week placements without accommodations are US$240. All prices include a donation to the project. Volunteers are responsible for their own meals.

Placement Length: Minimum of two weeks.

Language Requirements: Basic Spanish required.

Housing: Accommodations with VG are part of all two-week packages but are optional for volunteers committing four weeks or more. The volunteer guesthouse is in the heart of Buenos Aires, four blocks from the Plaza de Congreso, and has a fully equipped kitchen, TV, and wireless Internet; both shared and private rooms are available.

Operating Since: 2005

Number of Volunteers: 200-300 per year

INTERNATIONAL ORGANIZATIONS

The following international organizations support volunteer efforts in Argentina:

Habitat for Humanity International (toll-free U.S. tel. 800/422-4828, www.habitat.org), page 202.
Type of Work: community development

International Volunteer HQ (IVHQ) (toll-free U.S. tel. 877/342-6588, www.volunteerhq.org), page 203.
Type of Work: agriculture, children and youth, community development, education, environment, health, wildlife protection

Intern Latin America (ILA) (U.S. tel. 718/878-6393, www.internlatinamerica.com), page 205.
Type of Work: children and youth, community development, education, environment, health, wildlife protection, women's empowerment

TECHO (U.S. tel. 305/860-4090, www.techo.org), page 209.
Type of Work: community development

Wanderland Travel (toll-free U.S. tel. 866/701-2113, www.wanderland.org), page 212.
Type of Work: agriculture, children and youth, community development, education, environment

Essentials

BACKGROUND
Geography and Climate

Argentina is about the size of the United States east of the Mississippi River. Geographically, it can be divided into six main regions: the Pampas, fertile lowlands in central and eastern Argentina; the Mesopotamia, a lowland bordered by the Paraná and Uruguay Rivers; the Gran Chaco, semiarid lowlands in northern Argentina; Cuyo, the wine-producing, mountainous area of central-west Argentina; the Argentine Northwest; and Patagonia, a large plateau to the south.

With a climate that ranges from subtropical to subpolar, Argentina is home to a wide variety of flora and fauna. Some of the most notable species include big cats such as jaguar, puma, and ocelot; birds such as toucan, flamingo, and penguin; llamas and vicuñas; crocodiles; and orca whales.

Summer falls December-February and winter June-August. Buenos Aires has hot, sticky summers and mild, drier winters, making the shoulder months of October, November, March, April, and May the best months to visit weather wise. At the southern tip of the continent, the region of Patagonia is obviously Argentina's coolest, but summer days are long and warm (with cool nights), while winter temperatures often drop below freezing.

History and Economy

Argentina is a country of immigrants—its 35 indigenous groups make up less than 2 percent of the population, while the vast majority claim European roots.

Befitting Argentina's Italian flair, the first European to arrive on its shores was Amerigo Vespucci, in 1502. The Spanish quickly followed, however, establishing a colony in the 1500s that lasted until Argentina's independence in 1816. A series of civil wars took place in the subsequent years, until national unification in 1880. Populist Juan Domingo Perón won the presidency in 1946, and again in 1952,

thanks in part to his charismatic wife, Eva. His leadership, marked by extravagant government spending and squandering of post-World War II surplus, lasted until he was ousted in a military coup in 1955. Thus began three decades of brutal military dictatorships in Argentina, the worst of them the three-man junta led by Gen. Jorge Rafael Videla from 1976 until 1982. During that time, known as the Dirty War, more than 30,000 Argentines were killed, and thousands more tortured, imprisoned, or forced into exile. Constitutional government returned to Argentina in 1983, after the military's humiliating defeat in their attempt to take the Falkland (Malvina) Islands from British control.

Manufacturing is Argentina's largest single economic sector. It is one of the world's major agricultural producers, and the service sector (including tourism) accounts for more than 60 percent of the country's GDP. (According to the World Tourism Organization, Argentina was the most-visited country in South America in 2011.)

PREPARATION
Transportation

Flights from North America to Argentina are available through Air Canada, American Airlines, Delta, and United. **Ezeiza** (Ministro Pistarini, EZE, www.aa2000. ar), the international airport in Buenos Aires, is also serviced by numerous regional and global airlines. Flights are pricey, and more so around Christmas and New Year's and Holy Week (the week leading up to Easter). Domestic flights aren't cheap, but they're reasonable and a good way for travelers short on time to avoid long bus rides. It's a 16-hour bus ride from Buenos Aires to Iguazú Falls and a 20-hour ride to Bariloche, and prices for the comfortable buses aren't cheap, either. Bus service is frequent and comprehensive, however, and an excellent choice for shorter distances.

Passports and Visas

Visitors from the United States, Canada, and the EU do not need visas, but they are issued 90-day tourist cards upon arrival. U.S. citizens, Australians, and Canadians must prepay a "reciprocity fee" (equivalent to the fee Argentines are charged for a travel visa to those countries) and show proof of payment upon arrival to either of Buenos Aires's airports (required also at entry points by land or sea). At the time of this writing, the fee was US$160 for U.S. citizens (valid for 10 years), US$100 for Australians (single entry), and US$75 for Canadians (single entry, or US$150 for 5 years, multiple entry), payable online at www.migraciones.gov.ar.

Money

The Argentine currency is the **peso** ($) and bills come in denominations of $2, $5, $10, $20, $50, and $100. It is identified by the $ symbol, the same as U.S. dollars (which are widely accepted in Buenos Aires). Credit cards are widely accepted, although there are businesses that only accept American Express, as well as businesses that charge a fee of up to 10 percent for payments made by credit card (on the other hand, there are hotels that offer discounts for payments in cash). Businesses sometimes require that you show your passport when using your credit card. There are limits on the amount of cash that can be withdrawn at ATMs, as well as withdrawal fees of around US$4, in addition to whatever your own bank might charge (check with your bank—some charge hefty fees, while others will refund the fee charged to you overseas).

It's possible to change travelers checks in Buenos Aires, but it can be challenging elsewhere. There is a bank at the Buenos Aires airport offering excellent exchange rates, and it can be convenient to change dollars to pesos upon arrival. At the time of this writing, the exchange rate was US$1 to AR$4.85.

Health

With Argentina's high-quality health care, potable tap water, and few tropical diseases, there is little to advise would-be travelers about health. Should you, however, run into a health problem, head to a private clinic or hospital if possible, as public hospitals tend to be strained to capacity.

Safety

Crime rates are less of an issue in Argentina compared to the rest of the region. As *porteños* (Buenos Aires residents) tend to keep late hours, the city is fairly safe, even at night. Travelers should just take the precautions that are wise anywhere: stay alert, avoid deserted streets at night, and don't flash valuables.

CHILE

Long and lean, Chile stretches down the Pacific coast to the southern tip of South America, with a width of just 177 kilometers (110 mi) but a length of 4,270 kilometers (2,653 mi). Chile shares a border with Peru at its northern tip, and its western edge is shared with Bolivia and Argentina. Visitors will find modern cities such as the capital, Santiago, and Valparaíso, the colorful seaside town where Nobel Prize-winning Chilean poet Pablo Neruda passed the final years of his life. Amenities and transportation are well developed, ideal for exploring the country's renowned natural beauty—the steep mountains and green valleys of the Patagonia region or the icy blue waters of the Lake District.

Chile's gross national income per capita is the highest in all of Latin America (US$12,280 in 2011, per World Bank). But this high income hides pockets of great need—15 percent of the country's population lives beneath the poverty line. Of special note is the government-funded and Chilean-based organization, VOFAIR. They work with a number of organizations around the country (as well as in other places across Latin America) that address issues such as community development and education, and charge a minimal fee for access to their volunteer placements.

While Chile has only a few local volunteer organizations, conservation and wildlife protection efforts can always use a helping hand. Volunteers can help restore natural habitats (planting seeds), develop national

© PIERRE-YVES BABELON/123RF

parks (build trails), or assist with the rehabilitation of illegally trafficked monkeys. Fortunately, there are many placement agencies and international organizations with volunteer programs in Chile (see listings in the *International Organizations* chapter).

Local Organizations

CENTRO DE RESCATE Y REHABILITACIÓN DE PRIMATES

Peñaflor, tel. 56/2-2812-1020, www.macacos.cl

TYPE OF WORK: wildlife protection

The Primate Rescue and Rehabilitation Center began its work in 1994, when the Almazán-Muñoz family received an eight-month-old monkey. Since then, the family-run center has received over 175 monkeys that have been rescued from illegal trafficking. Some of the monkeys have arrived injured and/or diseased, and others have had addictions to alcohol or drugs. The center works to rehabilitate the monkeys both physically and behaviorally, and, when possible, release them to monkey sanctuaries.

Volunteers work 8:30am-6pm Monday-Friday and 8:30am-noon Saturday. Responsibilities include preparing the monkeys' food, cleaning the monkey habitat and the grounds, helping out at the monkeys' fruit and vegetable patch, and constructing and repairing the structures on-site. Veterinary students can help with checkups, but it is important to note that other volunteers cannot work directly with the monkeys.

Peñaflor is located 40 kilometers (25 mi) south of Santiago. In their free time, volunteers can head to Santiago, to the beach (for horseback riding, swimming, and surfing), or to the mountains.

Application Process: Send an email. Volunteers must be 18 or older.

Cost: US$1,200 per month, including accommodations, meals, and transportation to and from the Santiago airport and the center. The fee also includes a donation to the project.

Placement Length: Minimum of two weeks.

Language Requirements: None.

Housing: Accommodations are homestays with the Almazán-Muñoz family, and volunteers usually share rooms. All homes have wireless Internet, washing machines, and dryers, and one of the homes has a swimming pool that volunteers can use. Meals are usually beef or chicken with rice or potatoes, fresh fruit, and vegetables; vegetarians can be accommodated without problem.

Operating Since: 1996; began accepting volunteers in 2007

Number of Volunteers: five in 2012

CONSERVACIÓN PATAGONICA

Chacabuco Valley, U.S. tel. 415/229-9339, www.conservacionpatagonica.org

TYPE OF WORK: environment

Founded by Kristine Thompson, the former longtime CEO of the clothing company Patagonia, Conservación Patagonica's (CP's) mission is to "create national parks in Patagonia that save and restore wildlands and wildlife, inspire care for the natural world, and generate healthy economic opportunities for local communities." CP is a well-organized and prestigious organization with a high-profile board and highly qualified group of scientific advisors.

The volunteer program runs November-April, and volunteers come for three-week stints, camping and backpacking in the field (away from showers, cell phone coverage, and Internet). The work is focused on trail building and ecosystem restoration, and tasks include digging up plants, moving rocks, and planting seeds. While the work can be monotonous and tiring, volunteers are rewarded with spectacular scenery of snowy mountains and grassy valleys, crystal blue lakes and lagoons, Chilean flamingos and herds of guanacos (cousins of the llama).

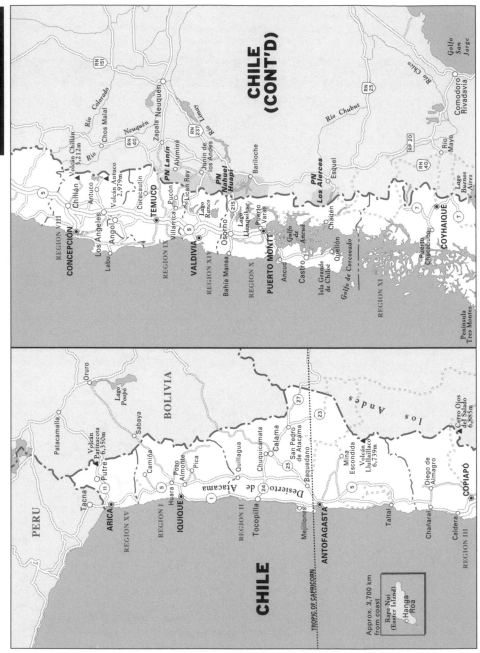

CHILE (CONT'D)

Golfo San Jorge

Río Chico

Comodoro Rivadavia

Río Chubut

RN 25

RP 20

Río Mayo

RN 40

Lago Buenos Aires

Esquel

PN Los Alerces

Chaitén

COYHAIQUE

7

Puerto Chacabuco

7

Puerto Cisnes

REGION XI

Peninsula Tres Montes

Golfo de Corcovado

Quellón

Isla Grande de Chiloé

Castro

Ancud

Golfo de Ancud

PUERTO MONTT

Puerto Varas

Lago Llanquihue

REGION X

Osorno

Lago Ranco

215

VALDIVIA

REGION XIV

Bahía Mansa

5

Lanco

Lican Ray

Villarrica

PN Nahuel Huapi

Bariloche

Junín de los Andes

RN 237

Aluminé

REGION IX

TEMUCO

Curacautín

Pucón

PN Lanín

Zapala Neuquén

Río Limay

RN 40

Neuquén

Chos Malal

Río Colorado

Volcán Antuco 2,979m

Antuco

Los Angeles

Angol

Lebu

CONCEPCIÓN

REGION VIII

5

Chillán

Volcán Chillán 3,212m

Río Malal

RN 151

PERU

Tacna

ARICA

REGION XV

Patacamaila

Volcán Parinacota 6,350m

Putre

11

Oruro

Lago Poopó

BOLIVIA

Sabaya

Camiña

Huara

5

Pozo Almonte

Pica

IQUIQUE

REGION I

Tocopilla

Mejillones

ANTOFAGASTA

REGION II

Quillagua

1

Desierto de Atacama

Baquedano

24

Chuquicamata

Calama

25

San Pedro de Atacama

27

23

Los Andes

Mina Escondida

Volcán Llullaillaco 6,739m

5

Diego de Almagro

Taltal

Chañaral

Caldera

COPIAPÓ

REGION III

Cerro Ojos del Salado 6,885m

CHILE

TROPIC OF CAPRICORN

Approx. 3,700 km from coast

Rapa Nui (Easter Island)

Hanga Roa

CHILE

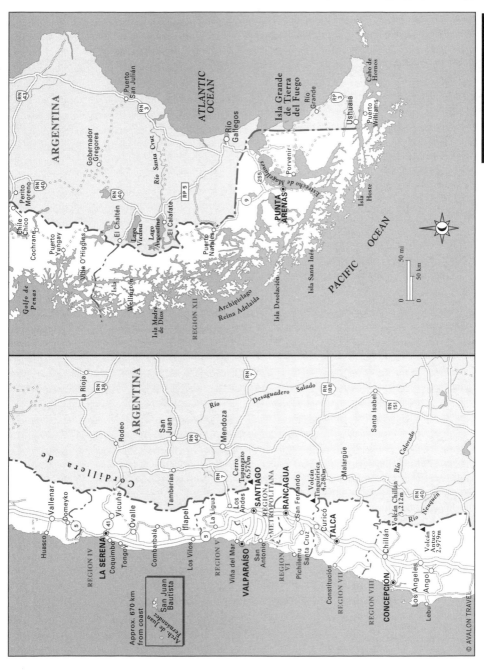

© AVALON TRAVEL

VOLUNTEER PERSPECTIVE

Brian Milton (age 58) is from the United Kingdom. He spent five weeks working at the **Centro de Rescate y Rehabilitación de Primates** (Peñaflor, tel. 56/2-2812-1020, www.macacos.cl).

I have worked for 24 years with monkeys in a sanctuary in the U.K., and I volunteered before with Primate Rescue and Rehabilitation Center for 10 weeks in 2002.

Volunteers should not expect to have direct contact with the monkeys; they will, however, get to know all about them, learn their histories, get to know their characters, etc. Volunteers typically collect and sort the monkeys' food, prepare their meals, and clean enclosures. Elba [the founder] will use any skills that volunteers bring – on this visit I spent a lot of time doing construction work.

Volunteers are extremely valuable there. The more that can be done by volunteers, the more the center can progress, as it enables Elba and her staff to move the center forward.

Elba's work is so important for many reasons. It is the only primate rescue center in Chile and where all rescued primates in that country end up. She works directly with the government there, which encourages them to enforce their laws properly and confiscate all monkeys found as pets, found in bad conditions, or smuggled into the country. She has a high profile in the Chilean media, which has led to a dramatic drop in monkeys trafficked into Chile. Her center is a good model for other South American countries, which, by following her example, could help stamp out the primate pet trade, which is so damaging to many species of monkeys, as well as their native forest homes. It is an extremely worthwhile project to anyone interested in primates or who cares about animals. The work Elba is doing is incredibly important for primates in Chile and South America in general.

Beyond enjoying the stunning surroundings, volunteers will have free time in the evenings and may want to bring a good book.
Application Process: Sometime before the beginning of the season (Nov.-Apr.), an application form is posted on CP's website. Slots fill up quickly, and volunteers should apply well in advance. Volunteers must be age 18 or older.
Cost: US$20 per day, including meals.
Placement Length: Three weeks.
Language Requirements: None.
Housing: Volunteers must bring their own tent, sleeping bag, and pad. Meals are provided by CP.
Operating Since: 2000
Number of Volunteers: 40-50 per season

SAVE THE WILD CHINCHILLAS
Illapel, www.wildchinchillas.org
TYPE OF WORK: environment, wildlife protection
Founded by resident expat Amy Deane, Save the Wild Chinchillas's mission is "to ensure that the endangered chinchillas and their ecosystem do not become extinct.... In order to meet this goal our objectives are to: educate people (of all ages) about conservation and sustainable living, collect funds to protect habitat, restore the degraded natural habitat of wild chinchillas [a rodent that looks something like a cross between a mouse and a squirrel], and promote studies that will carry this goal forward." Currently, the primary focus of their work is planting seeds in a plant nursery and

CHILE

© AMY DEANE

The endangered chinchillas of Chile feed on the flowers of the cardon plant.

transporting seedlings and planting them in the mountains. Save the Wild Chinchillas (SWC) also creates and distributes environmental educational materials and partners with the local community to develop support for local and global conservation.

Illapel is in northern Chile, half a day's travel by bus from the Santiago airport. It is a very small town (just three traffic lights). The work takes place in Aucó, 14 kilometers (9 mi) south of Illapel, outside of the National Chinchilla Reserve (volunteers need to get there on their own, but Amy will help explain how to hitchhike there). Volunteers can explore the reserve in their free time (there is a US$3 entry fee) and even stay the night in cabins there (US$15/night).

Application Process: Download their volunteer guide online, then apply by sending a short email to amy_deane@yahoo.com.
Cost: None. Volunteers are responsible for their own expenses.
Placement Length: No minimum.
Language Requirements: None.
Housing: There is a very small and simple wooden cabin in Aucó where volunteers can stay while working. It has a two-burner gas stove and a pit latrine. The only water is a stream outside, so volunteers may want to bring a water filter. They should also bring a sleeping bag.
Operating Since: 1996
Number of Volunteers: 25 in 2012

CHILE

INTERNATIONAL ORGANIZATIONS

The following international organizations support volunteer efforts in Chile:

A Broader View (U.S. tel. 215/780-1845, toll-free U.S. tel. 866/423-3258, www.abroaderview.org), page 193.
Type of Work: agriculture, children and youth, community development, education, environment, health, wildlife protection, women's empowerment

Earthwatch (U.S. tel. 978/461-0081, toll-free U.S. tel. 800/776-0188, www.earthwatch.org), page 196.
Type of Work: environment, wildlife protection

REI Adventures (toll-free U.S. tel. 800/622-2236, www.rei.com), page 208.
Type of Work: environment, wildlife protection

TECHO (U.S. tel. 305/860-4090, www.techo.org), page 209.
Type of Work: community development

VOFAIR (www.vofair.org), page 211.
Note that this organization is based in Santiago and has extensive listings for Chile.
Type of Work: agriculture, children and youth, community development, education, environment, health, wildlife protection, women's empowerment

Wanderland Travel (toll-free U.S. tel. 866/701-2113, www.wanderland.org), page 212.
Type of Work: agriculture, children and youth, community development, education, environment

Essentials

BACKGROUND
Geography and Climate
Despite a land area roughly twice that of the state of Montana, and a length that is equal to the distance between San Francisco and New York City, Chile's biodiversity has been limited by the geographic inaccessibility imposed by the Andean mountains, which run along its eastern border with Argentina. Mammals of note include the puma, or cougar, the llama-like guanaco, the small pudu deer, and the endangered chinchilla, which has been hunted nearly to extinction for its exceptionally soft fur.

Chile is home to a climate that varies from the world's driest (in the Atacamas desert), through moderate and subtropical, to glacial in the east and south. Seasons are fairly well defined, with summer December-February, fall March-May, winter June-August, and spring September-November. Rain in the capital of Santiago is heavily concentrated in the colder months of May-September, where daytime highs average around 15°C (60°F), even during the winter.

History and Economy
The original inhabitants of central and southern Chile are the Mapuche, an indigenous people whose members make up less than 5 percent of Chile's 17 million people. Roughly half of Chileans are of European descent, most commonly mixed, whose ancestors hail from Spain, Italy, Ireland, France, Greece, Germany, England, Scotland, Croatia, and Palestine. The rest of Chile's population are virtually all *mestizo,* or of mixed European and indigenous heritage. Like its neighbors, Chile was a Spanish colony, which proclaimed independence on September 18, 1810. Modern history has seen both highs, such as the election of its first female president, Michele Bachelet, in 2006, and lows, such as the brutally repressive tactics of the dictator Augusto Pinochet,

whose iron fist ruled the country from 1973 until 1990.

Chile's economy owes its strength in part to a stable financial sector, as well as to booming prices in copper in recent years. Wine, as you may know, is another of Chile's renowned exports—others include forestry and wood products, fresh fruit and processed food, and fish meal and seafood. Tourism is an ever-growing sector of the economy, with an estimated two million visitors arriving per year.

PREPARATION
Transportation
Given the central location of Chile's capital city, most travelers will arrive and depart from Santiago's **Arturo Merino Benítez International Airport** (SCL, www.aeropuertosantiago.cl), which is serviced by Air Canada, American Airlines, Delta, and United, as well as many regional and European airlines. Given the thousands of miles between Santiago and cities such as Arica in the north and Punta Arenas in the south (not to mention most other capitals in South America), long-distance travelers will want to skip the torturously long bus rides and take a flight to their final destination. From North America, Air Canada offers flights from Toronto, American from Dallas and New York, Delta from Atlanta, and Lan (Chile's excellent national carrier) from Los Angeles.

Intercity buses are usually both comfortable and punctual. Prices can vary significantly between companies, so be sure to shop around. Several even have websites with routes, timetables, and the possibility of purchasing tickets online, such as www.turbus.cl and www.pullman.cl. The company **Pachamama by Bus** (www.pachamamabybus.com) gears itself toward backpackers and offers routes to national parks and other points of interest.

Passports and Visas
While visas are not needed for most nationalities, Chile does charge a US$140 "reciprocity fee" to those arriving from the United States (US$132 for Canadians; US$95 for Australians), as a response to fees Chilean citizens must pay to apply for a visa. This is only charged to visitors arriving by air to Santiago and is valid for the life of the passport (payable in cash or by credit card). The latest information is available (in English) on the Santiago airport's website, www.aeropuertosantiago.cl.

Visitors will receive a tourist card at customs; keep it handy, as you can save yourself the 18 percent sales tax on hotels by brandishing it and paying in U.S. dollars.

Upon leaving Chile, visitors must pay a US$18 departure tax at the airport.

Money
The national currency of Chile is the **peso** ($), whose notes come in denominations $500, $1,000, $2,000, $5,000, $10,000, and $20,000. The latter two bills can be difficult to change, especially in small villages. Big cities and smaller tourist towns have international ATMs, which are much easier to use than travelers checks. Changing a few dollars into pesos is possible right at the airport upon arrival.

Health
Health care in Chile is of high quality, and no vaccines are required to visit—but some may be recommended, so check with your local travel clinic to see which ones.

Safety
Chile has one of the lowest violent crime rates in South America, but there is still plenty of pickpocketing and some mugging in the cities. Avoid flashing valuables and keep your wits about you when wandering the city streets.

INTERNATIONAL ORGANIZATIONS

International organizations are a widely diverse group, but all have volunteer programs in more than one country. Many have a depth of experience gained from years of working with thousands of volunteers in multiple countries. Others may be new or small, or both, with programs in two or more countries.

International organizations reflect a variety of arrangements—some are nonprofit, others are private companies, some are grassroots, others are corporately organized. Most (but certainly not all) have larger fees than local organizations and often cover more amenities, such as nicer accommodations, cultural activities and excursions, and a meet and greet at the airport.

Some International organizations, such as ACDI/VOCA and Global Communities: Partners for Good, are geared toward experienced professionals with valuable skills to share. They have no fees at all and actually pay expenses for the volunteer. Their opportunities require very specific skills sets (five or more years of professional experience in areas such as agriculture or women's empowerment). A few others, such as Biosphere Expeditions and Operation Wallacea, offer scuba diving as part of the volunteer experience. TECHO and VOFAIR are unique in that they originate from Chile, rather than from the United States or the United Kingdom.

Whether you choose to volunteer with an international organization or through a local one in a single location, be sure to examine the organization's philosophy to see if it is a good fit for your beliefs and expectations. What are

their goals and ideals? Who is behind the organization? Why do they send people abroad?

What these organizations all have in common is a serious commitment to delivering volunteer experiences that are not only effective, but also a heck of a lot of fun.

A BROADER VIEW

Elkins Park, PA, U.S. tel. 215/780-1845, toll-free U.S. tel. 866/423-3258, www.abroaderview.org
TYPE OF WORK: agriculture, children and youth, community development, education, environment, health, wildlife protection, women's empowerment
LOCATIONS: Belize, Chile, Colombia, Costa Rica, Ecuador, Guatemala, Honduras, Nicaragua, Peru

A Broader View (ABV) is a U.S.-based nonprofit organization founded by a Chilean American couple who had taken their own volunteer vacation in Chile and saw a need for an "affordable, safe and worthy" volunteer program.

ABV offers a large number of programs— from supporting children in orphanages to more unusual experiences like spending a month in Ecuador in a rural indigenous village. There are programs in HIV/AIDS awareness in Honduras, a home for elderly women in Guatemala, day care services for single mothers in Colombia, English lessons in Chile, therapy assistance for children and adults with special needs in Nicaragua, and a wild animal rehabilitation center in Peru, just to name a few. Medical programs are also available for medical professionals and medical and nursing students.

Upon arrival, volunteers will receive a four-hour Spanish-language refresher. Some locations have language immersion programs available, in which volunteers spend 20 hours per week studying Spanish and 20 hours per week volunteering. Volunteers normally work five days a week, eight hours per day. Cultural activities and excursions are arranged on the weekends and are included in the fee.

Note: A Broader View should not be confused with Abroad Reviews (www.abroad-reviews.com), which is a review website for volunteer programs.

Application Process: An application form is available online. Applicants must provide a personal reference and must disclose any criminal history. Email the completed application with your résumé and a copy of your passport. Individual volunteers must be age 17 or older. Families with children age 12 or older are welcome.
Cost: US$795-995 for one week; US$905-1,275 for two weeks, except in the Galapagos (US$1,695).
Placement Length: There is a minimum placement of one week for most programs and a two-week minimum for programs in Costa Rica and the Galapagos Islands.
Language Requirements: Varies by project. Basic conversational Spanish is required for most placements; proficient Spanish is required for medical placements. Spanish is not required for language immersion programs.
Housing: Most volunteers are placed with host families; a few locations offer a volunteer guesthouse. All meals are included.
Operating Since: 2007
Number of Volunteers: 1,215 in 2012, plus university groups totaling another 175 students

ACDI/VOCA

Washington DC, U.S. tel. 202/469-6000, www.acdivoca.org
TYPE OF WORK: agriculture, children and youth, community development, education, environment, health, wildlife protection, women's empowerment
LOCATIONS: Varies.

The Agricultural Cooperative Development International (ACDI; founded in 1963) and Volunteers in Overseas Cooperative Assistance (VOCA; founded in 1970) are two U.S.-based development organizations that merged in 1997. Their mission is to "promote economic opportunities for cooperatives, enterprises and communities through the innovative application of sound business practice." They work in some of the poorest countries around the globe, utilizing a combination of consultants and volunteers to provide development projects with business and technical advice with a humanitarian slant. Mid- to late-career professionals

INTERNATIONAL

volunteer their time to consult on projects in the areas of agriculture, climate change, community development, economic growth, women's empowerment, and more. Available opportunities are constantly changing; check the current database of volunteer and consultant positions online at www.acdivoca.org.

Application Process: Volunteers must register online and submit a résumé to apply. While there is no specific minimum age, volunteers should normally have 10 or more years of relevant experience.

Cost: None. ACDI/VOCA pays for all assignment-related expenses, including airfare (round-trip in coach), passports, visas, lodging, meals and incidentals, immunizations, and supplemental health insurance, and even covers the cost of emergency medical evacuation if required.

Placement Length: 2-4 weeks

Language Requirements: None. Interpreters are provided if needed.

Housing: Varies by project. In urban areas, volunteers are usually housed in hotels, guesthouses, or apartments leased by the project. In rural areas, volunteers may stay with the host or in more rustic settings. All meals are included.

Operating Since: 1997

Number of Volunteers: more than 10,000 volunteers since 1971

AMIZADE GLOBAL SERVICE LEARNING

Pittsburgh, PA, U.S. tel. 412/586-4986, www.amizade.org

TYPE OF WORK: agriculture, children and youth, community development, education, environment, health

LOCATIONS: Bolivia, Brazil, Mexico, Nicaragua

Amizade is a U.S.-based nonprofit whose mission is to "empower individuals and communities through worldwide service and learning." They follow a Fair Trade Learning model of volunteering, which includes community-driven development projects; fair compensation for in-country guides, drivers, homestay families, cooks, and community organizations;

and free or subsidized opportunities for overseas communities to engage in service-learning programs in the United States. As is fitting for an organization whose name means "friendship" in Portuguese, Amizade also emphasizes intercultural exchange.

Amizade works with many groups, in particular university groups, and offers alternative spring break trips. Other trips are organized in conjunction with Road Scholar (www.roadscholar.com), an organization particularly welcoming of senior travelers. In 2013, Amizade offered eight open group trips in Latin America; open group trips are perfect for individual travelers who enjoy the camaraderie of traveling and working with others. In addition to more typical volunteer trips, Amizade offers service-learning courses, which have both an online class component (through a partnership with West Virginia University) and a service trip of a week to one month. Service learning courses are open to students in good standing at any college or university, and some financial aid is available. Individual volunteer placements are also available.

Amizade works in specific communities in each country: Santarem in Brazil; in and around Cochabamba in Bolivia; the Yucatan in Mexico; and San Ramón in Nicaragua. Volunteer work might include caring for children at an orphanage in the mountain highlands of Peru, harvesting coffee at a cooperative in Nicaragua, or rehabilitating a beach in Mexico. Teaching English, working with the elderly, reaching out to at-risk youth, and providing health care to marginalized communities are other popular options. Doctors and dentists working with Amizade in Brazil receive a discounted rate on fees. Free time varies by location and might include cultural events and sightseeing trips to colonial cities, golden beaches, Mayan or Incan ruins, local markets, or natural wonders (such as the Bolivian salt flats).

Application Process: An application form is available online. All volunteers must agree to a background check at their own expense. There is no minimum age, and families are welcome.

Cost: Group trips are US$942-1,288 for one week and US$1,215-2,247 for two weeks. Individual placements cost approximately US$1,450 for two weeks and US$350-400 for each additional week. Housing, local transportation, airport pickup and drop-off, travel insurance, and multiple cultural and sightseeing activities are included.

Placement Length: There is a minimum placement of one week.

Language Requirements: Varies by placement; however, there are some programs with no language requirement.

Housing: Accommodations vary by location. Most programs have guesthouses, while homestays are possible in others. A couple of sites offer basic dorms. Meals are included.

Operating Since: 1994

Number of Volunteers: 552 volunteers in 2012

BIOSPHERE EXPEDITIONS

Longwood, FL, toll-free U.S. tel. 800/407-5761,
www.biosphere-expeditions.org

TYPE OF WORK: environment, wildlife protection

LOCATIONS: Honduras, Peru

Biosphere Expeditions organizes expeditions with authentic biological conservation content with the hope of making a "small but significant to our biosphere and at the same time bring enjoyment and fulfillment to our environment volunteer teams."

In Honduras, Biosphere Expeditions works with the Honduras Coral Reef Fund in Cayos Cochinos, a small archipelago off Honduras's northern coast, to offer diving trips where volunteers record the types of fish, invertebrates, and substrates. Volunteers have some free time between dives, and lectures are organized for the evenings. There are limited slots, and volunteers should sign up well in advance, although a wait list is maintained if the trip is full. Participants must have a PADI Open Water diving certificate (or equivalent) and should bring their own gear and wet suit. Equipment such as BCD, regulator, and weight belts can be rented at the research station dive center, and a few shorty wet suits are available for hire.

In Peru, volunteers head to the Amazon jungle outside of Iquitos, where they will work together with local biologists on a wildlife survey concentrating on cats, primates, and other important species, to aid community conservation efforts and the development of sustainable management strategies. Volunteers travel by foot and canoe on natural waterways through the jungle, recording species, setting camera traps, creating databases, and more, as part of the wildlife volunteer conservation project.

Biosphere Expeditions offers trips to various destinations around the world and has won awards and accolades for its trips, including "Best Volunteering Organisation" by the U.K.-based First Choice Responsible Tourism Awards.

Application Process: Application is online; passport number and a £300 (US$460) deposit is required. All ages are welcome.

Cost: approximately US$2,030 for Honduras; US$1,780 for Peru.

Placement Length: Two one-week trips per year, in consecutive weeks in May for Honduras, August for Peru.

Language Requirements: Spanish is not required, as the expedition and research are conducted in English.

Housing: Accommodations are in shared wooden cabins in Honduras, and a jungle lodge in Peru, and include all meals and research/park fees.

Operating Since: 1999

Number of Volunteers: about 500 around the world each year

CROSS-CULTURAL SOLUTIONS (CCS)

New Rochelle, NY (with offices also in Canada, the U.K., and Australia), toll-free U.S. tel. 800/380-4777,
www.crossculturalsolutions.org

TYPE OF WORK: children and youth, community development, education, health, women's empowerment

LOCATIONS: Brazil, Costa Rica, Guatemala, Peru

The mission of Cross-Cultural Solutions is to "to operate volunteer programs around the world in partnership with sustainable community initiatives, bringing people together to work side-by-side while sharing perspectives and fostering cultural understanding." CCS is one of the largest volunteer placement organizations in the field. It got that way by providing positive experiences with carefully selected volunteer opportunities that have been developed with local communities and have long-term sustainability. It is worth noting that all of CCS's in-country staff, including the coordinator resident at each volunteer guesthouse, are local.

CCS focuses on six main areas of work: improving children's education; assisting with the care of infants and children in orphanages or day cares; supporting the elderly with programs that include games, music, and physical activities; working with people with disabilities; supporting people with HIV/AIDS either directly or with the services of health; and working with physicians, administrators, support staff, patients, or families within the community. In Salvador, Brazil, volunteers support people living in favelas, or shantytowns. In Costa Rica, volunteers are placed in Cartago, a small colonial city that was the country's capital for more than 300 years. CCS's program in Guatemala is one of the few in the capital of Guatemala City, where need is great and volunteers few. In Lima, Peru, most volunteers work in Villa El Salvador, the shantytown that was a Nobel Peace Prize nominee for its community organization.

Exact programs may change from year to year. CCS can also find a different type of placement through their partner organizations on the ground—from microfinance to women's empowerment to utilizing specialized volunteer skills. CCS offers a variety of cultural activities in every location: city tours and excursions, Spanish (or Portuguese) lessons, cooking classes, visiting cacao farms or coffee plantations, horseback-riding, hiking, and salsa or samba dancing. Volunteers in Brazil and Costa Rica may also choose to spend their free time with nonprofits that work with sea turtle conservation.

Application Process: An application form is available online. and a US$275 deposit is required to reserve a spot. Individual volunteers must be age 18 or older; there is a special Teen Volunteer program for youth ages 15-17. Families with children age eight and older are welcome; approval must be obtained for families with children under age eight.

Cost: US$2,480 for one week up to US$4,244 for four weeks. Living expenses, ground transportation, cultural activities and in-country excursions, medical insurance, and language lessons are included. There are discounts for children, families, groups, CCS alumni, and enrollment in multiple programs. Program fees are tax-deductible for U.S. residents, and airfare may be tax-deductible as well.

Placement Length: Placement ranges 1-12 weeks. Fixed travel dates throughout the year are set well in advance, and some destinations have more travel dates than others.

Language Requirements: None.

Housing: Volunteers stay in guesthouses with communal living spaces. Most bedrooms are shared occupancy with 4-6 bunks, but double- or single-occupancy rooms may be available for an additional fee. All meals at the guesthouse are included. Meals outside the guesthouse are at the volunteer's expense.

Operating Since: 1995

Number of Volunteers: 2,400 volunteers in 2012

EARTHWATCH

Boston, MA, U.S. tel. 978/461-0081,
toll-free U.S. tel. 800/776-0188, www.earthwatch.org

TYPE OF WORK: environment, wildlife protection

LOCATIONS: Belize, Brazil, Chile, Costa Rica, Ecuador, Nicaragua, Peru

Earthwatch is a not-for-profit organization that seeks to achieve a sustainable environment. Their multipronged approach focuses on engaging people in scientific field research around the world, using research to inform policy and management of the environment, and engaging people in that research "to create understanding of environmental problems to inspire positive environmental action at home, at work, and in the community." Earthwatch also engages the local community with a capacity building program for scientists in developing countries.

Volunteer opportunities are organized in one- to two-week expeditions and typically include 6-10 participants. Trips are led by research scientists (usually employed by "major academic institutions, conservation groups, or other organizations with research missions"), and volunteers will join in undertaking field research to better understand and seek solutions for an environmental problem. Volunteer responsibilities vary widely and may include recording wildlife census and behavior, performing botanical identification, working with sea turtles, or assisting with archaeological findings. Volunteers are provided with both equipment and training to effectively conduct research. Expeditions require varying levels of physical fitness; check online to review offerings by fitness preference as well as location.

Expeditions vary from year to year: In 2013 there were 17 trips scheduled in Latin America, with another 6 in the Caribbean. A brief sample includes:

- investigating ancient agricultural practices and restoring the native forest on the Easter Island of Chile

- surveying bird and mammal species or studying caterpillars and climate change in the Ecuadorian Andes

- monitoring the movements of jaguar, puma, maned wolf, tapir, and giant anteater along the Araguaia River corridor in Brazil

- conducting research on conditions on coffee farms in Costa Rica

- observing dolphins, fish, river turtles, macaws, peccaries, tapirs, deer, monkeys, game birds, and caimans from a riverboat in the Peruvian Amazon

- evaluating volcanic activity on the surrounding plant, animal, and human communities in Nicaragua

- researching the famed Darwin's finches of the Galapagos Islands

A ROOM FOR YOUR LABOR

This guide focuses on organizations implementing worthwhile development or humanitarian projects. There are, however, additional opportunities for those simply seeking a free or low-cost roof over their head during their travels. **World Wide Opportunities on Organic Farms** (www.wwoof.org), or WWOOF, is a well-known network of organic farms that accept volunteers in exchange for labor on the farm. There are also hostels that use volunteers to help manage the front desk and hotel in exchange for room and board. If partnering with people and places in a developing country is a goal for your vacation, look carefully at how the farm or hostel is interacting with the local community before signing on. There are some, included in this guide, that have made an enormous commitment to the local community, providing services such as training in organic farming and permaculture or running programs for local children. Others may benefit only the farm or hostel owner at the same time that your volunteer efforts take a job away from a local, so choose carefully.

Expeditions are meant to be culturally immersive as well as educational. Free time activities vary by location but might include anything from shopping in the nearest town to hiking to enjoying a boat trip. However, not all optional activities or excursions are included in the program fee.

Application Process: To apply, call 978/461-0081 or 800/776-0188, or send an email for information. Volunteer advisors will provide details and help identify a suitable project. Individual volunteers must be age 18 or older. Teens (ages 15-17) may participate on a regular expedition if accompanied by a parent or guardian, or they can participate on a Teen Team, expeditions exclusively for 15- to 18-year olds.

INTERNATIONAL

Cost: US$1,875-4,525 (for 2013-2014 expeditions). Expedition prices vary by trip duration, local costs, and required equipment for research. Medical insurance and carbon offsetting are included in the program fee, as are housing and local transportation. Volunteers can establish an Expedition Fund with Earthwatch, where friends and family can make tax-deductible contributions to the volunteer trip. Occasionally, the minimum contribution is reduced in order to fill the trip.

Placement Length: 7-15 days

Language Requirements: None.

Housing: Accommodations are included in the program fee but vary widely by location. Volunteers should expect to travel, eat, and sleep like research scientists. Sleeping arrangements may be in hotels, live-aboard boats, wildlife lodges, student dormitories, field stations, or tents in a rainforest. Hot and/or running water and electricity may not be available. Meals are included, and special diets can often be accommodated.

Operating Since: 1971

Number of Volunteers: approximately 3,000 volunteers annually

EASTERN PACIFIC HAWKSBILL INITIATIVE (ICAPO)

San Diego, CA, U.S. tel. 619/818-0041, www.hawksbill.org

TYPE OF WORK: education, environment, wildlife protection

LOCATIONS: El Salvador, Nicaragua

The Eastern Pacific Hawksbill Initiative (ICAPO are the Spanish initials) is a project made up of more than 50 individuals and organizations in every country on the Pacific coast of the Americas—from the United States to Peru. Their aim is to "promote recovery of hawksbill turtles in the eastern Pacific." Of all sea turtles, the hawksbill is one of the most endangered on the planet. ICAPO has been instrumental in identifying its natural habitat and nesting grounds, as well as supporting its conservation.

Volunteers will: patrol beaches to encounter,

© DAVID MELERO

ICAPO helps conserve a critically endangered species, the hawksbill turtle, and sustains the well-being of local people in small communities in Nicaragua and El Salvador.

measure, and tag nesting hawksbill turtles; collect eggs for relocation to project hatcheries; monitor project hatcheries; patrol estuaries by boat to document hawksbill nesting; maintain station houses (sweeping, tidying, or washing dishes); and maintain the turtle hatchery and patrol structure. ICAPO proactively engages the local community in the turtle monitoring program, utilizing ex-poachers to help find turtle nests, and with community outreach. Volunteers can become involved with the community by teaching English, supporting environmental education and art programs, or participating in local tours. The volunteer program at ICAPO was initiated in 2012, but the team has been working with international volunteer programs across Latin America, all linked to sea turtle conservation projects, since 2001.

ICAPO also organizes day trips into the surrounding protected areas. Volunteers may spend their day off on affordable local tours (trekking, fishing, dining, dancing, horseback riding), available at both project sites, as well as at language exchange sessions with local staff.
Application Process: An application form is available online. Volunteers must be age 18 or older.
Cost: US$280 for one week, US$525 for two weeks, US$750 for three weeks, US$950 for four weeks, and US$200 for each additional week. Housing is included.
Placement Length: There is a minimum placement of one week. The volunteer program runs mid-April-mid-September.
Language Requirements: None.
Housing: Volunteers stay in cabins or a dorm. Living conditions are simple, but there is electricity and cold running water. Three meals are provided daily.
Operating Since: 2008; volunteer program initiated in 2012
Number of Volunteers: 17 in 2012

ELEVATE DESTINATIONS

Cambridge, MA, U.S. tel. 617/661-0203,
www.elevatedestinations.com
TYPE OF WORK: children and youth, community

development, education, environment, wildlife protection
LOCATIONS: Belize, Costa Rica, Honduras, Mexico, Peru

Elevate Destinations is a high-end adventure-travel operator that seeks to "go beyond sustainable tourism to what we call transformative travel." Trips benefit local communities and conservation efforts: 5 percent of the net costs of each trip go to nonprofit partners in the destinations visited, and carbon offsetting is provided for each trip.

Elevate Destinations offers many trips with a volunteer or service component, and volunteer components can be added to any trip. Suggested itineraries are available online. They will also customize or create trips to suit the preferences and priorities of individuals, families, and groups.

In 2013, Elevate Destinations offered service trips to:

• Peru, where volunteers could teach everything from English to surfing

• the Andean mountains, to support a boarding school for marginalized children or provide labor for infrastructure improvements

• a combination Amazon/Andes trip, where volunteers spend a couple of days at an animal shelter

• Magdalena Bay in Baja California, Mexico, where volunteers spend three days of a seven-day trip monitoring sea turtles

Application Process: An application form is available online. There is no age limit, and families are welcome.
Cost: Varies by trip. The aforementioned trips range US$2,500-4,000 for 7-10 days.
Placement Length: Most trips are 7-14 days, but travelers may choose the length of their trip. Volunteer placement ranges from half a day through the entire trip.
Language Requirements: None, although Spanish skills are always helpful.
Housing: Accommodations are specific to each itinerary and can range from campsites to a volunteer house to a top hacienda or ecolodge.

Meals vary by trip and traveler preference, and may include breakfast only or all meals.

Operating Since: 2005

Number of Volunteers: Elevate Destinations worked with approximately 130 travelers in 2012, about half of whom had a volunteer component on their trip (these figures exclude the trips organized for non-profit donors and for travel to Haiti).

GLOBAL COMMUNITIES: PARTNERS FOR GOOD

Silver Spring, MD, U.S. tel. 301/587-4700, www.globalcommunities.org

TYPE OF WORK: children and youth, community development, education, environment, women's empowerment

LOCATIONS: Colombia, Honduras, Mexico, Nicaragua, Peru

Global Communities: Partners for Good (formerly Foundation for Cooperative Housing, CHF International) has undergone a name change in order to better reflect its mission, which is no longer limited to housing but to be "a catalyst for long-lasting positive change in low- and moderate-income communities around the world." Global Communities is a highly regarded development organization with offices in 20 countries around the globe. The organization has projects in community and economic development, construction and infrastructure, microenterprise development, global health, nongovernmental organization capacity building, urban and municipal development, and local governance.

The Visiting International Professionals (VIP) Program was started in 1998, seeking to connect experienced professionals with development projects. Volunteers should have at least five years of experience in their area of expertise. (Areas of expertise may include information technology, youth outreach, public health, construction, and microfinance.) Past volunteers have included a former congresswoman, bank officers, private sector corporate executives, academic researchers, and graduate students. Volunteer expertise must be in alignment with a need that cannot be filled on-site, thus assignments are infrequent and require significant lead time.

Application Process: To apply, email your résumé to the VIP coordinator, who maintains a database of candidates. The coordinator then contacts candidates to discuss availability and check references when an opportunity arises.

Cost: None. Global Communities normally covers all assignment-related expenses, including round-trip airfare, visa fees, in-country transportation relating to the assignment, housing, meals, and incidentals.

Placement Length: Placement typically lasts three weeks.

Language Requirements: Spanish is required.

Housing: Accommodations are included and range from local economy hotels, hostels, and apartments to in-staff housing if available. Volunteers usually receive a small per diem toward meals and incidentals.

Operating Since: 1952

Number of Volunteers: two in 2012

GLOBAL VOLUNTEERS

St. Paul, MN, toll-free U.S. tel. 800/487-1074, www.globalvolunteers.org

TYPE OF WORK: children and youth, community development, education

LOCATIONS: Costa Rica, Ecuador, Mexico, Peru

The goal of Global Volunteers is to provide 12 essential services to partner communities worldwide: school and household gardens; child nutrition; micronutrient supplementation; improved stoves; health, nutrition, and hygiene education; malaria prevention; deworming; HIV/AIDS education; general education; the promotion of girls' education; potable water and sanitation facilities; and psychosocial support.

Global Volunteers organizes its programs as service trips in more than 100 host communities worldwide. This can be an advantage for solo travelers who enjoy traveling as a group, or a disadvantage if you would prefer to travel alone. Trips are generally friendly for families and seniors, and there are several trips that are exclusively for gays and lesbians. In all locations, volunteers are expected to work 40 hours per week.

While volunteers work on a short-term basis, they support long-term projects:

- In Costa Rica, volunteers work on community development projects such as renovating buildings, landscaping public spaces, painting classrooms, and improving ecotourism. Global Volunteers considers Costa Rica a particularly family-friendly destination.

- In Ecuador, volunteers work at a cooperative day care in Quito that supports children with working mothers. Volunteers may assist with child care, teach English, or engage in construction (continuing work on a new child care facility) and physical labor such as landscaping, painting, and masonry.

- In Mexico, Global Volunteers sends volunteers to the towns of Dolores Hidalgo and Queretaro to teach conversational English to college students (either individually or in small groups) for a few hours each day; no teaching experience is required.

- In Peru, Global Volunteers works with three partner organizations: a large children's home that serves 600 children, a 300-person boys' home, and a language center that provides English training for students and community members in agricultural and forestry studies. Volunteers may be involved in labor and construction, child care, tutoring, or teaching English.

Global Volunteers does not organize free-time activities for its volunteers, but team leaders are happy to recommend fun things to do. Depending on the location, volunteers may spend their free time exploring colonial centers or enjoying the beach.

Application Process: An application form is available online. Applications must be submitted at least 75 days prior to departure, and a nonrefundable US$350 deposit is required. Applications received less than 75 days prior to departure must include payment in full and a US$35 late fee. Minimum age requirements for families vary.

Cost: US$2,295-2,595 for one- to two-week trips. Global Volunteers is a 501(c)3 organization, and fees are tax-deductible.

Placement Length: 12 weeks

Language Requirements: None.

Housing: Accommodations are in shared rooms in simple hotels. Single rooms are available for an extra fee. All meals are included, although strict vegetarians should be prepared to supplement their diet.

Operating Since: 1984

Number of Volunteers: approximately 300 service-learning teams annually

GLOBAL VOLUNTEERS INTERNATIONAL

Boston, MA, toll-free U.S. tel. 888/653-6028, www.gviusa.com

TYPE OF WORK: children and youth, community development, education, environment, health, wildlife protection

LOCATIONS: Costa Rica, Mexico

For Global Volunteers International, the goal is to "provide support and services to international charities, non-profits and governmental agencies, through volunteering opportunities, internship programs, training and direct funding." Global Volunteers International focuses on the areas of environmental research, conservation, education, and community development, and they seek to create sustainable projects that result in long-term positive results. Unlike many of the large volunteer agencies that work with local partners, Global Volunteers International operates its own programs on the ground, but they work alongside prominent environmental and development organizations such as the Ministry of Education in Costa Rica and the U.K.-based nonprofit Rainforest Concern. In 2011, Virgin Holidays Responsible Tourism Awards named Global Volunteers International "Best Volunteering Organization"; 70 percent of all their funds go directly to projects.

Destinations and activities can vary. In 2013, trips to Costa Rica included volunteer opportunities working at a community center, teaching English and environmental education, leading art workshops and sports activities, tracking jaguars, monitoring birds, protecting sea turtles, and working on various construction projects. Most of the work is centered in or around the coastal town of Quepos, and volunteers have plenty of time to explore nearby Manuel Antonio National Park. Trips to Mexico were available in or near Playa del Carmen, on the Yucatan peninsula. Volunteers provide horse therapy to children with special needs or can earn a PADI diving certificate while conducting surveys of fish and coral along the barrier reef. Free time may be spent on the beach, swimming and snorkeling, or exploring nearby Mayan villages and ruins. Spanish lessons are available (for a fee) in both countries.

Application Process: An application form is available online, and it is possible to apply as little as two weeks prior to travel. The application is followed up by a phone call from Global Volunteers International, then a deposit from the volunteer. Volunteers must be age 18 or older, though trips for high school students can be organized through Global Volunteers International Foundations. Older volunteers are welcomed.

Cost: Varies by project. There are one-week projects from US$1,182 and four-week projects for US$1,947-3,052.

Placement Length: There is a minimum placement of one week, which varies by project.

Language Requirements: None.

Housing: Accommodations vary and include a volunteer house, huts on the beach, or a base camp in the jungle. Meals are included.

Operating Since: 1997

Number of Volunteers: approximately 1,500 in 2012

HABITAT FOR HUMANITY INTERNATIONAL

Americus, GA, toll-free U.S. tel. 800/HABITAT (800/422-4828), www.habitat.org
TYPE OF WORK: community development
LOCATIONS: Argentina, Bolivia, Costa Rica, Dominican Republic, El Salvador, Guatemala, Honduras, Nicaragua, Paraguay

Habitat for Humanity International is a nonprofit, nondenominational Christian housing ministry. Founded in 1976, Habitat for Humanity is a highly regarded organization with a massive outreach serving more than three million people worldwide. They have inspired several similar organizations around the globe and continue to be the global leader in providing housing to people in need. Their vision is simple: "That everyone has a decent place to live." They achieve this through work camps that build houses shoulder to shoulder with the beneficiaries (recipients invest "sweat equity" along with a financial commitment). The houses are sold at no profit to the beneficiary, who receives a low-interest loan for the mortgage.

Short-term volunteer opportunities are organized through the Global Village program, with one- to two-week trips to build sites around the world. Trip locations vary from year to year, and new trips are continually being organized. Volunteer responsibilities are related to construction—digging foundation trenches, sawing rebar, mixing and pouring cement, and laying bricks. Habitat for Humanity trips usually include a little free time for local sightseeing and a cultural activity. Those wishing to explore more can extend their in-country stay for a few days.

Alternatively, consider organizing your own trip with a group from your school, university, church, or other community group. All international trips take around six months to organize and must be led by Habitat for Humanity-certified group leaders. Volunteers can contact local offices directly. If you are already in the destination country, you may be able to organize or participate in a national brigade, to which different rules apply.

Application Process: An application form is available online. To apply, you will need contact information for your primary doctor and an emergency contact, the date of your last tetanus shot, and insurance information. The process is selective and is not on a first-come, first-served basis. Volunteers must be age 16 or older (or age 18 if required by the host country).

© AMY E. ROBERTSON

Volunteers, including the author, mix concrete at a Habitat for Humanity build.

INTERNATIONAL

Cost: US$1,450-1,900, depending on the destination and length of the build. Fees cover a donation to Habitat for Humanity, team coordination (such as on-the-ground coordination, translators, and team leader expenses), medical insurance, accommodations, meals, local transportation, and some local cultural activities.

Placement Length: 8-14 days

Language Requirements: None.

Housing: Accommodations are usually shared rooms in simple hotels or retreat centers. Meals are provided.

Operating Since: 1976

Number of Volunteers: 421 brigades in 2012

INTERNATIONAL VOLUNTEER HQ (IHVQ)

New Plymouth, New Zealand, N.Z. tel. 64/6758-7949, toll-free U.S. tel. 877/342-6588, www.volunteerhq.org

TYPE OF WORK: agriculture, children and youth, community development, education, environment, health, wildlife protection

LOCATIONS: Argentina, Brazil, Colombia, Costa Rica, Ecuador, El Salvador, Guatemala, Mexico, Peru

IVHQ's mission is to provide volunteer travelers with "quality, flexible, safe and highly affordable volunteering placements in developing countries" while ensuring the host communities benefit from volunteer skills, time, and expertise. Among the program goals are assistance to local communities and organizations, heightened awareness of issues in developing countries through firsthand experiences, and mutual learning between local communities and volunteers.

IVHQ works with locally based partner organizations in each country, believing that there is no one who will better know the needs of a community than its local population. IVHQ has a careful selection process for its partner organizations, ensuring that they offer effective volunteer opportunities, as well as adequate accommodations and services.

Responsibilities and work hours are tailored to the interests and expectations of the volunteer. Each locally based volunteer organization partners with local tourism companies to help organize activities and sightseeing excursions. This combination of personalization with a low price has paid off for IVHQ—former volunteers rave about their experiences.

- In Colombia, volunteers choose between working in Bogotá or a suburb. Work includes teaching English, caring for children or the elderly, feeding the homeless, and working on construction and renovation.

- In Costa Rica, volunteers might be involved with turtle or ecoagriculture conservation, teach English, work with children, provide health care, or work in construction and renovation.

- In Ecuador, placements are in Quito. Volunteers work with street children, teach English, or support schools and youth summer programs.

- In Guatemala, volunteers are placed in Antigua or a nearby town. Placements include teaching English, working in an orphanage or in child care, medical placement, construction and renovation, animal rights, working with the elderly, and conservation.

- In Mexico, volunteers are placed in and around the colonial city of Cuernavaca. Work ranges from teaching and tutoring to child care and conservation.

- In Peru, volunteers are based in either Lima or Cusco and can choose from teaching English, working with children or in an orphanage, medical placement, construction and renovation, or jungle conservation.

- In Brazil, volunteers must commit to at least two weeks. Placements are in or near Rio de Janeiro and include a sports program, building homes in favelas, working with children, teaching English, performing community development, and even a Carnival program (October-January), in which volunteers help make costumes for the famed parade.

At the time of this writing, Argentina and El Salvador were slated to have programs by the end of 2013.

Application Process: An application form is available online. Individual volunteers must be age 18 or older; those younger are welcome with chaperones or family members. Medical placements in any country require appropriate experience and degrees.

Cost: There is a US$249 registration fee, in addition to a program fee. US$180-360 for one week in the Spanish-speaking countries of Latin America; US$620-920 for two weeks in Brazil. Housing is included. Travel insurance is mandatory and is not included. The program fee covers volunteer accommodations, meals, and airport pickup and orientation.

Volunteers pay a registration fee (which goes to IVHQ) and a program fee. The program fee goes entirely to the partner organization, thus the volunteer's funds directly benefit the local community.

Placement Length: There is a minimum placement of one week in most locations and a minimum of two weeks in Brazil. Placements are limited and can fill during peak travel times. Some programs can start any day, while others have specific start dates.

Language Requirements: Varies by location and project. Some opportunities have no language requirements. If Spanish or Portuguese is required, language lessons will be compulsory for those without the requisite skills.

Housing: There are volunteer houses in all countries; some homestays are also available. Rooms are typically shared with one or two other volunteers, and meals are usually included; check each program description for details. Most volunteers live and work with other volunteers, although it is possible to request individual placement in an organization.

Operating Since: 2007

Number of Volunteers: more than 6,000 in 2012

INTERN LATIN AMERICA (ILA)

London, U.K., U.K. tel. 44/20-7193-4188,
U.S. tel. 718/878-6393, www.internlatinamerica.com

TYPE OF WORK: children and youth, community development, education, environment, health, wildlife protection, women's empowerment

LOCATIONS: Argentina, Colombia

Intern Latin America (ILA) is a British and Latin American joint venture whose goal is that participants: rapidly improve or perfect their Spanish, get a rewarding work experience in their area of interest or expertise, and have "a fantastic life experience." In addition to volunteer opportunities, ILA offers internships, medical elective projects, and Spanish courses. In Argentina, placements are in Buenos Aires; in Colombia, they are in Medellín. There are local offices in both countries.

Each volunteer placement is tailored to the individual. ILA prides itself on focusing on what the the participant learns, making the volunteer experience more of an "internship in an NGO"—nongovermental organization—in which key skills for any future career are developed. ILA offers placements in all types of NGOs, such as TECHO (an NGO that uses youth volunteers to create solutions for families living in slums). They also offer sports-based volunteering, in which local soccer teams take on volunteers as foreign assistant coaches. Responsibilities vary with each placement; while some might be more hands-on (interacting with people and communities), others might be more organizational (project management or marketing).

Spanish classes are an optional extra. In Argentina ILA partners with Expanish, and in Colombia they partner with EAFIT University, where participants gain access to lectures, sports facilities, and an extensive academic library. ILA offers weekly cultural activities as well as trips to museums, the countryside, art galleries, or the cinema, or a city immersion tour. In Colombia, volunteers watch a soccer game, while in Argentina they might enjoy a tango show.

A special note about Medellín, Colombia: Despite its reputation as the home of the late drug czar Pablo Escobar, it has made enormous strides in improving safety. ILA places its volunteers in safe areas, and the local staff provides guidance on safety. Volunteers are prohibited from visiting more marginalized zones after dark.

Application Process: An application form is available online. A résumé must also be uploaded online.

Cost: Argentina: US$1,420 for two weeks; US$2,200 for four weeks. Colombia: US$1,130 for two weeks; US$2,155 for four weeks. Accommodations and a few other perks— such as airport pickup, a mobile phone, and a cultural activity—are included. Volunteers are responsible for their own meals.

Placement Length: There is a minimum placement of two weeks. Start dates are every Monday year-round.

Language Requirements: None, although those with better Spanish skills can take on greater responsibilities.

Housing: Volunteers can choose from a family homestay, student residence, or shared apartment; each has a private bedroom, sheets and towels, and wireless Internet. There is a shared-room option in Colombia for those who are would like to trade privacy for price. All accommodations include access to a full kitchen; meals are the responsibility of the volunteer.

Operating Since: 2011

Number of Volunteers: Of the 300 worldwide bookings in 2012, approximately 5 percent were volunteer placements.

OPERATION WALLACEA

Lincolnshire, U.K., U.K. tel. 44/1790-763-194,
U.S. tel. 973/920-0487, www.opwall.com

TYPE OF WORK: environment, wildlife protection

LOCATIONS: Cuba, Ecuador, Guyana, Honduras, Mexico, Peru

Operation Wallacea (Opwall) runs a series of biological and conservation management research programs in remote locations across the world. The expeditions are designed with

PUTTING MEANING IN YOUR TRAVELS

If you've traveled before to a developing country, you've seen the people in need of jobs. There *is* someone local who can paint that fence, play with those kids, or build that house. Why should you travel thousands of miles and spend hundreds of dollars to do it instead of a local?

Anyone who has built a house or worked in an orphanage overseas can tell you: **What you will remember when you get home is not the project, but the people.** Meaningful travel doesn't come from handouts or patronage, it comes from solidarity. Without exception, the most valuable experience volunteers have on their service trips is the chance to get to know others who may live in very different conditions, yet share similar hopes and dreams.

That doesn't mean that there isn't a place for projects based on unskilled labor. Working side by side can enable those with a language barrier to share in an experience and communicate without words. Volunteers at environmental and wildlife projects help draw attention to issues that might not have been prioritized by the local community in the past. If you are considering a project based on unskilled labor, will community members be working with you? Will you or your group stay with community members, or in community-run accommodations? Is community outreach a component of the project?

There is also a genuine need for skilled service – environmental education, reforestation, sustainable agriculture, or even specialized service such as marketing assistance to community-based coffee or weaving cooperatives in promoting their products and connecting with international markets. Medical brigades that hand out aspirin to rural patients with cancer are of dubious value, but those that perform difficult surgeries, train local doctors to do the same, and leave behind the equipment and resources so that such care can continue are providing life-changing services.

No matter what type of service you hope to provide, just being in the community is one of the greatest benefits you can offer. You will eat their food, stay in their accommodations, purchase their handicrafts, and allow them to be your guides. Your stay gives locals the opportunity to be the tour operator; you will meet them on their own terms as representatives of their culture. This may not be the brick-and-mortar volunteer experience you originally envisioned, but it is just as valuable. It's called community-based tourism; the idea is that the community decides where they would like your support.

*Thanks to Tammy Leland of the educational nonprofit **Crooked Trails** (www.crookedtrails. com) for her observations about meaningful travel. Visit her website for more thought-provoking articles on sustainable travel, as well as environmentally and culturally sustainable travel opportunities.*

specific wildlife conservation aims, such as identifying areas that need protection and implementing and assessing conservation management programs. Unique to Opwall is the number of university academics (specialists in various aspects of biodiversity or social and economic studies) who participate in the expeditions, which gives volunteers the opportunity to work on a range of projects. Participants are typically university students volunteering as research assistants as part of their coursework or as part of a senior thesis or dissertation.

In Honduras, one of Opwall's partners is the Honduras Coral Reef Fund, which manages the Cayos Cochinos, a marine reserve 19 kilometers (12 mi) off the Honduran coast that consists of a small group of two main islands and 13 small cays within the Bay Islands archipelago, all surrounded by pristine reef. Volunteers can assist with a reef-monitoring program (collecting data via video while diving and analyzing it in the lab) or work on one of several ongoing research projects (studying a specific element of the marine environment in extensive detail either by diving, snorkeling, or kayaking). Opwall can also provide open-water PADI training at no additional cost, if needed.

Opwall places volunteers on Utila (June-August) and on the north coast of the Honduran mainland. Opwall also partners with FundAmazonia in Peru and with the University of Havana in Cuba. In Guyana, participants help monitor forest biodiversity, while in Mexico, volunteers might combine forest monitoring with reef surveys or participate in an entirely marine-based trip. A program in Ecuador is scheduled to begin in 2014.

Application Process: To apply, volunteers can either contact one of the 10 Opwall offices worldwide or complete the online form for "expressions of interest." Individual volunteers must be age 18 or older; 16- and 17-year-olds are welcome as part of high school groups.

Cost: US$1,750-5,500, depending on length of stay. Costs include everything except certain dive equipment.

Placement Length: Undergrad research assistants can choose their length of stay in two-week increments for up to eight weeks. Dissertation and senior thesis students choose a six- to eight-week stay.

Language Requirements: Research is conducted in English.

Housing: Included, and varies by project site. Accommodations may be in tents, dormitories, homestays, simple hotels, or even in a berth or on the deck of a research ship.

Operating Since: 1996, with volunteer expeditions in Latin America since 2003

Number of Volunteers: 700 in Honduras, 250 in Cuba, and 150 in Peru in 2011

PROWORLD

San Francisco, CA, toll-free U.S. tel. 877/429-6753, www.proworldvolunteers.org

TYPE OF WORK: children and youth, community development, education, environment, health, wildlife protection, women's empowerment

LOCATIONS: Belize, Brazil, Ecuador, Peru

ProWorld started as a Peru-based organization and eventually grew to cover programs in multiple countries around the world. ProWorld prides itself on long-term relationships with host communities. Projects vary year to year—even during the course of a year:

• In Brazil, volunteers support nurses and doctors in a rural health clinic, help develop local capacity in surf tourism in Salvador, and support after-school programs for disadvantaged children.

• In Ecuador, volunteers restore and protect natural habitats in the Amazon, the cloud forests, and the coastal mangroves. They work with children (whose families live at the city dump in Quito) and support education efforts for working children.

• In Peru, volunteers build schools, irrigation systems, and bridges; replant forests; help develop sustainable industries like agrotourism; construct water filters; and support a center for teenage mothers.

The majority of ProWorld's volunteers are college and grad school students, but older volunteers are very much welcome. Language classes are part of the package, but alternative activities—from Quechua lessons to capoeira or dance—are offered to those already fluent in the language. Cultural activities and excursions are offered at every site (a minimum of one weekend excursion), and there is a weekly dinner meeting with volunteers to discuss cultural issues and share experiences.

Application Process: An application form is available online. When applying, volunteers must choose two areas of interest. Placements will be confirmed only after the volunteer has been accepted and has placed a US$200 deposit. Individual volunteers must be age 18 or older; families are welcome.

Cost: US$1,345-1,545 for one week; approximately US$350 each additional week. Housing, local transportation, language courses, cultural activities and excursions, airport pickup and drop-off stipend, and health and travel insurance are included (as is a contribution to the project).

Placement Length: There is a minimum placement of one week.

Language Requirements: None.

INTERNATIONAL

Housing: Volunteers are usually placed in homestays, with a private bedroom; more than one volunteer may be placed in a home. Some locations may have a volunteer house. All meals are included.

Operating Since: 2000

Number of Volunteers: more than 6,000 globally since 2000

REI ADVENTURES

Sumner, WA, toll-free U.S. tel. 800/622-2236, www.rei.com

TYPE OF WORK: environment, wildlife protection

LOCATIONS: Chile, Peru

Best known for their top-notch outdoor equipment and clothing, REI is also in the travel business, offering volunteer vacations along with hundreds of other active adventures worldwide. REI Adventures's Torres del Paine Volunteer Vacation and Machu Picchu Volunteer Vacation trips are organized in conjunction with REI partner Conservation Volunteers International Program, a non-profit "dedicated to conserving iconic wilderness areas and cultural sites around the world."

In Peru, volunteers head to Machu Picchu to help maintain trails and restore archaeological features. Responsibilities include removing weeds, planting trees, collecting native seeds, or monitoring restoration study plots. Guided tours of colonial Cusco and Machu Picchu are included on the trip, as is a visit to a textile-weaving cooperative. In Chile, volunteers head to Torres del Paine National Park in Patagonia, where they team with park rangers to maintain and improve park trails. Volunteers may rehabilitate unauthorized or abandoned trails, out-slope trails with a pick or shovel and build water bars, clip vegetation to widen trails for safety, remove rocks from the trail to reduce tripping hazards, or move crushed rock to create a dry walking surface. Volunteers spend their free time relaxing at the mountain lodge or hiking.

Their Chile trip was selected by *National Geographic* as one of their "50 Tours of a Lifetime" for 2012 (so be prepared to book early!). Set departure dates are available online, but private departures can also be arranged (the cost may vary depending on the size of your group). Trips may vary from yar to year.

Application Process: An application form is available online, or call 800/622-2236 to apply. It is also possible (but not preferred) to mail a completed application with a US$400 nonrefundable deposit. Most trips require final payment two months before departure. Volunteers must be age 18 or older.

Cost: US$2,950 for either the Chile or Peru trip; single supplement US$300 in Chile, US$750 in Peru. Housing, park fees, and all transportation indicated in the itineraries are included. Travelers are responsible for expenses not indicated in the trip itinerary, including the reciprocity fee charged to some nationalities upon entry into Chile (US$160 for U.S. citizens at the time of this writing).

Placement Length: Typically 10-13 days.

Language Requirements: None.

Housing: Hotel accommodations, park fees, and most meals are included, as is all transportation indicated in the itinerary.

Operating Since: 1988

Number of Volunteers: There are three volunteer trips in Latin America scheduled for 2013, excluding private departures.

SPANISH AT LOCATIONS

toll-free U.S. tel. 877/268-3730, www.spanishatlocations.com

TYPE OF WORK: agriculture, children and youth, community development, education, environment, health, wildlife protection

LOCATIONS: Costa Rica, Panama

Spanish at Locations is a Spanish-language school and hostel with branches in Puerto Viejo and Turrialba, Costa Rica, and Bocas del Toro and Boquete, Panama.

- In Puerto Viejo, Costa Rica: Volunteers work at schools or in day cares; at an animal rescue center; or at a center for indigenous people, providing meals, tutoring for children, computer and English training for adults, and services for the elderly.

- In Turrialba, Costa Rica: Volunteers can choose from 11 different organizations in the areas of teaching, social work, agriculture, education, and recreation. Volunteers might teach English, lead games, or assist students with homework at an elementary school; read or play games with children in an orphanage or day care center; serve meals or help maintain the facilities at a home for the elderly; work with people with disabilities; or volunteer at the library or museum of a tropical agricultural research center.
- In Bocas del Toro, Panama: Volunteers lend a hand at day care centers or retirement homes, teach in an indigenous community, assist with administrative tasks at a medical clinic, or help with sea turtle conservation (March-June).
- In Boquete, Panama: Volunteers might work in schools, assist the Civil Protection Program (in the areas of humanitarian aid, emergencies, infrastructure, or health), work with disabled people of all ages, teach about recycling or support a recycling center, or work with animals (from household pets to rescued jungle animals).

There is plenty to keep volunteers busy during their free time. In addition to Spanish lessons, Spanish at Locations can arrange surfing, diving, rafting, kayaking, horseback riding, and rock climbing. The hostels attract many backpackers, so there are always plenty of people to hang out with, and the schools have a youthful vibe.

Application Process: To apply, call, Skype, or send an email for more information. There is no minimum age for volunteering, and families are welcome.

Cost: There is no cost if the volunteer stays at the hostel or takes Spanish lessons from Spanish at Locations. For all others, there is a placement fee of US$35. All-inclusive packages (Spanish lessons, hostel accommodations, and volunteer placement) run US$265 per week. Volunteering with sea turtle conservation in Bocas del Toro, Panama, requires a one-time fee of US$16 and costs US$20 per day for accommodations and food. Volunteering at the Animal Rescue Center in Puerto Viejo, Costa Rica, requires a US$50 fee, paid directly to the rescue center.

Placement Length: Varies by placement but starts with at least one afternoon.

Language Requirements: Varies with placement; however, there are some opportunities without language requirements.

Housing: Volunteers can arrange their own accommodations or stay in one of the school's hostels (dorm US$10/day, private room US$18-20/day). Homestays are available in Boquete, Panama, and Turrialba, Costa Rica. It is possible to rent a private room (US$18-25/night; varies for meals and laundry) in Bocas del Toro, Panama, and Puerto Viejo, Costa Rica. Volunteers must arrange their own meals, unless volunteering with the sea turtle conservation program.

Operating Since: 1998

Number of Volunteers: 1,000-1,500 students in 2012

TECHO

originally from Chile, with offices in 20 countries, U.S. tel. 305/860-4090, www.techo.org

TYPE OF WORK: community development

LOCATIONS: Argentina, Bolivia, Brazil, Chile, Colombia, Costa Rica, Ecuador, El Salvador, Guatemala, Honduras, Mexico, Nicaragua, Panama, Paraguay, Uruguay, and Venezuela

Founded by youth who dreamt of improving housing for people living in slums, TECHO (formerly Un Techo Para Mi País) is a civil society organization that seeks to overcome the situation of poverty in the slums of Latin America through the joint effort of local residents and youth volunteers. With the help of volunteers and potential residents, TECHO starts the development process by building transitional houses for people in need. Their model is similar to that of U.S.-based Habitat for Humanity, but with the idea that housing is transitional. The homes built by TECHO are simpler and cheaper, enabling the organization to reach people who are on even lower rungs of the economic ladder and thereby strengthening the community.

Volunteer responsibilities relate to housing construction—digging foundations, pouring cement, and sawing rebar. While construction brigades are the most common activity, volunteers with more time (at least one month) may become involved with housing evaluation and project assignment, participation in TECHO's work plans (in the areas of health, education, productive development, and microcredit), or participation in and monitoring of community-organizing committees.

Timing varies from country to country, so interested volunteers should get in touch with national offices to obtain details and apply. (The "Participate" page at www. techo.org includes information about upcoming builds and events across the region. Country-specific information is also available online.) In the Caribbean, TECHO has programs in Haiti and the Dominican Republic, and it also has a U.S. office that works on volunteer management, partnerships, and fundraising.

While youth from any country are welcome to participate in a TECHO build, the organization's focus is on calling local youth to volunteer. This means that international volunteers have to organize their own accommodations, meals, and other logistics. The trade-off is working with teams that are likely to be comprised entirely of nationals of the host country.

Application Process: A registration form is available online for each country (in Spanish, or for Brazil, in Portuguese). Volunteers ages 18-29 are encouraged to apply.

Cost: Varies.

Placement Length: Placement ranges 1-5 days, with a few longer options (office volunteers can make a longer commitment). Volunteers interested in activities such as the community-organizing committees should commit to a month or more.

Language Requirements: Volunteers must be able to communicate in Spanish or in Portuguese (in Brazil) with the local office, as well as with other volunteers and build leaders.

Housing: Volunteers are responsible for making their own arrangements.

Operating Since: 1997

Number of Volunteers: 60,500 in 2012

UBELONG

Washington DC, U.S. tel. 202/250-3706, www.ubelong.org

TYPE OF WORK: agriculture, children and youth, community development, education, environment, health, wildlife protection, women's empowerment

LOCATIONS: Bolivia, Ecuador, Paraguay, Peru

UBELONG's mission is threefold: to improve the socioeconomic conditions of disadvantaged populations by placing volunteers in grassroots organizations that address locally identified needs; to mobilize volunteers of all backgrounds and provide flexible and affordable placements; and to bring people together in order to advance cross-cultural learning, understanding of international development issues, and civic engagement. The organization's founders have 20 years of international development, management, and teaching experience between them.

UBELONG breaks its experiences into two categories: Immersion and Expeditions. Within Latin America, UBELONG only has Expedition programs in Peru. Immersion experiences are fixed in a single location, and are offered in Bolivia, Ecuador and Peru. In La Paz, Bolivia, volunteers are involved with caregiving and choose between working in a center for abused children, in a public hospital with disabled children, or at a public orphanage. There is also a need for volunteers with expertise or interest in art therapy to work at these facilities. In Ecuador, volunteers might help care for children, the elderly, or mentally disabled persons; teach baking, cooking, carpentry, or other vocational skills to at-risk youth; help reforestation efforts in a cloud forest reserve; or help to remove invasive plant species from a nature reserve on the Galapagos islands. In Peru, volunteers might teach English at an elementary school, provide sports training to underprivileged youth, or lead workshops for women on topics ranging from nutrition to how to make handicrafts or run a small business.

Expeditions are traveling placements, and while they include a volunteer component, the emphasis is on learning. Expeditions have a full agenda of activities including project visits, class instruction, tutoring and mentoring, volunteer service and social outings. Prices for these trips include in-country travel. In Paraguay the focus of the experience is business development as an anti-poverty mechanism. In Peru UBELONG offers two Expeditions, one described as an "Introduction to International Development," the other with a focus on development research in a shantytown of Lima.

Application Process: An application form is available online. Once your application is received, UBELONG will respond within 72 hours. If the application is accepted, the volunteer must sign and return a liability waiver and code of conduct along with a US$200 deposit. If the scheduled placement starts within 60 days, the entire payment is due within 48 hours. Volunteers must be age 18 or older.

Cost: A US$200 placement fee is required. Expeditions placements run US$1,800-1,900. Immersion placements run US$150-US$300 for one week, US$240-590 for two weeks, and each additional week is US$75-120.

Placement Length: There is a minimum placement of 2 weeks for Expedition placements and 1-4 weeks for Immersion placements.

Language Requirements: Varies by placement and location.

Housing: Volunteers live in homestays or in a volunteer guesthouse, depending on location. While applicants can sign up individually, volunteers will always be living and working with other volunteers. All or most of the meals are provided.

Operating Since: 2009

Number of Volunteers: approximately 1,000 in 2012; 2,000 volunteers expected in 2013

VOFAIR

Santiago, Chile, www.vofair.org

TYPE OF WORK: agriculture, children and youth, community development, education, environment, health, wildlife protection, women's empowerment

LOCATIONS: Chile, Ecuador, Guatemala, Peru, Venezuela

VOFAIR stands for Volunteering Fairly, and their aim is to be a clearinghouse for fair and verified volunteer projects in Chile and other places in South America. The organization was funded by a grant from the Chilean government; assistance from partner organizations with psychologists, an environmental specialist, and a veterinarian informs their certification process. VOFAIR is based in Chile's capital of Santiago, but volunteer opportunities are around the country and region.

VOFAIR's projects ensure that any accompanying services must be priced fairly, strictly verifying that any charges for accommodations, transportation, and food are market price. Other criteria for certification include: (1) the project brings change; (2) the volunteer does not cause damage nor is exposed to unnecessary risks; (3) an appropriate recruitment process is assured; (4) the hosting organization is open to suggestions for improvement; and (5) the hosting organization has not and does not break the law.

At the time of this writing, VOFAIR had just launched its volunteer database with 15 certified projects in Chile, Colombia, and Ecuador. They anticipate having 50 certified projects within the following weeks. VOFAIR works with organizations across Latin America, and has received expressions of interest from organizations in Guatemala, Peru, and Venezuela as well. Project listings describe volunteer tasks and responsibilities, as well as information about accommodations and meals (if included), and any charges for those services.

Application Process: Varies according to the project selected by the volunteer.

Cost: VOFAIR charges US$5 to access its database for one month. Organizations certified

by VOFAIR do not charge a fee to volunteer. Some may have fees for accommodations and meals, which VOFAIR verifies to ensure they are fair market prices.
Placement Length: Anywhere from a day to a year, depending on the organization.
Language Requirements: Varies according to project.
Housing: Varies according to project.
Operating Since: 2012
Number of Volunteers: VOFAIR launched just as this guide was going to press, and did not yet have numbers to report.

WANDERLAND TRAVEL

Prescott, AZ, toll-free U.S. tel. 866/701-2113, www.wanderland.org
TYPE OF WORK: agriculture, children and youth, community development, education, environment
LOCATIONS: Argentina, Chile, Costa Rica, El Salvador, Mexico

Wanderland is a nonprofit organization whose mission is to "provide educational travel that reveals and respects geography, culture, and history, while responsibly supporting and re-investing into local economies and environmental protection." Wanderland Travel has a deep-seated commitment to fair trade principles, which they believe are a natural partner with travel in community development. They operate primarily in the sectors of educational travel and voluntourism. Along with service trips, Wanderland Travel runs custom trips to the American Southwest, educational treks in Costa Rica, and bicycle "edventures" (educational adventures) in the Lake Districts of Chile.

While the founders of Wanderland Travel have more than 20 years' experience in the field, as a business it is in the early stages of development. They intend to develop additional trip options for individuals, couples, and families, and destinations may vary as the programs develop. Currently, group volunteer trips are offered, some of which have a heavy educational component, but custom trips can be developed at any time. Some examples:

• 10 days in Argentina: Lots of sightseeing, with a day or two spent volunteering at a rural school in Patagonia to install organic gardens and to provide English-language practice.

• 15 days in Costa Rica: Two days intensive training at an ecolodge, followed by 10 days on an organic farm engaged in farming and seed collection. (The other two days are for travel.)

• 10 days at a rural village in the Atacama desert, Chile: Volunteers construct and maintain paths to a local archaeological site, develop infrastructure for visiting ancient petroglyphs, and learn about llama breeding.

Application Process: An application form is available online to discuss interests and priorities. This process should be initiated 6-8 months prior to the desired travel dates. Volunteers must be age 14 or older; Wanderland Travel has developed protocols with GPS messaging and email to keep minors in close contact with parents if traveling as part of a youth or student group.
Cost: Varies, but ranges US$2,700-3,000 according to group size. Housing is included.
Placement Length: 10-15 days
Language Requirements: None.
Housing: Accommodations are provided in lodges or homestays, and occasionally tents with air mattresses. Meals are included.
Operating Since: 2010
Number of Volunteers: Wanderland Travel was in the field for 25 weeks in 2012 on a variety of trips, including one volunteer service trip to Costa Rica and El Salvador with 20 high school students.

RESOURCES

Transportation

AIRFARE

Some airlines offer discounts on selected international routes for those traveling for humanitarian reasons. **Fly for Good** (www. flyforgood.com) helps volunteers find those discounts and offers the lowest published fares for routes that do not have a special discount. Note that discounted humanitarian fares are mostly available on flights to Africa and Asia.

Carbon Off-Setting

The ethics of carbon off-setting are often debated, and rightly so: Flying less is really the most effective way to reduce your carbon footprint. However, once you've made the choice to fly, there are companies that have more highly regarded carbon-offsetting programs than others (with savvier approaches than planting a tree or handing out energy-saving light bulbs to a developing country). Certainly, doing something is better than doing nothing at all. In addition to protecting rainforests, there are projects to harness wind power, distribute fuel-efficient cooking stoves, and reduce the greenhouse gases emitted by farm animals.

For more information about carbon off-setting programs, contact any of the following organizations:

© ACHIM BAQUE/123RF

atmosfair (www.atmosfair.de/en/home), based in Germany
Carbon Retirement (www.carbonretirement. com), based in the United Kingdom
Climatefriendly.org (www.climatefriendly. org), based in Australia
myclimate (www.myclimate.org), based in Switzerland
NativeEnergy (www.nativeenergy.com), based in the United States

TRAVEL INSURANCE
If you have health insurance, check to see if your insurer includes coverage outside the United States. Many health policies (including Medicare) don't pay for medical expenses outside the U.S. border. If you're not covered, consider purchasing a policy that includes emergency evacuation coverage. If you might extend your trip overseas, make sure the policy you are considering allows this. Some providers to consider include:

InsureMyTrip (www.insuremytrip.com)
QuoteWright (www.quotewright.com)
Travel Insurance Center (www.travelinsurancecenter.com)
USI Travel Insurance Services (www.travelinsure.com)
WorldNomands.com (www.worldnomads.com)

Tips for Volunteers

HEALTH CONCERNS
Most visitors to Latin America will travel without any health incident. The best way to try to be one of those travelers is by taking a few precautions.

Digestion
Stomach trouble is the most likely nuisance you may encounter. Be vigilant about water and ice cubes, eat only fruit you peel yourself, and avoid raw vegetables such as salads (unless you have prepared them yourself) to avoid issues on a short trip. I'm an enormous fan of Pepto-Bismol for light stomach trouble, while Immodium will get you through that next bus ride without needing to make a break for the bathroom.

Malaria and Dengue
Travelers to the tropics will face mosquito-borne diseases such as malaria and dengue. The strains of malaria prevalent in Latin America are rarely fatal, and antimalarial medications are easily obtained. Malaria is characterized by 24-hour cycles of chills, headaches, fatigue, and fever; dengue symptoms include the latter three, particularly high fever. When asking your doctor about prophylactic drugs to prevent malaria (which you take before, during, and after your trip), also ask about adverse reactions. Alternatively, be vigilant about the use of insect repellent; try to pick up an environmentally friendly repellent before embarking on your trip.

Dengue, also known as the "bone-breaking disease," can be miserable, but it is rarely fatal. However, always seek medical attention for aches and high fevers, as the hemorrhagic strain can be a rapid killer. There are no prophylactics for dengue.

Yellow Fever
Yellow fever lasts several days and usually presents as fever, chills, lack of appetite, nausea, muscle pain, and headache. In some patients, a toxic phase can follow, in which jaundice and liver damage can occur and lead to death. There is no known treatment, but the vaccine is generally regarded as safe and effective. Ninety percent of yellow fever cases occur in Africa; whether the vaccine is recommended for travel in South America depends largely on where in the country you'll be traveling. Mosquitoes do not live at high altitudes, so if, for example, you'll be sticking to coastal and Andean Ecuador or Peru, you are unlikely to need the

vaccine. Note that some countries require the yellow fever vaccination if you are coming from another where the disease is endemic, in which case you will need to present your yellow fever vaccination card. Current information can be found online at the **Centers for Disease Control and Prevention** (www.cdc.gov).

Altitude Sickness

While exploring the mountain peaks of South America, travelers may find themselves suffering from altitude sickness. The most common symptoms are mild nausea and headaches, which usually disappear after a day or two as your body adjusts to thinner air. The best preventative is to take it easy during your first day or two in the mountains and to limit alcohol intake. Locals in Bolivia and Peru swear by a cup of coca leaf tea to help adjust. Should you face more severe symptoms, such as extreme nausea or a stroke-like reaction, seek help from a local doctor immediately. The most common treatment for a severe reaction is the use of an oxygen tank while you transition to the new climes.

SAFETY

Always ask what the security situation is like at the volunteer site and surrounding area. Safety can be a big concern in Latin America's big cities and a nonissue in a small town an hour away. In less-secure areas, volunteers should be perfectly safe if following the safety recommendations given to them by the volunteer coordinators on the ground. Whether locally based or international, volunteer organizations use their local contacts to determine safety concerns and make any necessary recommendations. Please follow them.

Leaving valuables at home, keeping an eye on your belongings, and taking a taxi after dark are three universal ways to boost your travel smarts.

CONDUCT AND CUSTOMS

Volunteer organizations have worked hard to earn their reputation within the local community—communities that are frequently much more conservative than the ones volunteers

come from. As such, organizations often have guidelines on dress and behavior, which almost always include no drugs and no drunkenness. Depending on the organization and project, guidelines may also include no drinking in front of children, no alcohol at all, no romantic relationships with members of the local community, and/or no romantic relationships with other volunteers. Dress codes may include no shorts, no tank tops, no multiple piercings, no visible tattoos, and no baseball caps worn backward (the latter three are strongly associated with gangs in Central America). Rather than considering it an affront to your personal freedoms, remember that you are serving as a representative of the organization and as a model for local youth, and respect the guidelines that have been given to you.

I wish it could go without saying, but according to reports in the field it apparently needs to be said: Do not engage in drugs while on a volunteer vacation. The drug trade in Latin America is responsible for the deaths of thousands of people each year. This includes innocent bystanders who are caught by the escalated levels of violence related to the drug trade. Don't be part of the problem.

Photo Etiquette

While the colorful fabrics and cultural heritage of places like Bolivia and Guatemala make for fantastic photographs, it is important to be respectful. Remember to always ask permission before taking pictures of people. Some indigenous groups consider photos highly offensive and in conflict with their spiritual beliefs, so tread carefully. Once asked, however, many are willing to grant permission—especially if you offer to send them a copy of the photo.

ACCESS FOR TRAVELERS WITH DISABILITIES

Anyone with a disability traveling in Latin America will quickly realize that allowances made for anyone less mobile are few and far between. International chain hotels in the major cities are the best bets for wheelchair-friendly rooms, although travelers may find a few exceptions here and there. Internal travel by plane or bus can be a challenge, although flight and bus attendants are usually accustomed to helping those with physical disabilities on and off. Hiring a driver with a van or car that is suitable for you may be the easiest option, albeit not the most economical.

Now for the good news. **Mobility International USA** (www.miusa.org) is an organization dedicated to the empowerment of people with disabilities "to achieve their human rights through international exchange and international development." Their website offers resources for travelers with disabilities, including a database of organizations that welcome volunteers with disabilities (http://volunteerabroad.miusa.org).

TRAVELING WITH CHILDREN

Planning on travelling with young children? With its opportunities for exploring and learning, traveling with children in Latin America can be a wonderful experience—especially since discounts are often given on domestic flights and in hotel rooms, making it more affordable as well. Latin Americans are generally very accepting of children in restaurants or elsewhere, and young kids often become icebreakers between travelers and locals.

If you will be traveling with teens, safety may be greater or less than what you are used to at home, depending on your destination. Check with locals about what is appropriate (for example, should you allow them to go for a walk by themselves?) and how to be street smart.

WOMEN TRAVELING ALONE

Women traveling alone may draw unwanted attention in Latin America. One way to discourage this is to avoid wearing shorts or miniskirts, which are inappropriate at most volunteer destinations except those on the beach. Sundresses and tank tops are usually perfectly fine in the cities; however, in rural communities sleeveless shirts may be frowned upon. On average, dress in Latin America is more conservative and formal, although this is becoming less true for

younger generations. Unfortunately, it doesn't seem to matter what you wear or look like: Foreign women can be sure to attract a few catcalls if walking alone, but it is a custom that is more annoying than harmful.

SENIOR VOLUNTEERS

Seniors considering a volunteer vacation will find plenty of options in Latin America. There's a reason why places like Panama and Costa Rica—boasting a combination of fabulous weather and first-rate medical care—are popular with retirees. While there is ever-growing interest in volunteer travel across the age spectrum, it is still dominated by adults in the 18-25 age bracket, so if it is important to you that your organization has experience with older travelers, ask about the ages of their past volunteers. If the volunteer experience you're interested in requires physical work, ask the organization if it is a suitable opportunity for seniors. You may be surprised. My own retired parents participated on a house-construction volunteer project with me, and while my father led the trench digging, my mother was put to good use cutting wire and sawing rebar, tasks that didn't require as much physical strength. The senior-specialized travel organization ElderHostel has been revamped and is now **Road Scholar** (www.roadscholar.org). While it no longer caters exclusively to seniors, it still has extensive experience working with older travelers and offers many programs that combine volunteering and learning, searchable by level of physical activity. Many of the international organizations listed in this guide reach out to seniors; look for further information on their websites. Note that Medicare does not cover health care outside of the United States.

GAY AND LESBIAN VOLUNTEERS

Gay and lesbian travelers should be aware that in most of Latin America, homosexuality is back in the closet. There are few resources for gay and lesbian travelers, and the attitude of many locals toward homosexuality is strongly informed by antigay religious or *machista* (hyper-masculine) perspectives. That said, attitudes are often more tolerant toward foreign travelers. While public displays of affection are likely to attract serious trouble, a same-sex couple asking for a hotel room with a double bed (*cama matrimonial*) usually won't face any issues. Same-sex relations are legal in all the countries included in this guide.

Argentina is a regional leader in its treatment of gays and lesbians. In July 2010, it became the first country in Latin America to legalize same-sex marriage. Buenos Aires has an active gay scene. Argentines are also demonstrative by nature—women hold hands, and men give each other a kiss on the cheek. That said, even in Argentina there have been cases of police harassment (and worse) of members of the LGBT community. If in doubt, discretion may be the safer choice.

FAITH-BASED VOLUNTEERS

Religion is a significant source of inspiration for many organizations and volunteers alike. Some of the organizations in this guide have strong religious principles; volunteers are generally required to respect those beliefs, but not necessarily share them. Likewise, religiously inspired volunteers shouldn't exclude organizations from consideration simply for being secular. A great way to turn a volunteer vacation into a mission trip is to pick an inspiring cause and organize a volunteer opportunity through your church, synagogue, mosque, or youth group.

VEGETARIANS

Herbivores planning a trip to Latin America may find the local love of meat a challenge, but sticking to a vegetarian (and even vegan) diet is certainly not impossible. Rice and beans are staples across the entire region—just double-check what kind of fat was used to cook them. Most of the time it is *manteca,* and 99 percent of the time that means vegetable shortening, but it can also refer to pig fat (lard). To make sure, ask if *manteca vegetal* was used or *manteca animal.* Just don't be surprised if they look confused; given the cheap price of vegetable shortening, anyone using animal lard for cooking is a rarity. Many cooks are happy to cook without *manteca* if you ask them—it just never occurs to them that people might like it that way!

Vegetables are often presented as a condiment rather than a substantial part of the meal, but luscious fresh fruit is available just about everywhere and is often sold by street vendors cut and ready to eat.

Vegetarians should keep in mind that meat may be an expensive luxury for many of the people they encounter in Latin America and that the philosophy behind vegetarianism is not widely understood or embraced. Rather than explaining your reasons for not eating meat and possibly offending someone (who may have offered you something they consider special), it may be easier to simply say that you cannot eat meat because it makes your stomach hurt.

Suggested Reading and Internet Resources

The magazines **Afar** (www.afar.com), **Transitions Abroad** (www.transitionsabroad.com), and **Verge** (www.vergemagazine.com) all focus on less-traditional destinations and experiences.

Travel as a Political Act (www.travelasapoliticalact.com), by renowned travel writer Rick Steves, is a good read for those who have not yet traveled overseas, especially to a developing country. Rick's personal travel experiences illustrate the point of how to travel more purposefully, how to be open to new perspectives, and how people-to-people connections enrich travel immeasurably.

VOLUNTEER REVIEWS AND OPPORTUNITIES

If this guide has whetted your appetite for more, there are plenty of resources, especially online, to search for additional volunteer opportunities, as well as reviews by former volunteers. Be savvy when checking reviews, as there are some dishonest organizations that post either positive reviews about themselves or negative reviews about their competition. Reviews that describe specifics about the volunteer's experience are more likely to be authentic. If you want to dig deeper to find out more about the organization you're considering, try these tips:

Use your favorite search engine and enter the organization's name within brackets. Then add first the word *forum,* try again with the word *feedback,* and then *review* and *experience.* For organizations that are based in the United States or have a U.S. counterpart with 501(c)3 (nonprofit) certification, you can search for their tax records online (http://guidestar.org). Look for their most recent 990 forms and check line 12 on the first page of the 990 for the organization's total revenue for that year. Line 13 lists the amount of grants they made.

Abroad Reviews
www.abroadreviews.com

This review site has more than 1,000 reviews of over 200 volunteer programs. Any organization can be listed, but those marked as "verified" have submitted their business registration to Abroad Reviews (AR) for one verification seal, had their emails and phone numbers tested by AR for a second seal, and have at least one review on AR from a verified legitimate participant for the third seal.

Catholic Volunteer Network
www.catholicvolunteernetwork.org

Catholic Volunteer Network offers a searchable online database of volunteer opportunities with Catholic organizations around the world. Volunteers do not necessarily have to be Catholic or Christian.

Go Overseas
www.gooverseas.com

Go Overseas has reviews of overseas volunteer programs, as well as study abroad, internships, teaching abroad, and gap year programs, together with articles on all these topics. They also offer scholarships for volunteer travel; there are no restrictions of age, nationality, or whether the applicant is a student or not. There are more than 500 applicants per year, so it is highly competitive.

Idealist
www.idealist.org

This site has a massive database of nonprofit organizations worldwide, including volunteer, internship and job listings.

Omprakash
www.omprakash.org

Omprakash seeks to "build partnerships with grassroots health, education, and environmental projects around the world, and connect them with volunteers, donors, and classrooms that can learn from and support their work." Volunteer opportunities listed on the site do not charge a placement fee, but the cost of transportation, food, and lodging will vary by volunteer site. There are volunteer reviews, as well as a volunteer database that enables site visitors to connect with other volunteers who have spent time at the organization they are interested in.

South American Explorers
www.saexplorers.org
This institution of backpacker travel in South America has an online database of nonprofit organizations and volunteer opportunities in the region. Access to the site is limited to club members; individual memberships start at US$60/year (access to the clubhouses in Buenos Aires, Cusco, Lima, and Quito included). Volunteer listings are primarily in the countries where South American Explorers has clubhouses.

Volunteering Info
www.volunteeringinfo.org
This site has volunteer opportunities, organization reviews, and volunteer stories. Unlike many review sites, Volunteering Info makes an effort to get in touch with a former volunteer from every organization it lists in order to limit who is on its site to reputable organizations. Their focus is on small organizations with small fees.

Volunteers for Prosperity
www.volunteersforprosperity.gov
Volunteers for Prosperity (VfP) is a resource created by the U.S. government development agency USAID, designed to connect professionals with volunteer opportunities that can utilize their skills. Sought-after professionals include doctors, nurses, teachers, engineers, economists, computer specialists, financial sector professionals, business executives, and others with specialized technical expertise and significant practical experience. The VfP website has links to vetted partner volunteer organizations, where those interested can search for an opportunity that fits their skill set and interests. There is also a search engine that enables volunteers to search

for opportunities with multiple organizations at once.

Requirements are that the volunteer must: (1) be a U.S. citizen; (2) be at least 18 years old; and (3) have at least three years of professional experience in a related field.

Vounteer South America
www.volunteersouthamerica.net
This website is a gold mine of free and low-cost volunteer opportunities in South America. Not all the opportunities are development oriented, however; a few are simply volunteering at a farm or hostel in exchange for room and board, so read carefully if you're hoping to make a difference through your volunteer time.

VOUNTEER STORIES AND INSPIRATION
Five Point Five
www.FivePointFive.org
Five Point Five was launched by four passionate travelers who hope to inspire others to travel with a difference and maybe even make travel a lifestyle. The website features articles and blog posts about volunteer opportunities, travel experiences, and people who are creating positive change.

Journeys For Good
www.journeys4good.com
Husband and wife production team Steve and Joanie Wynn have traveled the world together, producing stories for Travel Channel, History Channel, Discovery, HBO, and Conservation Corporation Africa. They launched Journeys For Good as a way to "spread the message of volunteer travel." The site includes blog and vlog posts on volunteer experiences and interviews with organizations that promote volunteer travel.

FUNDRAISING
There are websites which offer products for group fundraising, which can be a great way to raise money toward service trips with

BRINGING IT HOME

The impact of your volunteer experience can be greatly enhanced in two very important ways: by sharing your experience with others and by continuing your commitment to the cause.

SHARING THE EXPERIENCE

This may be something you begin to do while you are volunteering, sharing stories and photos via email or a blog. Or you may document as you go, and upon your return do the same. It is surprisingly easy to make videos (out of either video footage or still images) that you can upload to YouTube and share with friends, as well as with others who might stumble upon them. But you don't have to stop there.

Have friends over for coffee or a drink to share pictures and tell stories – you might have souvenirs to show or music from the country to play. While Internet communication is great, there is nothing like sharing your enthusiasm for the project and its impact firsthand.

Write an article about the experience, to share in your school newspaper, church newsletter, or local paper. There are websites where volunteers can submit stories about their experiences. If you are working, perhaps you can organize a brown bag lunch where you share images and talk about the experience; maybe you belong to a professional association and can place an article in their newsletter.

CONTINUING YOUR COMMITMENT

A volunteer vacation does not have to be a one-off commitment. If you come home feeling passionate about the work you did, there may be other ways to keep supporting the organization from home. Financial donations are one obvious way. Besides giving your own money, you can also consider organizing an annual fundraiser, such as a bake sale, walkathon, or hosted dinner. Can you provide writing and editing skills, translations, or website design by connecting virtually?

Take a step back to consider what you have learned about the larger issues that created the need for the organization you helped in the first place. Are they issues of poverty or criminality? Consider what role your home country might play in other nations, and take a look at their stance on issues such as trade and the drug wars. Do you think it is helping the problem or making it worse? Make a call or send an email to your politicians and let them know what you think about the issue.

Another way to continue your commitment is by using the skills you acquired during your vacation with an organization at home. Did you improve your Spanish? Learn about social injustice? Perhaps there is an immigrant-outreach organization in your hometown where you can build on your newly acquired knowledge. Did you learn about organic or permaculture farming practices? What about supporting or creating a community garden near where you live? Were you working with animals? Your local zoo might have a way for you to support wildlife protection. You may also have learned general skills related to grassroots organizing, activism, community outreach, and nonprofit management that you can put to use in any kind of organization that captures your attention at home.

---

schools, churches, synagogues, mosques or youth groups:

All Fundraising Companies Directory
www.fundraisingweb.org

Fund-Raising.com
www.fund-raising.com

Fundraising 101
www.fundraising.ca

These three websites link to companies that offer products which groups can sell for project or event fundraising. All Fundraising Companies Directory works with companies in the U.S. and Canada. Fund-Raising.com has articles and tips on fundraising. Fundraising 101 is exclusively for Canada.

Crowdfunding

Crowdfunding refers to online networking and fundraising. An individual (or organization) proposes a project to be funded and a "crowd" of people financially back the project. Crowdfunding is supported by an organization (the "platform") which brings together the project initiator and the crowd. Listed are several platforms which volunteers may find suitable for funding their volunteer work and travel.

FirstGiving
www.firstgiving.com

Note that First Giving charges their site fee to the nonprofit, while other crowd-funding sites charge the fee to the volunteer.

GoFundMe
www.gofundme.com

GoFundMe charges a 5 percent fee on all donations, in addition to the 2.9 percent and US$0.30 per transaction charged by its financial processer WePay (PayPal for international donors).

Kickstarter
www.kickstarter.com

This fundraising platform is an all-or-nothing affair, where you must raise your entire goal or no funds will be released to you. Funds must be earmarked for a creative project—perfect for those planning to make a video or write an article about their volunteer experience.

Volunteer Forever
www.volunteerforever.com

Volunteer Forever (VF) is a one-stop shop offering listings of opportunities, reviews of volunteer experiences, a fundraising platform for volunteers, a blog space that volunteers can use to tell contributors and friends about their trip, and links to articles about volunteering overseas. VF charges 5 percent per transaction to conduct fundraising through the site, and PayPal will also charge 2.9 percent and $0.30 for each donation. VF has an option for donors to make an additional $5 donation to cover transaction fees, to help volunteers offset these costs.

RESPONSIBLE TOURISM
International Centre for Responsible Tourism
www.icrtourism.org

Founded in 2002, ICRT is a community of "Responsible Tourism Practitioners" in the business, government, and non-profit sectors. They seek to support the use of tourism "to make better places for people to live in and better places for people to visit."

The International Ecotourism Society (TIES)
www.ecotourism.org

Founded in 1990, TIES is a non-profit association "committed to promoting responsible tourism practices that benefit conservation and communities." Travelers can join TIES for free, and receive emails with advice on traveling responsibly, and on ecotourism destinations and experiences. They have a publication called "Volunteer Guidelines" aimed at sending organizations that gives in-depth information about what kinds of standards the organization should be upholding.

COUNTRY-SPECIFIC RESOURCES

The following websites offer general tourist information. Detailed destination information is also available on www.moon.com.

For information about indicators such as gross national income per capita and poverty and literacy rates, visit **The World Bank Data** (http://data.worldbank.org).

Argentina

www.argentina.travel
www.bue.gove.ar

Bolivia
www.boliviabella.com
www.bolivia.travel

Brazil
www.visitbrasil.com

Chile
www.chile.travel

Colombia
www.colombia.travel

Costa Rica
www.visitcostarica.com

Ecuador
www.ecuador.travel
www.quito.com.ec

Guatemala
www.visitguatemala.com

Honduras
www.honduras.com

Mexico
www.oaxaca.travel
www.visitmexico.com

Nicaragua
www.visitnicaragua.us

Panama
www.visitpanama.com

Peru
www.limaeasy.com
www.visitperu.com

General Index

agriculture: 13; see also Type of Work Index
air travel: 8-9, 11, 17; see also specific place
airfare: 9, 11, 17, 213
altitude: 9, 10, 146, 215; see also specific place
Amazon rainforest: 8, 110, 113, 116-118, 121, 124, 125, 130, 135, 141, 147, 150, 160, 195, 197, 199, 207
Amerindians: 100, 145, 158
Andes: 110, 123, 139, 155, 179, 197, 199
Antigua (Guatemala): 38, 41, 45, 204
application process: see specific place
Arajuela (Costa Rica): 82
Arequipa (Peru): 130, 142
Argentina: 172-183, 202, 203, 204, 209, 212; map 174-175
Atlantic Forest: 160, 164-166
Aymara: 147, 155, 156, 158
Aztecs: 21, 32
Baja California: 28, 199
balboa: 101
Baños (Ecuador): 118, 122
Bariloche (Argentina): 179
Bay Islands (Honduras): 11, 50-51, 58, 206
Becari Q.R.: 28
Belize: 193, 196, 199, 207
Boaco (Nicaragua): 68, 72
Bocas del Toro (Panama): 96-98, 208-209
Bogotá (Colombia): 102, 109, 204
Bolivia: 147-159, 194, 202, 209, 210; map 148-149
Bolivian Ministry of Foreign Relations: 159
bolivianos: 159
Boquete (Panama): 98, 208-209
Brazil: 160-171, 194, 195, 196, 203, 207, 209; map 162-163
Buenos Aires (Argentina): 173, 176, 177, 180, 205
CA4: 63, 78
Canoa (Ecuador): 126
carbon off-setting: 213-214
Carnival: 161, 204
Cartagena (Colombia): 102, 103
catrach: 50
Cayos Cochinos (Honduras): 195, 206
Centers for Disease Control: 215
Central America: 8, 9
Central Valley (Costa Rica): 86
Chacabuco Valley (Chile): 185
Chan Chan: 130, 138

Chapare (Bolivia): 150
Chiapas: 27, 29, 31, 33
chicken buses: 48
children and youth: 13, 15 see also Type of Work Index
children, traveling with: 216
Chile: 184-191, 193, 196, 208, 209, 211, 212; map 186-187
chinchillas: 188
Chortí: 56
Ciudad Dario (Nicaragua): 76
Civil Protection Program: 209
climate: 9-10; see also specific place
clothing: 11-12
Cochabamba (Bolivia): 150, 152, 153, 154, 155, 194
Cocinas Mejoradas: 139
coffee farm: 29, 39, 56, 70, 138, 194, 197
Cofradía: (Honduras): 54
colón: 91
Colombia: 102-112, 193; 200, 203, 204, 209; map 104-105
community development: 15; see also Type of Work Index
conduct and customs: 215
Copán: 50, 54, 56, 63
cordoba: 78
Coroico (Bolivia): 151
Correa, Rafael: 128
Costa Rica: 79-92, 193, 195, 196, 199, 200, 201, 202, 203, 208, 209, 212; map 80-81
costs: 17, 20; no fee organizations 17-18; fee-based organizations 18; see also specific place
Cotachachi-Cayapas Reserve: 123
crime and safety: 39; see also specific place
Crooked Trails: 206
crowdfunding: 19, 221
Cuba: 205, 207
Cuellaje (Ecuador): 123
Curimana (Peru): 135
Cusco (Peru): 130, 131, 136, 139, 204, 208
dengue fever: 49, 63, 78, 92, 112, 139, 171, 214
digestion: 214
disabled travelers: 215-216
Dominican Republic: 65, 202, 210
Easter Island: 197
economy: see specific place

Ecuador: 113-129, 193, 196, 200, 203, 205, 207, 209, 210, 211; map 114-115
education: 15; *see also* Type of Work Index
El Progreso (Honduras): 60
El Salvador: 198, 202, 203, 209, 212
engineers: 18, 41
Escobar (Argentina): 176-177
Escobar, Pablo: 205
Escuela de Agroecología y Permacultura Tierra Linda: 29
environment: 15; *see also* Type of Work Index
Estelí (Nicaragua): 69
faith-based organizations/volunteers: 44, 54, 83, 141, 202, 217, 218
FARC (Revolutionary Armed Fores of Colombia): 111
favelas: 160, 161, 171, 196, 204
Flamingo Beach (Costa Rica): 83, 84
fees: see costs
Fly for Good: 213
FundAmazonia: 207
fundraising: 19, 219-221
Galapagos Islands: 113, 116, 121, 122, 124, 193, 197, 210
Garífuna: 50
gay and lesbian travelers: 216-217
geography: *see specific place*
Gorgona (Colombia) 103, 106
Granada (Nicaragua): 65, 71, 72
Guanacaste (Costa Rica): 79, 88
Guapi (Colombia): 103
Guarani: 155, 158, 177
Guatemala: 34-49, 193, 195, 202, 203, 209, 211; map 36-37
Guatemala City (Guatemala): 40, 196
Guayaquil (Ecuador): 117, 129
Guyana: 8, 18, 205, 207
Haiti: 210
health: 16; *see also* Type of Work Index
health concerns: 214-215
history: *see specific place*
holidays: 9-10
homestays: 14; *see also specific place*
Honduras: 50-63, 193, 195, 199, 200, 202, 205, 209; map 52-53
housing: 17; *see also* homestays; *specific place*
Huanchaco (Peru): 138
Huarez (Peru): 131, 139
Huehuetenango (Guatemala): 44
hurricanes: 9, 32, 43, 47, 62, 77
iguanas: 60-62
Illapel (Chile): 188
Incan archaeological sites: 130, 135, 137

Instituto Cultural Oaxaca: 26
Intag (Ecuador): 123
international organizations: 192-212
internet resources: 218-222
inverno: 10, 91, 128, 158, 169
Iquitos (Peru): 195
Isla de la Plata (Ecuador): 116
Jiquillo (Nicaragua): 74
Jinotega (Nicaragua): 68
Jutiapa (Guatemala): 35
kayaking: 28, 74, 88, 97, 207, 209
La Casa en el Arbol: 27
ladino: 50
La Esperanza (Honduras): 55
language requirements: 11, 20; *see also specific place*
language schools: 24, 26, 27, 28, 31, 40, 54, 56, 83, 98-99, 120, 155, 161, 173, 208
La Paz (Bolivia): 153, 154, 156, 159, 210
Las Tolas (Ecuador): 125
Lazy Dog Inn: 131
lempira: 63
Lenca: 55, 62
León (Nicaragua): 65, 68
lesbian and gay travelers: 216-217
Lima (Peru): 137, 139, 141, 196, 204, 211
Lobitos (Peru): 143
macaws: see parrots
Machu Picchu: 130, 208
malaria: 49, 63, 78, 92, 112, 171, 214
Managua (Nicaragua): 64, 69
manteca: 217
Mapuche: 178, 190
Masaya (Nicaragua): 65
Matagalpa (Nicaragua): 68, 72
Maya: 8, 21, 34, 47, 62
Mayan archaeological sites: 21, 27, 34, 38, 47, 50, 54, 56, 130, 137, 138, 194
Medellín (Colombia): 205
medical professionals: 18, 38, 56, 152, 193, 204
Mera (Ecuador): 125
mestizo: 50, 64, 79, 100, 102, 113, 158, 190
Mexico: 8, 9, 21-33, 194, 199, 200, 201, 203, 205, 209, 212; map 22-23
Mexico City (Mexico): 30
Minas Gerias (Brazil): 164, 165
Minca (Colombia): 108
money: *see specific place*
Monte Albán: 24
Monteverde (Costa Rica): 83, 84
Morales, Evo: 158
morenada: 157
Nauhatl: 21

new sole: 146
Nicaragua: 64-78, 194, 193, 196, 198, 200, 202, 209; map 66-67
Nicoya Peninsula (Costa Rica): 82, 87, 89
Oaxaca (Mexico): 24, 26, 27, 30
Ocotal (Nicaragua): 70
Ollantaytambo (Peru): 130, 135
Ometepe (Nicaragua): 73
orchids: 93, 96
organizations: 16-20; see also Organizations Index
packing tips: 11-12
Pacuare Nature Reserve: 85
Palenque: 27
Panama: 93-101, 208, 209; map 94-95
Panama Canal: 100
Panajachel (Guatemala): 43
Paraguay: 8, 18, 202, 209, 210
Parismina (Costa Rica): 83-84
Parque Ambue Ari: 150
Parque Jacj Cuisi: 150
Parque Machía: 150
parrots: 82, 141, 197
passports: 10-11; see also specific place
Patagonia: 178, 179, 180, 182, 208, 212
Peñaflor (Chile): 185, 188
Peru: 130-146, 193, 195, 196, 199, 200, 203, 205, 207, 208, 210, 211; map 132-133
Perutí (Argentina): 177-178
peso: 33, 112, 183, 191
photo etiquette: 215
Playa Malena (Panama): 99
Portuguese: 11, 161
Programa de Asistencia al Turista: 48, 49
placement length: 19; see also specific place
Puerto Lopez (Ecuador): 116, 119
Puerto Maldonado (Peru): 141
Punta Pargos (Costa Rica): 87
Quechua: 8, 11, 135, 145, 147, 155, 158
quetzal: 48
Quetzaltenango (Guatemala): 35, 40, 46
Quito (Ecuadar): 116-118, 121, 124, 129, 201, 204, 207
Rainbow Centre: 137
reading, suggested: 218
real: 170
religion: 83, 217, 218
research tips: 16-19
responsible tourism: 139, 195, 201
Rio de Janeiro (Brazil): 160, 161, 167, 171, 204
Río Dulce (Guatemala): 38
Río Muchacho Community Environmental School: 126

Rivas (Nicaragua): 72
Road Scholar: 68, 194, 216
Roatan (Honduras): 56-58, 63
Sacred Valley (Peru): 130, 135, 137, 146
safety: 215; see also specific place
Salasaca (Ecuador): 120
San Cristobal de las Casas (Mexico): 27
Sandinista revolution: 77
San Joaquín de Flores (Costa Rica): 83
San José de Cusmapa (Nicaragua): 69
San Juan Comalapa (Guatemala): 41
San Juan del Sur (Nicaragua): 72
San Martín (Argentina): 176
San Miguel de Allende (Mexico): 24
San Pedro Sula (Honduras): 51
Santa Marta (Colombia): 107
Santiago (Chile): 184, 185, 190, 211
scuba diving: 51, 57, 61, 98, 106, 108, 120, 192, 195, 202, 205, 206-207, 209
sea turtles: 28, 35, 51, 58, 83-89, 98, 99, 103, 119, 196, 197, 198, 199, 202, 204, 209
seasons: 9-10
seniors: 200, 216
Sierra (Ecuador): 120, 122, 123, 124, 125, 129
snorkeling: 51, 57, 61, 87, 88, 97, 98, 99, 106, 120, 202, 207
Sopacachi (Bolivia): 153
South America: 8-10
spring break: 9
students: 18, 51; high school 28, 30, 55, 85, 103, 202, 207; middle school 28; university 85, 87, 161, 193, 194, 207
Sucre (Bolivia): 150
surfing: 74, 88, 96-98, 130, 138, 143, 161, 167, 199, 207, 209
Tayrona National Park: 108, 109
Tegucigalpa (Honduras): 51, 54
tips for volunteers: 214-217
Tortuguero (Costa Rica): 86
Trancoso (Brazil): 166
transportation: 11; see also specific place
travel insurance: 17, 214
turtles: see sea turtles
type of work: see Type of Work Index
Uruguay: 8, 209
U.S. Department of State: 33
U.S. dollar: 129
UNESCO World Heritage Site: see World Heritage Sites
Uribe, Alvaro: 111
Urubamba (Peru): 136
Utila (Honduras): 51, 61, 207
vaccinations: 11

Valle de Anton (Panama): 96
Valparaíso (Chile): 184
vegetarians: 43, 56, 74, 121, 126, 127, 166, 185, 201, 217
Venezuela: 8, 209, 211
verano: 9, 10, 91, 111, 145, 158
veterinarians: 18
visas: *see specific place*
Visiting International Professionals (VIP): 200
volunteer experience: 25, 42, 58, 75, 84, 97, 106-107, 118-119, 140, 155, 165, 177, 188, 218-219, 220
volunteer reviews: 218-219

WaaW: 136
wildlife protection: 16; *see also* Type of Work Index
women's empowerment: 16; *see also* Type of Work Index
women travelers: 216
World Heritage Sites: 24, 26, 103, 135, 138, 142, 151
Yachayhuasi Learning Centre: 142
yellow fever: 11, 112, 129, 146, 159, 171, 214-215
Yungas (Bolivia): 151
Yurac Yacu Centro de Desarollo: 134

Organizations Index

A Broader View: 193
ACDI/VOCA: 192, 193-194
Akazul: Community, Conservation & Ecology: 35
Aldea Yanapay: 131
Amizade Global Service Learning: 194-195
Andean Alliance: 131, 134-135
APROVACA: *see* Association of Orchid Producers of El Valle and Cabuya
Ara Project, The: 82-83
Association of Orchid Producers of El Valle and Cabuya (APROVACA): 96
Association Save the Turtles of Parismina: 83, 84
ASTOP: *see* Association Save the Turtles of Parismina
Awamaki: 135
Bay Islands Conservation Association: 51
Becari: 24
Biosphere Expeditions: 195
Bridges to Community: 65, 68
Casa de Cultura de La Boquilla: 103
Casa de los Ángeles: 24-26
Casa Guatemala: 38, 106
Casa Hogar Luz Alba Orphanage: 142
CCS: *see* Cross-Cultural Solutions
CEN CINAI Huacas: 84
Central American Children's Institute: 60-61
Centro de Investigacion para el Manejo Ambiental y Desarrollo (CIMAD): 103, 106-107
Centro de Rescate y Rehabilitación de Primates: 185, 188
Centro Educativo de Preservación de la Flora y Fauna: 99

Christian Veterinary Mission: 18
CIMAD: *see* Centro de Investigacion para el Manejo Ambiental y Desarrollo
Cofradía Bilingual School: 54
Comunidad Inti Wara Yassi: 150
Condor Trekkers: 150-151
Conservación Patagonica: 185, 188
Constru Casa: 38-40
CPI Spanish Immersion School: 83-85
Cross-Cultural Solutions (CCS): 195-196
Doctors Without Borders: 18
Earthwatch: 196-198
Eastern Pacific Hawksbill Initiative (ICAPO): 198-199
Ecuador Volunteer Foundation: 116-117
EcuaExplora: 117-119
El Hogar Projects: 54-55
El Maestro en Casa: 55
El Nahual Community Center: 40
El Porvenir: 68
Elevate Destinations: 199-200
Emergency Response Services for Latin America (ERSLA): 68-69
En Vía Foundation: 26
Endangered Wildlife Trust: 85-86, 106
English Volunteers for Change in Costa Rica: 86
Equilibrio Azul: 119-120
Escuela Katitawa: 120-121
Esperanza Verde: 135-136
EVOLC (English Volunteers for Change in Costa Rica): 86
Expanish: 173, 176
Fabretto Children's Foundation: 69-70
FairPlay: 136
FAM: *see* Fundación Arte del Mundo

FIMRC: see Foundation for International Medical Relief for Children
FivePointFive: 106-107, 219
FMA: see Fundación Mariposas Amarillas
Food Bank Foundation: see Fundación Banco de Alimentos
Foundation Bolivar Education: 121-122
Foundation for International Medical Relief for Children (FIMRC): 18
Fundación Arte del Mundo (FAM): 122
Fundación Banco de Alimentos (Food Bank Foundation): 176
Fundación Guía: 150
Fundación Mariposas Amarillas (FMA): 106, 107-108
Fundación Por La Madre: 108-109
Fundación Salvación: 44-45
Galapagos ICE: 122-123
Give and Surf: 96-98
Global Brigades: 18
Global Communities: Partners for Good: 192, 200
Global Volunteers: 200-201
Global Volunteers International: 201-202
Guacamaya: 56
Guardabarranco, S.A.: 70-71
Habitat for Humanity International: 202-203
Habla Ya Panama: 98-99
Hogar Miguel Magone: 40-41
Honduras Coral Reef Fund: 195, 206
ICAPO: see Eastern Pacific Hawksbill Initiative
IHVQ: see International Volunteer HQ
Iko Poran: 161, 164
ILA: see Intern Latin America
IntagTour: 123-124
Intern Latin America (ILA): 205
International Volunteer HQ (IHVQ): 203-204
Iracambi: 164-166
Island Friends–Roatan Charities: 57-58
Jatun Sacha: 124-125
Kiya Survivors: 136-137
La Casa de Maria de la Esperanza: 176-177
La Esperanza Granada: 71
La Senda Verde: 151-152
Las Tolas Community: 125
LIFE: see Luchemos para una Infancia Feliz y con Esperanza
Light and Leadership Initiative, The: 137-138
Long Way Home: 41-43
Luchemos para una Infancia Feliz y con Esperanza (LIFE): 177-178
Mano a Mano Internacional: 152-153
Mayan Families: 43

Médecins Sans Frontières: 18
Merazonia: 125-126
More Than Compassion / Fundación Salvación: 44-45
Ñanta: 150
Nataté: 27
Nicaragua Children's Foundation: 72
Niños de Guatemala: 45-46
Oaxaca Streetchildren Grassroots: 27-28
Operation Wallacea: 205-207
Otra Cosa Network: 138-139
Parques Nacionales Naturales de Colombia: 109-110
Partners in Education–Roatan (PIER): 57
Patagonia Volunteer: 178-179
PIER: see Partners in Education–Roatan
Playa Malena Conservation Association: 99-100
Power to the People: 72-73
Project Bona Fide: 73-74, 75
Project Hope: 18
Protective Turtle Ecology Center for Training, Outreach and Research (ProTECTOR): 58-59
ProTECTOR: see Protective Turtle Ecology Center for Training, Outreach and Research
ProWorld: 207-208
Rancho Esperanza: 74
RDLC: see Roatan Daycare and Learning Center
RED Sustainable Travel: 28-29
REI Adventures: 208
REMAR Bolivia: 153
Respons Sustainable Tourism Center: 139-141
Río Muchacho: 126-127
Roatan Daycare and Learning Center (RDLC): 57-58
Santa Martha Foundation / Villa Martha Home for Children: 141
Save the Wild Chinchillas: 188-189
Scope Volunteer in Brazil: 166
Sea Turtle Conservancy: 86-87
Sea Turtles Forever: 87-88
Seeds of Learning: 76-77
Sexto Sol Center for Community Action: 29
SiKanda: see Solidaridad Internacional Kanda A.C.
Solidaridad Internacional Kanda A.C. (SiKanda): 30
Spanish at Locations: 208-209
Spanish in Bariloche: 179-180
Spirit of the Andes: 153-154
Students Helping Honduras / Central American Children's Institute: 60-61

Sustainable Bolivia: 154-156
Tambopata Macaw Project: 141-142
TECHO: 209-210
TRAMA Textiles: 46
Traveller Not Tourist: 142-143
Tropical Adventures: 88-89
Turtle Trax: 89
Two Brothers Foundation: 167
UBELONG: 210-211
Up Close Bolivia: 156-158
Utila Iguana Conservation Project: 61-62
Veterinarians Without Borders: 18
Villa Martha Home for Children: 141
VIMEX: see Voluntarios Internacionales
    Mexico A.C.

Viva Rio: 167-168
VOCA: 193-194
VOFAIR: 211-212
Voluntario Global: 180-181
Voluntarios Internacionales Mexico A.C.
    (VIMEX): 30-31
Volunteer Optometric Services to Humanity: 18
Wanderland Travel: 212
WAVES for Development: 143-145
WOOF: see World Wide Opportunities on
    Organic Farms
World Vets: 18
World Wide Opportunities on Organic
    Farms: 197

Type of Work Index

AGRICULTURE
general discussion: 13

MEXICO
Nataté: 27
Sexto Sol Center for Community
    Action: 29
Solidaridad Internacional Kanda A.C.
    (SiKanda): 30

GUATEMALA
Casa Guatemala: 38, 106

HONDURAS
Guacamaya: 56

NICARAGUA
Guardabarranco, S.A.: 70-71
Project Bona Fide: 73-74, 75
Rancho Esperanza: 74

ECUADOR
Ecuador Volunteer Foundation: 116-117
Escuela Katitawa: 120-121
IntagTour: 123-124
Las Tolas Community: 125
Río Muchacho: 126-127

PERU
Otra Cosa Network: 138-139

BOLIVIA
Mano a Mano Internacional: 152-153

BRAZIL
Iko Poran: 161, 164

ARGENTINA
Patagonia Volunteer: 178-179
Spanish in Bariloche: 179-180

INTERNATIONAL
A Broader View: 193
ACDI/VOCA: 193-194
Amizade Global Service Learning: 194-195
International Volunteer HQ (IHVQ):
    203-204
Spanish at Locations: 208-209
UBELONG: 210-211
VOFAIR: 211-212
Wanderland Travel: 212
World Wide Opportunities on Organic
    Farms: 197

CHILDREN AND YOUTH
general discussion: 13-14

MEXICO
Becari: 24
Casa de los Ángeles: 24-26
En Vía Foundation: 26
Nataté: 27
Oaxaca Streetchildren Grassroots:
    27-28
Solidaridad Internacional Kanda A.C.
    (SiKanda): 30

Voluntarios Internacionales Mexico A.C. (VIMEX): 30-31

GUATEMALA
Casa Guatemala: 38
El Nahual Community Center: 40
Hogar Miguel Magone: 40-41
Long Way Home: 41-43
Mayan Families: 43
More Than Compassion / Fundación Salvación: 44-45
Niños de Guatemala: 45-46

HONDURAS
Cofradía Bilingual School: 54
El Hogar Projects: 54-55
Guacamaya: 56
Island Friends–Roatan Charities: 57-58

NICARAGUA
Bridges to Community: 65, 68
Fabretto Children's Foundation: 69-70
La Esperanza Granada: 71
Nicaragua Children's Foundation: 72
Rancho Esperanza: 74

COSTA RICA
CPI Spanish Immersion School: 83-85
Tropical Adventures: 88-89
Turtle Trax: 89

PANAMA
Give and Surf: 96-98
Habla Ya Panama: 98-99

COLOMBIA
Casa de Cultura de La Boquilla: 103
Fundación Mariposas Amarillas (FMA): 106, 107-108
Fundación Por La Madre: 108-109

ECUADOR
Ecuador Volunteer Foundation: 116-117
EcuaExplora: 117-119
Equilibrio Azul: 119-120
Escuela Katitawa: 120-121
Foundation Bolivar Education: 121-122
Fundación Arte del Mundo (FAM): 122
Galapagos ICE: 122-123
IntagTour: 123-124
Jatun Sacha: 124-125
Las Tolas Community: 125

PERU
Aldea Yanapay: 131
Andean Alliance: 131, 134-135
Awamaki: 135
FairPlay: 136
Kiya Survivors: 136-137
Light and Leadership Initiative, The: 137-138
Otra Cosa Network: 138-139
Respons Sustainable Tourism Center: 139-141
Santa Martha Foundation / Villa Martha Home for Children: 141
Traveller Not Tourist: 142-143
WAVES for Development: 143-145

BOLIVIA
Condor Trekkers: 150-151
REMAR Bolivia: 153
Spirit of the Andes: 153-154
Sustainable Bolivia: 154-156
Up Close Bolivia: 156-158

BRAZIL
Iko Poran: 161, 164
Two Brothers Foundation: 167
Viva Rio: 167-168

ARGENTINA
Expanish: 173, 176
La Casa de Maria de la Esperanza: 176-177
Luchemos para una Infancia Feliz y con Esperanza (LIFE): 177-178
Patagonia Volunteer: 178-179
Spanish in Bariloche: 179-180
Voluntario Global: 180-181

INTERNATIONAL
A Broader View: 193
ACDI/VOCA: 193-194
Amizade Global Service Learning: 194-195
Cross-Cultural Solutions (CCS): 195-196
Elevate Destinations: 199-200
Global Communities: Partners for Good: 200
Global Volunteers: 200-201
Global Volunteers International: 201-202
International Volunteer HQ (IHVQ): 203-204
Intern Latin America (ILA): 205
ProWorld: 207-208
Spanish at Locations: 208-209
UBELONG: 210-211
VOFAIR: 211-212
Wanderland Travel: 212

COMMUNITY DEVELOPMENT
general discussion: 14

MEXICO
En Vía Foundation: 26
Nataté: 27
Sexto Sol Center for Community
    Action: 29
Solidaridad Internacional Kanda A.C.
    (SiKanda): 30
Voluntarios Internacionales Mexico A.C.
    (VIMEX): 30-31

GUATEMALA
Casa Guatemala: 38, 106
Constru Casa: 38-40
El Nahual Community Center: 40
Long Way Home: 41-43
Mayan Families: 43
TRAMA Textiles: 46

HONDURAS
El Hogar Projects: 54-55
Guacamaya: 56
Island Friends–Roatan Charities: 57-58
Students Helping Honduras / Central
    American Children's Institute: 60-61

NICARAGUA
Bridges to Community: 65, 68
El Porvenir: 68
Emergency Response Services for Latin
    America (ERSLA): 68-69
Guardabarranco, S.A.: 70-71
La Esperanza Granada: 71
Nicaragua Children's Foundation: 72
Power to the People: 72-73
Project Bona Fide: 73-74, 75
Rancho Esperanza: 74
Seeds of Learning: 76-77

COSTA RICA
CPI Spanish Immersion School: 83-85
Tropical Adventures: 88-89
Turtle Trax: 89

PANAMA
Give and Surf: 96-98
Habla Ya Panama: 98-99
Playa Malena Conservation Association:
    99-100

COLOMBIA
Fundación Mariposas Amarillas (FMA): 106,
    107-108

ECUADOR
Ecuador Volunteer Foundation: 116-117
EcuaExplora: 117-119
Escuela Katitawa: 120-121
Foundation Bolivar Education: 121-122
Galapagos ICE: 122-123
IntagTour: 123-124
Jatun Sacha: 124-125
Las Tolas Community: 125
Río Muchacho: 126-127

PERU
Aldea Yanapay: 131
Andean Alliance: 131, 134-135
Awamaki: 135
Otra Cosa Network: 138-139
Respons Sustainable Tourism Center: 139-141
WAVES for Development: 143-145

BOLIVIA
Condor Trekkers: 151-152
Mano a Mano Internacional: 152-153
Spirit of the Andes: 153-154
Sustainable Bolivia: 154-156
Up Close Bolivia: 156-158

BRAZIL
Iko Poran: 161, 164
Scope Volunteer in Brazil: 166
Two Brothers Foundation: 167
Viva Rio: 167-168

ARGENTINA
Expanish: 173, 176
Fundación Banco de Alimentos (Food Bank
    Foundation): 176
Luchemos para una Infancia Feliz y con
    Esperanza (LIFE): 177-178
Patagonia Volunteer: 178-179
Spanish in Bariloche: 179-180
Voluntario Global: 180-181

INTERNATIONAL
A Broader View: 193
ACDI/VOCA: 193-194
Amizade Global Service Learning: 194-195
Cross-Cultural Solutions (CCS): 195-196
Elevate Destinations: 199-200
Global Communities: Partners for Good: 200

Global Volunteers: 200-201
Global Volunteers International: 201-202
Habitat for Humanity International: 202-203
International Volunteer HQ (IHVQ): 203-204
Intern Latin America (ILA): 205
ProWorld: 207-208
Spanish at Locations: 208-209
TECHO: 209-210
UBELONG: 210-211
VOFAIR: 211-212
Wanderland Travel: 212

EDUCATION
general discussion: 14

MEXICO
Becari: 24
Casa de los Ángeles: 24-26
En Vía Foundation: 26
Nataté: 27
Oaxaca Streetchildren Grassroots: 27-28
Sexto Sol Center for Community Action: 29
Solidaridad Internacional Kanda A.C.
    (SiKanda): 30
Voluntarios Internacionales Mexico A.C.
    (VIMEX): 30-31

GUATEMALA
Casa Guatemala: 38, 106
El Nahual Community Center: 40
Hogar Miguel Magone: 40-41
Long Way Home: 41-43
Mayan Families: 43
More Than Compassion / Fundación Salvación:
    44-45
Niños de Guatemala: 45-46

HONDURAS
Bay Islands Conservation Association: 51
Cofradía Bilingual School: 54
El Hogar Projects: 54-55
El Maestro en Casa: 55
Guacamaya: 56
Island Friends–Roatan Charities: 57-58
Students Helping Honduras / Central American
    Children's Institute: 60-61
Utila Iguana Conservation Project: 61-62

NICARAGUA
Bridges to Community: 65, 68
Fabretto Children's Foundation: 69-70
La Esperanza Granada: 71
Nicaragua Children's Foundation: 72

Rancho Esperanza: 74

COSTA RICA
CPI Spanish Immersion School: 83-85
Endangered Wildlife Trust: 85-86, 106
EVOLC (English Volunteers for Change in Costa
    Rica): 86
Tropical Adventures: 88-89
Turtle Trax: 89

PANAMA
Give and Surf: 96-98
Habla Ya Panama: 98-99

COLOMBIA
Casa de Cultura de La Boquilla: 103
Fundación Mariposas Amarillas (FMA): 106,
    107-108
Fundación Por La Madre: 108-109

ECUADOR
Ecuador Volunteer Foundation: 116-117
EcuaExplora: 117-119
Equilibrio Azul: 119-120
Escuela Katitawa: 120-121
Foundation Bolivar Education: 121-122
Fundación Arte del Mundo (FAM): 122
Galapagos ICE: 122-123
IntagTour: 123-124
Las Tolas Community: 125

PERU
Aldea Yanapay: 131
Andean Alliance: 131, 134-135
FairPlay: 136
Kiya Survivors: 136-137
Light and Leadership Initiative, The: 137-138
Otra Cosa Network: 138-139
Respons Sustainable Tourism Center: 139-141
Santa Martha Foundation / Villa Martha Home
    for Children: 141
Traveller Not Tourist: 142-143
WAVES for Development: 143-145

BOLIVIA
Condor Trekkers: 151-152
REMAR Bolivia: 153
Sustainable Bolivia: 154-156
Up Close Bolivia: 156-158

BRAZIL
Iko Poran: 161, 164
Scope Volunteer in Brazil: 166

Two Brothers Foundation: 167
Viva Rio: 167-168

ARGENTINA
Expanish: 173, 176
La Casa de Maria de la Esperanza: 176-177
Luchemos para una Infancia Feliz y con
    Esperanza (LIFE): 177-178
Patagonia Volunteer: 178-179
Spanish in Bariloche: 179-180
Voluntario Global: 180-181

INTERNATIONAL
A Broader View: 193
ACDI/VOCA: 193-194
Amizade Global Service Learning: 194-195
Cross-Cultural Solutions (CCS): 195-196
Eastern Pacific Hawksbill Initiative (ICAPO):
    198-199
Elevate Destinations: 199-200
Global Communities: Partners for Good: 200
Global Volunteers: 200-201
Global Volunteers International: 201-202
International Volunteer HQ (IHVQ): 203-204
Intern Latin America (ILA): 205
ProWorld: 207-208
Spanish at Locations: 208-209
UBELONG: 210-211
VOFAIR: 211-212
Wanderland Travel: 212

ENVIRONMENT
general discussion: 14

MEXICO
Nataté: 27
RED Sustainable Travel: 28-29
Sexto Sol Center for Community Action: 29
Solidaridad Internacional Kanda A.C.
    (SiKanda): 30
Voluntarios Internacionales Mexico A.C.
    (VIMEX): 30-31

GUATEMALA
Akazul: Community, Conservation &
    Ecology: 35
Long Way Home: 41-43
Mayan Families: 43

HONDURAS
Bay Islands Conservation Association: 51

Island Friends–Roatan Charities: 57-58

NICARAGUA
Bridges to Community: 65, 68
Guardabarranco, S.A.: 70-71

COSTA RICA
CPI Spanish Immersion School: 83-85
Sea Turtles Forever: 87-88
Tropical Adventures: 88-89
Turtle Trax: 89

PANAMA
Association of Orchid Producers of El Valle and
    Cabuya (APROVACA): 96
Give and Surf: 96-98
Habla Ya Panama: 98-99
Playa Malena Conservation Association:
    99-100

COLOMBIA
Centro de Investigacion para el Manejo
    Ambiental y Desarrollo (CIMAD): 103,
    106-107
Fundación Por La Madre: 108-109
Parques Nacionales Naturales de Colombia:
    109-110

ECUADOR
Ecuador Volunteer Foundation: 116-117
EcuaExplora: 117-119
Equilibrio Azul: 119-120
Foundation Bolivar Education: 121-122
Galapagos ICE: 122-123
IntagTour: 123-124
Jatun Sacha: 124-125

PERU
Esperanza Verde: 135-136
Otra Cosa Network: 138-139
Respons Sustainable Tourism Center: 139-141
WAVES for Development: 143-145

BOLIVIA
Condor Trekkers: 151-152
Sustainable Bolivia: 154-156
Up Close Bolivia: 156-158

BRAZIL
Iko Poran: 161, 164
Scope Volunteer in Brazil: 166
Viva Rio: 167-168

ARGENTINA
Patagonia Volunteer: 178-179
Spanish in Bariloche: 179-180

CHILE
Conservación Patagonica: 185, 188
Save the Wild Chinchillas: 188-189

INTERNATIONAL
A Broader View: 193
ACDI/VOCA: 193-194
Amizade Global Service Learning: 194-195
Biosphere Expeditions: 195
Earthwatch: 196-198
Eastern Pacific Hawksbill Initiative (ICAPO):
    198-199
Elevate Destinations: 199-200
Global Communities: Partners for Good: 200
Global Volunteers International: 201-202
International Volunteer HQ (IHVQ): 203-204
Intern Latin America (ILA): 205
Operation Wallacea: 205-207
ProWorld: 207-208
REI Adventures: 208
Spanish at Locations: 208-209
UBELONG: 210-211
VOFAIR: 211-212
Wanderland Travel: 212

HEALTH

general discussion: 15

MEXICO
Becari: 24
Nataté: 27
Sexto Sol Center for Community Action: 29
Solidaridad Internacional Kanda A.C.
    (SiKanda): 30
Voluntarios Internacionales Mexico A.C.
    (VIMEX): 30-31

GUATEMALA
Casa Guatemala: 38, 106
Mayan Families: 43

HONDURAS
Guacamaya: 56
Island Friends–Roatan Charities: 57-58

NICARAGUA
Bridges to Community: 65, 68

Fabretto Children's Foundation: 69-70
La Esperanza Granada: 71
Nicaragua Children's Foundation: 72

COSTA RICA
CPI Spanish Immersion School: 83-85

PANAMA
Habla Ya Panama: 98-99

ECUADOR
EcuaExplora: 117-119
Foundation Bolivar Education: 121-122
Galapagos ICE: 122-123
Jatun Sacha: 124-125

PERU
Otra Cosa Network: 138-139

BOLIVIA
Condor Trekkers: 151-152
Mano a Mano Internacional: 152-153
REMAR Bolivia: 153
Spirit of the Andes: 153-154
Sustainable Bolivia: 154-156

BRAZIL
Iko Poran: 161, 164
Viva Rio: 167-168

ARGENTINA
Luchemos para una Infancia Feliz y con
    Esperanza (LIFE): 177-178
Spanish in Bariloche: 179-180
Voluntario Global: 180-181

INTERNATIONAL
A Broader View: 193
ACDI/VOCA: 193-194
Amizade Global Service Learning:
    194-195
Cross-Cultural Solutions (CCS): 195-196
Global Volunteers International:
    201-202
International Volunteer HQ (IHVQ):
    203-204
Intern Latin America (ILA): 205
ProWorld: 207-208
Spanish at Locations: 208-209
UBELONG: 210-211
VOFAIR: 211-212

WILDLIFE PROTECTION
general discussion: 16

MEXICO
Nataté: 27
RED Sustainable Travel: 28-29
Voluntarios Internacionales Mexico A.C.
    (VIMEX): 30-31

GUATEMALA
Akazul: Community, Conservation &
    Ecology: 35

HONDURAS
Bay Islands Conservation Association: 51
Island Friends–Roatan Charities: 57-58
Protective Turtle Ecology Center for Training,
    Outreach and Research (ProTECTOR): 58-59
Utila Iguana Conservation Project: 61-62

COSTA RICA
Ara Project, The: 82-83
Association Save the Turtles of Parismina:
    83, 84
CPI Spanish Immersion School: 83-85
Endangered Wildlife Trust: 85-86, 106
Sea Turtle Conservancy: 86-87
Sea Turtles Forever: 87-88
Tropical Adventures: 88-89
Turtle Trax: 89

PANAMA
Habla Ya Panama: 98-99
Playa Malena Conservation Association:
    99-100

COLOMBIA
Centro de Investigacion para el Manejo
    Ambiental y Desarrollo (CIMAD): 103,
    106-107

ECUADOR
Ecuador Volunteer Foundation: 116-117
EcuaExplora: 117-119
Equilibrio Azul: 119-120
Foundation Bolivar Education: 121-122
Galapagos ICE: 122-123
Jatun Sacha: 124-125
Merazonia: 125-126

PERU
Esperanza Verde: 135-136
Tambopata Macaw Project: 141-142

BOLIVIA
Comunidad Inti Wara Yassi: 150
La Senda Verde: 151-152

BRAZIL
Iracambi: 164-166

CHILE
Centro de Rescate y Rehabilitación de
    Primates: 185, 188
Save the Wild Chinchillas: 188-189

INTERNATIONAL
A Broader View: 193
ACDI/VOCA: 193-194
Biosphere Expeditions: 195
Earthwatch: 196-198
Eastern Pacific Hawksbill Initiative (ICAPO):
    198-199
Elevate Destinations: 199-200
Global Volunteers International: 201-202
International Volunteer HQ (IHVQ):
    203-204
Intern Latin America (ILA): 205
Operation Wallacea: 205-207
ProWorld: 207-208
REI Adventures: 208
Spanish at Locations: 208-209
UBELONG: 210-211
VOFAIR: 211-212

WOMEN'S EMPOWERMENT
general discussion: 16

MEXICO
En Vía Foundation: 26

GUATEMALA
Mayan Families: 43
TRAMA Textiles: 46

COSTA RICA
CPI Spanish Immersion School: 83-85

COLOMBIA
Fundación Mariposas Amarillas (FMA): 106,
    107-108

ECUADOR
Foundation Bolivar Education: 121-122

PERU
Andean Alliance: 131, 134-135
Awamaki: 135
FairPlay: 136
Light and Leadership Initiative, The: 137-138
Otra Cosa Network: 138-139

BOLIVIA
REMAR Bolivia: 153
Spirit of the Andes: 153-154
Sustainable Bolivia: 154-156

BRAZIL
Iko Poran: 161, 164

ARGENTINA
Voluntario Global: 180-181

INTERNATIONAL
A Broader View: 193
ACDI/VOCA: 193-194
Cross-Cultural Solutions (CCS): 195-196
Global Communities: Partners for Good: 200
Intern Latin America (ILA): 205
ProWorld: 207-208
UBELONG: 210-211
VOFAIR: 211-212

www.moon.com

DESTINATIONS | ACTIVITIES | BLOGS | MAPS | BOOKS

MOON.COM is ready to help plan your next trip! Filled with fresh trip ideas and strategies, author interviews, informative travel blogs, a detailed map library, and descriptions of all the Moon guidebooks, Moon.com is all you need to get out and explore the world—or even places in your own backyard. While at Moon.com, sign up for our monthly e-newsletter for updates on new releases, travel tips, and expert advice from our on-the-go Moon authors. As always, when you travel with Moon, expect an experience that is uncommon and truly unique.

KEEP UP WITH MOON ON FACEBOOK AND TWITTER
JOIN THE MOON PHOTO GROUP ON FLICKR

**MOON VOLUNTEER VACATIONS
IN LATIN AMERICA**
Avalon Travel
a member of the Perseus Books Group
1700 Fourth Street
Berkeley, CA 94710, USA
www.moon.com

Editor: Sabrina Young
Copy Editor: Justine Rathbun
Production and Graphics Coordinator:
  Lucie Ericksen
Cover Designer: Lucie Ericksen
Map Editor: Mike Morgenfeld
Cartographer: Paige Enoch, Mike Morgenfeld

ISBN-13: 978-1-61238-641-6
ISSN: 2327-3844

Printing History
1st Edition — November 2013
5 4 3 2 1

Front cover photo: underwater data collection © Biosphere Expeditions
Title page: photo courtesy of the ARA Project
Other color photos: page 4: © Robert Lerich/123RF; page 5: © Elultimodeseo/Dreamstime.com; page 6: inset © Luis Louro/123RF, bottom © Brian Lasenby/Dreamstime.com; page 7: top left: © hadynyah/iStock.com, top right: © Tomas Hajek/123RF, bottom left © Joshua Berman, www.joshuaberman.net, bottom right © Ashley Mihle; page 9: © holgs/istockphoto.com; page 10: photo courtesy of Biosphere Expeditions; page 12: © William Friar, www.panamaguidebooks.com; page 13: © Serena Star Leonard, www.FivePointFive.org; page 15 and 17: © Amy E. Robertson; page 20: photo courtesy of ProWorld

Printed in Canada by Friesens

MAP SYMBOLS

▱ Expressway	⬛	Highlight	✗	Airfield	⚑	Golf Course
▱ Primary Road	○	City/Town	✈	Airport	Ⓟ	Parking Area
▱ Secondary Road	◉	State Capital	▲	Mountain	▲	Archaeological Site
▱ Unpaved Road	⊛	National Capital	✦	Unique Natural Feature	⚰	Church
▱ Trail	★	Point of Interest			⛽	Gas Station
▱ Ferry	•	Accommodation	⟆	Waterfall		Glacier
▱ Railroad	▼	Restaurant/Bar	▲	Park		Mangrove
▱ Pedestrian Walkway	■	Other Location	◻	Trailhead		Reef
▱ Stairs	⋀	Campground	✗	Skiing Area		Swamp

CONVERSION TABLES

°C = (°F - 32) / 1.8
°F = (°C x 1.8) + 32
1 inch = 2.54 centimeters (cm)
1 foot = 0.304 meters (m)
1 yard = 0.914 meters
1 mile = 1.6093 kilometers (km)
1 km = 0.6214 miles
1 fathom = 1.8288 m
1 chain = 20.1168 m
1 furlong = 201.168 m
1 acre = 0.4047 hectares
1 sq km = 100 hectares
1 sq mile = 2.59 square km
1 ounce = 28.35 grams
1 pound = 0.4536 kilograms
1 short ton = 0.90718 metric ton
1 short ton = 2,000 pounds
1 long ton = 1.016 metric tons
1 long ton = 2,240 pounds
1 metric ton = 1,000 kilograms
1 quart = 0.94635 liters
1 US gallon = 3.7854 liters
1 Imperial gallon = 4.5459 liters
1 nautical mile = 1.852 km

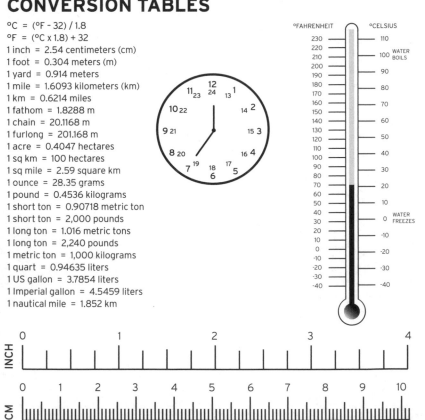